Mennonite Disaster Service

Mennonite Disaster Service

Building a Therapeutic Community after the Gulf Coast Storms

Brenda D. Phillips, Ph.D.

LEXINGTON BOOKS
Lanham • Boulder • New York • Toronto • Plymouth, UK

Published by Lexington Books
A wholly owned subsidiary of Rowman & Littlefield
4501 Forbes Boulevard, Suite 200, Lanham, Maryland 20706
www.rowman.com

10 Thornbury Road, Plymouth PL6 7PP, United Kingdom

British Library Cataloguing in Publication Information Available

Library of Congress Cataloging-in-Publication Data
Phillips, Brenda.
Mennonite Disaster Service : building a therapeutic community after the Gulf Coast storms / Brenda
Phillips.
pages cm.
Includes bibliographical references.
ISBN 978-0-7391-8545-2 (cloth : alk. paper)—ISBN 978-0-7391-8546-9 (ebook)
1. Mennonite Disaster Service. 2. Disaster relief. 3. Disaster relief—Gulf Coast (U.S.) 4. Hurricane
Katrina, 2005. 5. Hurricane Rita, 2005. 6. Hurricane Ike, 2008. I. Title.
BX8128.W4P45 2014
363.34'92280882895—dc23
2013031566
ISBN 978-1-4985-1520-7 (pbk : alk, paper)

Printed in the United States of America

To Frank and Mary Jane Phillips

Contents

Foreword

This book is personal. In the days following Hurricane Katrina, my home along with 80 percent of New Orleans flooded as levee after levee collapsed or breached. To come back to see your belongings mud soaked, your house smelling of mold and mildew; it was hard to find a road back. But for some of us, there was a path, strewn with false starts, obstacles, and incompetence. We are here today in our rebuilt home, with the help of our friends and family. Rebuilding is not a task to do alone; it requires a community. In so many ways, Brenda Phillips was part of my rebuilding community helping with knowledge, resources and an understanding of the tasks ahead.

It is with this sense of knowledge and understanding that she allows the story of the Mennonites to emerge. The recovery of the Gulf Coast from Hurricanes Katrina and Rita is far from over; the unevenness of the recovery continues. As the government at all levels struggled in its response to these catastrophic events, others rushed to Gulf Coast to help. What this help looked like and how it was received will be written about for decades to come. The story of the Mennonites and this recovery provide a roadmap to understand how aid might be organized in future disasters.

It is easy to imagine that the events described in this book as a movie, a work of fiction. Traditionally dressed Mennonites, "plain people," from a farm in Pennsylvania come to the Gulf Coast. Photos show a young Mennonite woman in modest dress and bonnet working on a roof on a bayou of a Native American community in lower Jefferson Parish, Louisiana. At any point in this interaction, there are places for misinterpretation, mistrust and confusion. Throughout this book, we learn about this interaction and how surprisingly, based on faith, organization, and labor, the Mennonites built homes and communities.

The story of this aid, and much aid after Hurricanes Katrina and Rita, cannot be told without writing about the faith of those involved. Often academics are cynical about faith, standing from a distance recording without understanding. This is not the perspective of Brenda in this book; faith is not tangential to this story—it is central. Nor is it simple. The faith that guides the lives and the work of the Mennonites has a historical specificity that is the subtext here. Their faith sustains the organization itself, the staff and the volunteers.

The Gulf south has a diverse religious history; a strong combination of Protestant and Roman Catholic. In many ways, the Mennonites found themselves in homes and communities where prayer was part of every-day life. It might not be their way to worship, but the Mennonites devel-oped a common language with these communities as evidenced in the house blessing ceremonies. The relationships based on faith deepened the Mennonites understanding of where they were and who they were work-ing with.

The Mennonites, despite their efforts to do their work and remain "the quiet in the land," leave a legacy about how to "volunteer" In reading this book, I am not sure that "volunteer" captures the work of the Men-nonites in this disaster. First, they access the community in a way that builds partnership. After the storms, many people came to help, but few understood that they needed to use local knowledge and personnel. The Mennonites knew that as important as the process of creating a building was to create a relationship with local agencies and whenever possible, the homeowners themselves.

In each community they entered, the Mennonites were assigned the most vulnerable in the community—the elderly, disabled, or single par-ents. As the recovery progressed, the families with the more difficult situations were still struggling. A good example is the community of Grand Bayou in Louisiana. The ownership of their traditional lands was in dispute and the ability to obtain building permits nearly stopped the process completely. The Mennonites showed that they were there for the long term, spending the years it took to get the permits and build careful-ly constructed raised houses.

The commitment that the Mennonites showed to the Gulf Coast is also a key ingredient to their success in the area. They came to stay. They are still here. More than six years after the storms, they are still doing work. And, the work that they are doing is well done. What we know happened after the storm was that many well-intentioned volunteers came down to help out and did not have the skills. The organization and skill level of the Mennonites moved them far beyond the 'volunteer.'

This book should be read carefully. Within these chapters are the ways in which we might as a country think about helping people and communities in disasters—you come when you are needed, you do good work, you take care of yourself and others, and you honor the people you serve.

Pam Jenkins
University of New Orleans

Acknowledgments

This ethnographic study of a faith-based organization delves deeply into the historical, cultural, and theological reasons for volunteer efforts after disaster. Most studies of volunteerism rely on quantitative surveys and, while informative, fail to tap into the experiences and personal impacts of volunteering for both actors and beneficiaries. This qualitative study aims to fill such a gap in our understanding of the lived experience of volunteering in a faith-based and post-disaster context.

I first heard about Mennonite Disaster Service (MDS) in the 1970s, as a student at Bluffton College in Ohio. I came to know MDS as a student of E. L. Quarantelli, who co-founded the Disaster Research Center at The Ohio State University. As a disaster researcher for 30 years, I have been asking emergency managers, elected officials, and community leaders "who has been the most helpful to you since the disaster?" Mennonite Disaster Service has consistently been identified as "most helpful," over and over. In this study, I try to explain why.

I came to know the current executive director of MDS, Kevin King, prior to Katrina. We met at a conference convened by Church World Service and afterwards Mr. King asked for input on developing a disaster management program at Hesston College in Kansas. He called me again in 2005, the night before Katrina struck, and we worried together about the potential impact on the U.S. Gulf Coast. MDS became busier than ever in the following years, in an effort documented in this volume. Internally, MDS worried about their level of growth and activity: would it change their organization? I wondered as well: would people continue to speak of MDS as the best in the business? In 2010, Mr. King and MDS asked if I would help them evaluate their work and I agreed to do so if rigorous academic standards could be used and if the results could be published independently. Details of the methodology can be found in Appendix A.

I would like to thank a number of people and organizations who made this unique look into MDS possible. First, I want to acknowledge that Mennonites practice humility. For Mennonites who may feel uncomfortable in a spotlight that analyzes their standout reputation, I suggest that the analysis written here sheds light on best practices for those who want to help when disaster strikes. People want and need to know what is helpful in a post-disaster context and those who shared their experiences in this book did so in good faith that it would help those impacted by future events. I especially thank those who agreed to be interviewed for this book, particularly storm survivors and community leaders tasked with the daunting task of reconstruction.

Within MDS, I thank the entire staff in the United States and Canada who provided warm hospitality and participated in the research process. In particular, I thank Kevin King, Arleta Martin (at MDS in the U.S.) and Lois Nickel (formerly at MDS in Canada and now at Canadian Mennonite University) as well as the entire staff of MDS (past and present). The research team involved students from Canadian Mennonite University including Malory Shack and from Hesston College including Jake Ressler, Andreia Dück, Amber Repp, Jordan Penner, and So Young Choi. Their work was exceptional. I especially thank fellow researcher Ron Dueck for his partnership, insights, and collegiality during our many trips to the coast. A number of people including Russ Gaeddert (Hesston College) and Paul Unruh (MDS) read early versions of the manuscript and provided valuable feedback. I appreciate the time spent with former MDS director Lowell Detweiler who shed insight into MDS history. I am indebted to the many people who hosted me in Akron, Pennsylvania and Winnipeg, Canada and on MDS project sites. They gave openly to help an outsider understand MDS and Anabaptism.

This research was possible because of a sabbatical leave from Oklahoma State University and through support provided by the College of Arts and Sciences, the Department of Political Science, the Fire and Emergency Management Program, and the Center for the Study of Disasters and Extreme Events. I especially thank my colleague and husband sociologist David M. Neal who provided invaluable disaster research consultation. Mike Thompson, OSU Professor of Religious Studies, read early drafts and deepened my understanding of Anabaptist theology. Additional colleagues who provided crucial insights and feedback include Pam Jenkins, Shirley Laska and Kris Peterson from the University of New Orleans and Walt Peacock from Texas A&M University. Several archivists spent countless hours hunting down documents, photographs, film, microfiche, and microfilm for this study. In particular, I thank archivist Colleen McFarland from Mennonite Church USA. Her enthusiasm for this project kept me going during long days poring over rare documents. I am equally grateful for the spirit of service found in Frances Griffin who shared personal photographs from the social justice origins of MDS. Frances also edited this manuscript multiple times. Beth Hewett, an extraordinary writing coach, pushed me across the finish line.

On a personal level, I greatly appreciate my parents, Frank and Mary Jane Phillips, who understood the many long weeks away from home and who provided steadfast support. My students also practiced patience in allowing me time away from the office. They listened to presentations of the data several times and provided useful feedback. With appreciation, I also thank Amy King and the entire production team at Lexington

Books who saw worth in ethnographic analysis of voluntary service in a religious context. The findings presented in this work are my own and do not necessarily reflect anyone named here. I extend a sincere regret to anyone I missed in these acknowledgements.

Brenda D. Phillips, Ph.D.
Ohio University
Chillicothe, Ohio

ONE

The Gulf Coast Storms

This is home.
—Coastal Resident

AUGUST 29, 2005

Marking time for millions of people, hurricane Katrina severed life into "before" and "after." Numbers defy the lived experience of the storm. Many residents assumed they would be safe after experiencing Hurricane Camille in 1969, a storm that ranked at the top of the most destructive events in U.S. hurricane history. As the warnings to evacuate came in 2005, thousands remained forcibly in place without assistance to reach safety. Residents suffered horrific, slow deaths, life-threatening injuries, and soul-numbing efforts to survive. They waited for help on their rooftops, in makeshift shelters, on overpasses, and in agony. People died from exposure scant miles from food, water, shelter, and medical care. Strangers worked frantically to save each other, offer first aid, cover the body of an elder who passed, and cool babies suffering from heat. For many in Louisiana, Mississippi, and Alabama, help simply came too late.

When help did arrive, families and neighbors became separated. First responders, exhausted and overwhelmed, passed by hundreds of people they could not help while desperately triaging those with greatest need. Focused on human life, rescue officials refused to take along beloved pets that died alone. Flown or bused to safety in faraway cities, people with medical needs arrived without wheelchairs, medical equipment, prescriptions, or caregivers. Evacuees gathered around computers in public shelters, searching satellite maps to see what, if anything, remained of homes, neighborhoods, schools, and jobs.

Worldwide attention focused on a situation unimaginable in such a powerful nation. A collective agony captured all who watched events unfold, impotent to render aid. Traumatized family members called frantically to phones that no longer worked, unable to ascertain if their loved ones had lived or died. Criticism pounded government officials at all levels as helicopters rescued those still living and transferred bodies to makeshift morgues. Television stations organized efforts to identify and reunite children separated from parents. Shelter workers searched the Internet for hours, trying to find missing kin. Relatives drove hundreds of miles to retrieve someone from a shelter, with tearful reunions in parking lots as arms closed around someone thought to have perished.

Surviving trauma requires the support of meaningful social relationships (Norris et al. 2002a and 2002b). Such interpersonal connections emanate from primary groups that include partners, spouses, children, and friends and also from broader social networks like neighbors, faith families, and work colleagues. For many survivors, hurricane Katrina cut off such connections. In Mississippi, people could not get home to broken communities for a very long time or left forever. In Louisiana, mandatory evacuations in Orleans and Plaquemines Parishes separated blood and chosen kin who had supported each other through prior events. Churches, mosques, and synagogues destroyed by the storms lost their clergy to geographic distance, and congregations struggled to reunite. In a context where government help was not a given, where social ties had been fractured, and where communication infrastructure remained severely compromised, people experienced profound trauma.

Hurricane Katrina was just the first of multiple storms that pummeled Louisiana, Mississippi, Alabama, and East Texas from 2005 to 2008. Personal and community experiences during and after Hurricanes Katrina, Rita (2005), and Ike (2008) established the context for the work of many faith-based organizations as they moved through the debris and devastation to repair, rebuild, and restore hope. Mennonite Disaster Service (MDS), one such organization, quietly moved into affected areas to fulfill a mandate dictated by faith to "bear ye one another's burdens and in so doing, fulfill the law of Christ" (Galatians 6:2). This volume sheds light on how faith-based organizations, through the lens of Mennonite Disaster Service, served those affected by Katrina, Rita, and Ike. The story unfolds through the perspectives of community partners, clients, and MDS volunteers and staff as they meet in the aftermath of historic disasters. To start, this chapter describes the challenges faced by recovery organizations seeking to serve those affected by the storms. Prior to Superstorm Sandy in 2012, the top three costliest hurricanes in U.S. history were, in order: Katrina, Rita, and Ike. To illustrate their effects, this chapter situates readers into communities where Mennonite Disaster Service would establish projects.

HURRICANE KATRINA

Meteorologists measure hurricanes in terms of intensity, ranking them from category 1 (the lowest, winds from 75 to 94 mph) to category 5 (the highest, winds over 155 mph). Hurricanes make landfall differently; some are wind-born events while others push seas onto land through a storm surge. Camille, a category 5 storm that occurred in 1969, generated a storm surge of 24.6–feet into the small community of Pass Christian, Mississippi. Located in western Hancock County, Pass Christian endured landfall winds estimated at 200 miles-per-hour as Camille devastated residences, businesses, agriculture, and infrastructure. Over five thousand people lost their homes with another 11,667 facing major damage. At least five hundred businesses did not survive the storm. Across the affected areas, railways, bridges, and roads failed and critical waterway channels that served as transportation and portage routes became unnavigable. In the Mississippi River alone, 94 vessels sank and out in the Gulf, oil industries dealt with toppled drilling rigs. In Mississippi, 139 died with 76 missing; as Camille moved inland, heavy rain and flooding claimed another 108 in Virginia and West Virginia (Hearn 2004; ESSA 1969).

The devastation from Katrina surpassed that wrought by Camille. Reaching a category 5 status in the Gulf, powerful 175 mile-per-hour winds produced massive swells, including the highest wave ever recorded (55 feet) near Dauphin Island, Alabama. Katrina made landfall on Plaquemines Parish below New Orleans on August 29, 2005. Although the storm had fallen to a category 3 level (winds from 111 to 130 mph), the storm had already generated a historic storm surge. Survivors spoke of waves towering thirty to forty feet, well over treetops. The storm then moved east of downtown New Orleans, sparing most of the city initially. St. Bernard Parish, southeast of New Orleans, experienced a 15 to 19 foot storm surge that destroyed neighborhoods and business sectors. In western New Orleans, a 10 to 14 foot surge pressed in. Hancock County in Mississippi bore the landfall brunt as Katrina moved inland, bringing a 24 to 28 foot surge twenty miles wide and as far as six miles inland. State route 90 along the beach disappeared and waters crossed parts of Interstate 10 nearly 12 miles from shore. As Katrina moved east, Mobile Bay in Alabama observed surges ranging from 8 to 12 feet, with the inflow affecting bays and rivers twenty miles farther inland. Life changed in communities along the coast.

The Grand Bayou, Plaquemines Parish, Louisiana

The Grand Bayou, located in the middle of Plaquemines Parish, Louisiana, lies south of New Orleans. The small community can be found just outside and west of two tall, parallel levees that stretch southward along the length of the Parish. About 100 residents live in Grand Bayou and many claim ancestry from the Attakapa-Ishaak tribe of Native Americans. Before saltwater intruded into their wetlands, their ancestors could step across the meandering bayou that runs through the community to visit and care for each other. More recently, massive and extensive coastal erosion has widened the bayou and made it impossible to care for family without a boat. Children travel in a locally owned boat to the shoreline to be picked up for school. Residents enjoy a close set of relationships in the bayou where they take care of each other, the land, and the water.

Life in Grand Bayou is familiar and comfortable, a place where loved ones gather for Fourth of July events, to worship in the small church with its handmade wooden pews, and to earn a livelihood. Faith is strong here, with local residents sharing their love of God through weekly worship and daily witness. Loving the land and water, many extract a living from the sea by shrimping and fishing. Some work on land, for parish government or industry, but all come home to the bayou and to each other. Outsiders, sometimes promising help, have ultimately always left. Residents are concerned about area development, seeing outsiders as bringing undesirable behaviors into the bayou and extracting marsh resources for sport. They fear intrusion of those not respectful of environmental riches or of ancestral and cultural resources in nearby burial mounds. But they watch out even for outsiders, rescuing the perishing from capsized boats while out on fishing runs. For Grand Bayou residents, shrimping, oystering, and trapping remain their way of life. Talented cooks live here too, "dressing" shrimp from a fresh catch with tomato, lettuce, and mayo for a savory "po'boy" sandwich. Despite hardship, residents care for each other, with elders living into their eighties. They check on each other, watch over the bayou, and staunchly advocate for a disappearing way of life.

Residents have endured repeated inundations from tropical storms that poured water into their homes, the church, and the shared community center. In the years just prior to Katrina, tropical storms Lili, Isidore, and Bill pushed water into their community. Each time, residents moved their boats to safety, mucked out each other's homes, repaired the church, and carried on, always taking care of each other and always surviving. Katrina destroyed The Grand Bayou.

The Lower Ninth Ward, New Orleans, Louisiana

Thinking they had dodged a bullet, residents of New Orleans went outside after the storm to look around, pick up debris, walk dogs, and talk to neighbors. Yet the powerful storm surge generated far out in the Gulf strained a levee system protecting a major port city lying below sea level. Overtopping of levees occurred east of New Orleans in Orleans and

St. Bernard Parishes. Water pushed into the Intracoastal Waterway and Industrial Canal. Multiple breaches and failures turned levees into massive, destructive waterfalls flooding eighty percent of the City of New Orleans (Graumann et al. 2005; Knabb et al. 2005). One of those neighborhoods was the Lower Ninth Ward.

In contrast to externally generated images of an impoverished and troubled community, the Lower Ninth Ward has an historic legacy with strong social ties among its residents. Its history tells how that happened. The Lower Ninth rose out of a cypress swamp originally populated by poor African Americans and Irish, Italian, and German immigrants unable to afford more adequate land for housing (GNOCDC 2002). Problematic infrastructure, including drainage issues, plagued the area and development languished.

Nonetheless, people from the Lower Ninth Ward have always stood firm in supporting their community and each other. In 1892, a Committee of Citizens (also called the Free People of Color of New Orleans) supported a free African American, Homer Plessy, when he refused to move to a segregated railroad car. The resulting court case, Plessy v. Ferguson, failed to support their claims to equal rights but laid the foundation for later and more successful court challenges to segregation. Community groups emerged in the 1950s to secure improvements, laying a foundation to expand small businesses. A simultaneously occurring civil rights movement led to school desegregation by the 1960s.

A continuing lack of economic and political will failed to address deteriorating conditions and stubbornly entrenched problems including affordable housing, low incomes, high crime rates, inferior education, and more (Cutter 2006). By 2005, census data revealed historic patterns of segregation, with the area approximately 98 percent African American. The area also included a higher percentage of residents over the age of fifty than other neighborhoods. Of the older residents, 57.6 percent served as caregivers for grandchildren, compared to 42 percent nationally. Among those over the age of fifty, 26.8 percent lived alone. As age increases, so does the prevalence of disability (National Council on Disability 2009). Not surprisingly, the Lower Ninth Ward reported a higher percentage of older residents with disabilities than the rest of New Orleans and the United States. As an indicator of ability to evacuate and rebuild, data show that 39.1 percent of Lower Ninth Ward residents over 65 experienced mobility challenges compared to 28.6 percent nationwide.

Income also influences abilities to prepare for and recover from a disaster. In the Lower Ninth, the average household earned $27,499 compared to $56,644 across the country. As a reflector of the older population, over one-third lived on social security income in contrast to one-fourth across the nation. Three times as many people in the Lower Ninth, compared to state averages across the United States, relied on supplemental security income. Katrina would cost the area disproportionate deaths, injuries, and property losses consistent with research on age, disability, race, and income (Sharkey 2007; Dash 2013; Peek 2013; Clive et al. 2013).

Prior to Katrina, the Greater New Orleans Community Data Center (2002) described the Lower Ninth Ward as "rich with small businesses, barber and beauty shops, corner stores, eateries, gasoline stations, day care centers, as well as public schools," and numerous churches. Historic, shotgun style homes, where you could see from the front door through to the back, characterized local architecture. The Holy Cross Historic Neighborhood, nestled adjacent to the Lower Ninth Ward, hosted annual Easter egg hunts, holiday caroling, and community festivals. Together, residents created the Delery Street Riverfront Playground so that children could play safely and under neighbor supervision. Locals characterized the area as a "neighborhood where people work for a living" and "not a hoity toity place" (Preservation Resource Center, no date).

Dedicated service characterized neighborhood associations, community organizations, and the faith community. Residents worked collectively to overcome embedded patterns of segregation and to address health needs, children's education, affordable housing, crime rates, and inadequate political representation (GNOCDC 2002). It seemed for many that the Lower Ninth Ward and Holy Cross were on the verge of moving forward in many positive directions. Despite the challenging living conditions and reports of official neglect, the Lower Ninth was *home*.

Nonetheless, this area along the river remained at risk for repetitive flooding, evidenced when hurricane Betsy flooded 80 percent of the area in 1965. The Lower Ninth remained "one of the most congested and dangerous [areas] of the entire river" (Preservation Resource Center, no date). Hurricane Katrina arrived at the end of the month as residents waited for their hard-earned government entitlement checks for disability and elderly support. Many could not afford to evacuate, or were unable to do so, because they lacked transportation. Water overtopped the levee that protected the area and shoved buildings off their foundations for blocks, contorting them into a bizarre post-disaster landscape. Hundreds died in their attics or on rooftops awaiting rescue. Devastation brought national attention as allegations arose over neglect based on race and poverty. Devastation was so complex that residents, displaced across the U.S. for years, might never be neighbors again.

Pass Christian, Mississippi

Pass Christian lies along the Mississippi Gulf Coast, about 65 miles east of New Orleans. A community of 6,000 prior to Katrina, this coastal fishing town and commercial harbor is proud of its long history and small town feel. The "Pass" tracks its heritage as far back as 1699, when French explorer d'Iberville came ashore. A French map dated 1732 marked the area as "Oyster Pass" or Basudre aux Huistres, a commercial opportunity that remained healthily in place for centuries. The French ceded the area to the British in 1763 through the Treaty of Paris. The area joined the U.S. through the Louisiana Purchase of 1803 (Ellis 2005). Consistent with broader trends, an 1805 treaty mandated that the "Southeast Indians" (probably Creeks) relinquish their coastal lands (Ellis 2005).

Local residents raised the U.S. flag formally following the creation of Hancock County and joined in the Battle of New Orleans in 1815 (Ellis 2005). Mississippi became a state in 1837; four years later, Harrison County formed out of Hancock County and in 1848 the town was chartered formally as Pass Christian (Ellis 2005). The town embraced its French legacy by naming streets after explorers like (Jean Baptiste) Saucier Street. Its antebellum history is also reflected in classic worker housing and larger beachfront homes with a number of homes on the National Register of Historic Places.

Local culture reflects an important heritage: "many citizens of Pass Christian originated from descendants of the first settlers, most of whom were Black . . . not slaves, but *freemen* which is considered unique in state history" (Ellis 2005, his emphasis). Freemen were reported in Pass Christian about 1810. In 1835, a formerly enslaved African, Charles Asmard, passed downtown and residential property to his heirs (Ellis 2005; 2001a). By doing so, Asmard created opportunities for African American business development and community leadership, unusual opportunities both prior to and after the Civil War. By 1850, census data show that 39 percent of the Harrison County population was African American (Ellis 2001a). However, despite the exceptional contributions of early African Americans, the town passed an "Ordinance of 1858" restricting the activities of both freemen and those enslaved, including "unlawful assembly" and gun ownership. The ordinance also curtailed social life as well by instituting night-time curfews, regulating public worship, and disallowing private dances, gambling, drinking, and buying liquor. Further, "white fraternization was punishable by a fine and/or jail" (Ellis 2001a). After seceding during the Civil War, Mississippi rejoined the United States in 1869. Many neighborhoods in the Pass still reflect land use marked by race.

Disaster in the form of yellow fever first struck the area in 1853, 1867, and 1878 followed by another epidemic in 1897 and the devastating influenza pandemic of 1918. Hurricanes hit in 1915 and again, with a 13.4-foot storm surge, in September of 1947. A 1948 hurricane destroyed the Dunbar Dukate Oyster Cannery (Ellis 2005). Pass Christian rebuilt its city hall after a fire in 1959 but on September 9, 1965, Hurricane Betsy slammed into the coast. Four years later, Camille took the lives of 131 along the coast with Pass Christian suffering the loss of 78 (Ellis 2005). Despite it all, Pass Christian residents would rebuild their homes and lives over and over.

Before Katrina, Pass Christian residents enjoyed short walks to the beach, small locally owned businesses, and a beautiful shoreline. The dock thrived with commercial fishermen bringing in their harvest for local tables, restaurants, and tourists. Along the white sand beaches, built after the 1947 hurricane to protect the coastal highway, dolphin pods bobbed along at predictable times of day. Artists captured flora, fauna, and sea life, selling jewelry, paintings, and memories to those who stayed and those who passed through. Tourists enjoyed antebellum homes converted into bed and breakfast hotels. Echoing its long-term residency patterns, the Pass in 2000 remained home to a population 28 percent African American and 65 percent white. About 3 percent of the population reflected Asian ancestry, primarily Vietnamese Americans with 1.7 percent Hispanic. Residents lived in approximately 2,672 housing units with a median value of $99,500. Some homes had passed down through families for several generations, with kin still living nearby.

In 1972, local resident George T. Watson, a vital African American leader, became principal of the Pass Christian high school and later city-wide superintendent. In 1995, he said, "I think Pass Christian, today, has finally reached where we were prior to Camille. Camille set us back so far. Needless to say, we have a long, long way to go. However, there's an attitude of moving forward and there is a togetherness to go forward" (Ellis 2001b). But during Katrina, those who stayed in the Pass thought they would die, and dozens did. In the days that followed, the National Guard would have to cut their way through debris-filled roads to reach those alive. Residents who returned found that little had survived. All they could see was rubble.

Bayou la Batre, Alabama[1]

A small fishing village named Bayou La Batre lies southwest of Mobile, Alabama along the Gulf Coast. A land grant originated the community formally in 1786, providing permission to fish and plant corn. However, historians suggest occupation of the land goes back "nearly eight thousand years" as a hunting and fishing area for Native Americans (Gaillard 2007, p. 858). The coastal area has lured outsiders since then as proximity to sea and land allowed for growth. Over time, the area became known as the "seafood capital of Alabama." By the end of the twentieth century, the local Chamber of Commerce could boast of generating $80 million for the state's economy. Being connected to the larger land mass enabled the area to survive hurricanes in 1906 and 1916, though a fledgling tourist industry did not (Bayou la Batre Chamber of Commerce 2010). The storm of 1906 took 135 lives and lingers still in community memories (Gaillard 2007).

With an elevation of 13 feet and a population of 2,313 in 2000, the community perched precariously on the eastern edge of an area that

Katrina would impact. A diverse community, the population before the storm included Asian Americans (33.3 percent of the total population), African Americans (10.3 percent), Hispanics (1.9 percent), whites (52.4 percent) and a few Native Americans. Seventeen percent were foreign born. Nearly one-third spoke a language other than English at home, often Cambodian or Vietnamese. Having fled war in their home countries, they found familiar work along the Alabama coastline.

Just over half of the population had earned a high school diploma or GED with 3.6 percent holding a bachelor's degree. Earning a living in a predominantly fishing village meant that the per capita income in 2000 was a meager $9,928 with a median below $25,000 (Gaillard 2007); 28 percent fell below the official poverty line. The town's 864 homes in 2000 had a median value of $44,400. Typically, such housing values indicate considerable vulnerability to disasters. Such economic challenges had resulted in discussions with a developer to erect high-rise condominiums in Bayou la Batre (Gaillard 2007).

In contrast to the rest of the Gulf Coast and to the 1906 hurricane, no one died in Bayou la Batre in 2005. But Katrina's 16-foot storm surge destroyed 75 percent of the housing and left 1,700 people homeless. Similar to The Grand Bayou, residents bravely endured the storm to save fishing boats as their primary means to feed their families, but the downtown was lost along with the local school and the library. Damage to the sewage system resulted in bay contamination and local residents endured dangerous bacterial infections (Elliot 2006; Callaway and Moore 2010; Marus 2010). The first help they got from outside the area came when Mennonite Disaster Service and Mennonite Central Committee arrived with food and blankets more than a week after Katrina's landfall.

HURRICANES RITA AND IKE

Hurricane Rita followed on the heels of Katrina, making landfall on September 24, 2005, near Galveston Island, Texas. As a category 5 with 175 mph winds, Rita compelled massive evacuations inland. A 15-foot storm surge rolled through Cameron Parish, Louisiana, but advance evacuation reduced directly attributable deaths to seven residents. Though the winds dropped to 150 mph upon arriving at the coast, tropical force winds were felt as far north as the Louisiana, Texas, and Arkansas borders. Debris made roads impassable in affected areas across Louisiana and Texas (NOAA 2005). Hurricane Rita dropped to tropical storm status, with winds below 75 mph, but still caused damage inland, emerging as the second costliest hurricane in U.S. history. Lake Charles, Louisiana suffered as did the Sabine Pass area in East Texas. The Sabine Pass area along the Texas-Louisiana border, which experienced a 9.4-foot storm surge from Hurricane Audrey in 1957, saw a 9.8-foot surge from Rita.

Occurring so closely after Katrina, people affected by Rita felt forgotten. They would sense further neglect when, three years later, another hurricane named Ike moved into Texas and then crossed into Louisiana.

Hurricane Ike occurred September 13, 2008, making landfall as a category 2 on Galveston Island, Texas. Though the intensity level seemed far less than that of Katrina and Rita, the massive wind field proved destructive. Ike measured 450 miles wide less than 48 hours before coming ashore. The storm reached as far as 275 miles out from its center, comparable to a category 4 storm (FEMA 2010). And to the east of Galveston, Ike's right front quadrant surged through the bay and into the Sabine River, heavily damaging homes, schools, and public buildings (Kraus and Lin 2009). Louisiana did not escape Ike either, with 7–9 feet of water pushing into Cameron, Vermilion and Calcasieu Parishes. Becoming the third costliest storm in U.S. history, Ike ravaged parts of East Texas and then moved east, adding insult to injury in Cameron Parish, Louisiana.

Hurricane Rita, Cameron Parish, Louisiana

Cameron Parish, in the southwestern corner of Louisiana, stretches slowly out to the Gulf, from the urban center of Lake Charles into rural farm and fishing communities just above sea level. With a population slightly under 10,000 people, the coastal parish enjoys both environmental riches and economic challenges. Rice pans out in sea-level fields, in an economy supplemented by oil and gas industries. Trucking brings land and sea crops inland. Cattle herds dot the area as well. In the off-season, commercial fishers rely on trapping to bring in money. People living in Cameron Parish before Rita earned a $15,348 per capita income with a median household income of $35,998 (Tootle 2007). Environmentally, the parish features some beautiful stretches of beach as well as wetlands resplendent with wildlife. Visitors enjoy the Creole Nature Trail National Scenic Byway which meanders through the parish. They can stop at the Southwest Louisiana National Wildlife Refuge and also the Cameron Prairie National Wildlife refuge, where 9,621 acres of marsh and prairie (some formerly rice fields) host migratory flocks. Driving along, one can easily spot roseate spoonbills and white ibis rising from a field, with neotropic cormorants, anhingas, yellow-crowned night herons, tri-colored herons, and ospreys luring avid birdwatchers. Annually, about 30,000 people visit area nature spots (U.S. Fish and Wildlife Service, no date). Sport fishing also lures tourists, with 66 charter boats operating out of Cameron, resulting in $12,947,178 in annual retail sales not including food and lodging (Louisiana Speaks, no date). Cameron Parish is a beautiful, though challenging, place that local residents call home.

Long-time residents know the destructive power of hurricanes. An early season category 4 hurricane named Audrey aimed itself at Cameron Parish in June 1957 and ultimately claimed about 525 lives with one third under the age of nine. Audrey destroyed 60 percent to 80 percent of the parish's built environment (Keim and Muller, 2009; Post 2007). Maximum sustained winds for Audrey are unknown but estimated to have potentially reached 100 mph. In contrast, Rita held 77 mph sustained winds with gusts to 120 mph. Further inland, Lake Charles (about 25 miles from the heart of the parish) felt 75 mph sustained winds and 97 mph gusts from Audrey compared to 76 mph sustained winds and 96 mph gusts from Rita. The storm surge from Audrey in Cameron Parish measured 10.6 feet in comparison to 16.2 feet for Rita (NOAA 2009).

Rita devastated Cameron Parish. Water covered the roads, pushed oil into the refuges and took the buildings. In the parish seat, only the water tower and courthouse remained. The parish lost three of six schools, medical and dental facilities, five fire stations, four community recreation centers, four libraries, the school board office, and police facilities. Six water districts sustained damage along with sand intrusion into the sewer system. At least 250 commercial fishing boats were damaged, with few being insured sufficiently to return to the sea. Most of the churches in the heavily Baptist area suffered badly. Rita also caused massive damage to housing. Of the 3,500 pre-storm housing units, about 90 percent sustained damage. Assessing structures in the area, the U.S. Army Corps of Engineers deemed 2,691 private property structures (homes and outbuildings) to be "unsound." The Sabine National Wildlife Refuge suffered saltwater intrusion along with building debris that contained hazardous materials. Calcasieu Lake took a hit as well, with an unknown amount of debris pushing into the 27,000 hectare body of water. Thousands of 100-year-old live oak trees were lost (Louisiana Speaks, no date).

Advance warning and evacuations proved valuable as no deaths occurred during Rita. However, residents have struggled to recover, a particular challenge "given the rurality and depressed socioeconomic conditions" (Tootle 2007, p. 13). Even in the parish seat of Cameron, one local said, "It is hard for the kids; there is no place to play." The high school graduated 70 seniors every year before Rita, a number reduced to 20 in 2006. Everything took a hit: "We are hoping we can keep the football team; it's important to Cameron Parish." In the parish's smaller towns obliterated by Rita, it would take years to seem normal again. Hackberry, with an 8 feet storm surge, and Johnson Bayou, dealing with 12.4 feet of surge, faced long waits for aid in the shadow of Katrina.

Hurricane Rita, East Texas

Small towns, named for early white settlers (Bon Weir, Weirgate, Newton, Burkeville), dot both Newton and Jasper countries which lie along the Texas-Louisiana border. Newton County emerged from Jasper County, Texas in 1846, though locals have uncovered spearheads dating back 5,000 years. Rich timber resources have spurred growth in the area, coupled with the navigable Sabine River. Texas cowboys once drove distinctive longhorn cattle through Newton County en route to Louisiana. Steamboats and ferries moved along the Sabine River, transporting both people and merchandise to and from a coastal port and railway (Newton County Historical Commission 1996).

Today, rural roads (unpaved and paved), lead travelers into smaller towns, isolated neighborhoods and farms. The county motto, "Friendly people, fresh water, and clean air," suggests a close connection to area resources (Newton County Historical Commission, no date, 1986, 1996). Fishing, boating, and bird-watching lure locals and outsiders. Local timber distinguishes the area as part of the Piney Woods of Texas. A 30,000 acre virgin tract of yellow pine could once produce 500,000,000 feet of lumber. However, heavy logging nearly depleted the once-abundant timber used to make homes, churches, bridges, and cypress shingles and to heat homes, produce maple sugar, and earn a livelihood (Newton County Historical Commission 1996). Despite a replanting program in the 1950s, the timber supply ultimately tumbled again.

Economic disparities characterize the area: "this is one of the second or third poorest counties in Texas," explained an area resident. Economic struggles stem from continued, uneven access to livelihoods, especially in Newton County. "Economically if you own your own land you can make money," said another local resident, "but most is owned by companies. The work here is hard, hot, and dirty. A trucker can make some money but there are no benefits for anyone." A member of the clergy added, "you would swear it is the third world here. Homes are shacks here. They are tumbledown; snakes fall through the holes in the roof. The floors are not sealed. Housing is abysmal here. We were on the precipice of falling and the hurricane pushed us off."

In East Texas, Rita hammered both coastal and inland counties. Newton County lost 55 single family homes, with major damage to another 355 and minor damage to 1000; 60 mobile homes were lost along with major damage to 175 more and minor damage to over 400. Sabine County lost 20 homes with major damage to another 99 and minor damage to 508; 40 mobile homes were destroyed with major damage to another 255 and problems with a remaining 582. Tyler County lost 150 homes with major damage to 375 and minor to 459; 131 mobile homes were lost to Rita with major damage to 450 and minor damage to 650 (Texas Department of Emergency Management 2005). Because of the attention paid to the recent damage of Katrina, many survivors and county officials thought of Rita as "The forgotten hurricane." A faith-based partner noted, "The area was devastated, the eye passed through Newton. It was a category 3 here, 115 mph; people can't believe it but it is true. Trees and poles were down. The place looked like it was bombed out."

Even though respondents in this area described themselves as "forgotten" after Rita, faith remains. The first Methodist minister in Texas had been assigned to Newton in 1834 with a church built around 1850. Baptists built a church in 1844 and the Biloxi C.M.E. church met first in 1870. When Mennonite volunteers arrived to clean up debris, start demolition, repair, and rebuild homes after Rita, "They found my wedding dress which was moldy," one interviewee offered, adding in amazement, "but my Bible was not damaged—at all."

Hurricane Ike

Ike, in 2008, poured salt water into a wound opened by Rita, as explained by a west Louisiana client who said, "Rita took the boat, Ike took our doublewide." Though Cameron Parish suffered again, so did parishes farther north and inland in both western Louisiana and east Texas. As observed by a Louisiana community official, "Water pushed up through the canal into other canals and bayous. It coincided with a high tide and heavy rain, the worst we've ever had." Inland communities in and around New Iberia, Louisiana (about 40 miles north from the coast) sustained flood damage, which was particularly severe in the homes of the poor, seniors, and people with disabilities. Routine home maintenance, which people on low or restricted incomes could ill-afford, had been long deferred, resulting in roof damage when tropical force winds passed through. A community partner explained the situation as "not so much hurricane damage, but when you took off the shingles to put on new, you realized the whole house was rotten." Federal funds do not typically allow for such repairs, and those living in such residences faced permanent displacement.

Believing that Ike would miss them, many in East Texas remained in their homes only to be traumatized into near-immobility by the fearful winds. Huge trees came down on homes and blocked access into neighborhoods. In the words of an East Texas partner, "Ike grazed us to the west or it would have been the end of Newton." The material possessions, representing safety and economic security, were not the only treasures lost. A MDS client, whose husband had died several years earlier, missed the flowers he planted at their home when "Ike took them." The first thing she would do in her rebuilt home would be to plant rose bushes.

WHY DO PEOPLE LIVE "THERE"?

Given the extraordinary risks coastal residents face with hurricanes, why do people want to return? Answers can be found by understanding why and how people form attachments to places. Socially, psychologically, and economically, places give us a sense of identity and connection. We know who we are because of where we are. We are Americans, Canadians, African American, Native American or Acadians/Cajuns with a distinct sense of culture, history, and heritage linked to the land, environment, and surroundings. The music we know, the food we eat and the way we greet each other are all influenced by where we come from. Even when we move far away from "home," we still carry an accent, a taste for familiar spices, the sound of birds, a view of the bayou, the smell of the sea, or the liveliness of urbanism in our collective memories.

Different kinds of ties link us to places (Hummon 1986, 1990; Phillips 2009). *Orientational ties* help us find our way around. Tourists become lost in the complexity of New Orleans, which locals know as a series of familiar, adjacent neighborhoods with distinct boundaries. Although architecture, culture, and economic status vary across the neighborhoods, people remain linked by common history and heritage. *Place role ties* tell us how to act, such as whether to make eye contact when greeting a Native American from a particular Louisiana tribe. *Communal ties* include chosen kin, those not related by legal or ancestral connections who help us survive stress. *Value ties* are defined as links to places we find desirable. We may prefer to live in a bayou where we feel connected to the land and animals, emerging from that experience as guardians of place. Or perhaps we prefer a small coastal town where our families have fished and shrimped for decades, built homes alongside each other, and raised children.

Disasters cause us to reflect on those ties and to make conscious decisions about why we should return. Leaving can undermine our entire identity and sense of connection to people, places, history, and culture. Rebuilding in a new location requires more than physical materials: we have to start over by constructing new identities in unfamiliar locations. The process of recovery can be disconcerting and traumatic (Norris et al. 2002a, 2002b; Phillips 1996; Garrison 1985). Ultimately, though, we all want the same thing: to go home to a familiar place with nearby family, neighbors, friends, churches, schools, and livelihoods. We just want to go home.

NOTE

1. I am indebted to Jake Ressler for research on Bayou la Batre.

TWO

Disaster Recovery

This one is different.
—Voluntary Organization, FEMA Joint Field Office, 2005

INTRODUCTION

Hundreds of thousands of coastal residents contacted the government for assistance after Katrina, many of them for the first time in their lives. Cell phones did not work in most affected areas, sometimes for several weeks. Calls to the Federal Emergency Management Agency (FEMA) did not go through or a damaged cellular infrastructure dropped calls. Overwhelmed by the numbers of those affected, online aid systems timed out or crashed. Surviving the event transitioned into yet another ordeal: to make it through the aid application process and start the journey back home. Then came Rita, and later Ike, compounding the misery.

In major disasters, FEMA opens a Joint Field Office (JFO) where people and organizations coordinate under the National Response Framework (NRF). Most voluntary organizations collaborate under the NRF's Emergency Support Function (ESF) #6 to deliver mass care, emergency assistance, housing, and human services (see FEMA, no date a). Facilitated by FEMA's Voluntary Agency Liaison (VAL), the organizations attend to a wide range of interests and resources. About two weeks after Katrina, FEMA VALs convened voluntary organizations at a local Catholic church in Baton Rouge. Dozens of organizations then fanned out to extend resources to survivors.

But the effort felt overwhelming even to experienced organizations, many dealing with a catastrophic event that taxed capacities at all levels (Quarantelli 2006). Any potential project felt meager in contrast to the physical damage and human pain wrought by the storm. In Mississippi and Alabama, debris that blocked entry, along with damage to bridges and roads, made needs assessments difficult. Water that lingered from the levee breaches in Plaquemines, St. Bernard, and Orleans parishes made it impossible to enter the area for over a month—and even then going into the area felt dangerous: muck, insects, and concern over a "toxic brew" of oil and chemicals spread through contaminated flooding. Most disaster voluntary organizations start by finding those most vulnerable to the impact of disasters. But with public officials stretched beyond exhaustion and community leaders scattered across the country, voluntary organizations found it nearly impossible to establish initial contact and say "we're here to help."

SOCIAL VULNERABILITY

Disasters are not equal opportunity events. Predictably, some populations simply have far more trouble, revealing deeply embedded social problems (Barton 1970). Many low-income homes cannot resist area hazards. Affordable housing tends to be located in or near floodplains, locations which subject lower-income families to flooding. Older homes, where lower-income families and senior citizens live in higher concentrations, fail to meet more recent and stringent building codes. Understandably, people living in homes less likely to survive disasters are more likely to suffer property losses, sustain injuries, and die at higher rates, as happened in areas hit by Katrina (Sharkey 2007).

Vulnerability theory explains that social, economic, and political contexts produce inequitable effects (Phillips and Fordham 2010; Wisner et al. 2004). For those facing disaster, race and ethnicity, age, disability, medical conditions, and gender rank among the factors considered most important (Thomas et al. 2013; Heinz Center 2002; Cutter 1996). Embedded patterns of discrimination further limit opportunities to earn incomes that allow those marginalized to secure safer housing (Dash 2010; Bolin 2006). Historic patterns of segregation mark racial and ethnic relations and place people at risk for disasters (Cutter 2006). Native Americans and African Americans, pushed onto flood-prone lands others did not want, may endure repetitive losses. New immigrants may move into areas familiar economically (such as for fishing) but vulnerable physically. Because of the presence of important historic and cultural elements, such as burial grounds or buried resources, people stay in meaningful places and lay claim to ancestral legacies. Such is the case in Grand Bayou, where Atakapa-Ishaak descendants safeguard their past and advocate for environmental preservation. Louisiana Cajuns, French-speaking people displaced centuries ago from Canada, cling tenaciously to a clear identity and cultural way of life despite stereotypes. Similar circumstances exist in New Orleans, where neighborhoods populated historically by African Americans have struggled with poverty, predatory lending, and unemployment while simultaneously working together to improve schools, reduce crime, build playgrounds, and support neighborhood businesses.

Not surprisingly then, low-income and minority households are more often subject to disaster damage (Bolin 1994; Bolin and Bolton 1983). Lower incomes result in a household unable to maintain their homes or to afford to repair damage from previous storms (Peacock, Dash and Zhang 2006). Pre-disaster inequalities also influence the battle to secure post-disaster resources. After Hurricane Andrew in 1992, minority neighborhoods faced slower recoveries when insurance companies underwrote coverage and African Americans received less government assistance (Peacock and Girard 1997; Dash et al. 1997; Lu et al. 2007). Post-disaster sales and property abandonment rates also increased at a faster rate in low-income and minority areas leaving minorities worse off while others recovered (Lu et al. 2007; Zhang and Peacock 2010). One long-term study of Andrew found that some minority families affected by Andrew never recovered, living in units still lacking electrical power ten years after the storm (Dash, Morrow, and Mainster 2007).

Societal inability to reasonably accommodate people with disabilities also worsens disaster impacts. Problems with evacuation, public shelters that lack appropriate resources, inaccessible temporary housing, disrupted access to health care, and a lack of affordable, post-disaster housing means that people with disabilities take longer to recover (National Organization on Disability 2005; National Council on Disability 2009). Medical conditions that prevent people from participating in recovery efforts make it more difficult to rebuild (Fernandez et al. 2000). Elderly residents find assistance applications frustrating and may fail to access available aid. Helping such populations requires experienced case managers who know where to turn for resources, with both in short supply after a catastrophic event (Stough and Sharp 2008; Fernandez et al. 2000).

Gender also influences disaster experiences (Heinz Center 2002). Further, a majority of single parents are female with nearly half of them below the poverty line. After Hurricane Andrew struck southern Florida in 1992, single mothers living in public housing struggled to recover (Enarson and Morrow 1997). Other stressors, such as abuse, pregnancy, lack of child care and job loss complicate efforts to participate in recovery (Phillips, Jenkins, and Enarson 2010; Jenkins and Phillips 2008, 2009; Enarson, Fothergill, and Peek 2006; Wilson, Phillips, and Neal 1998; Webb et al. 2000).

Katrina hit all of these populations especially hard. In the U.S., recovery depends on a combination of private savings, insurance, and government aid. The economically marginalized may have neither private savings nor insurance; therefore government aid may represent their only post-disaster resource. But traditional disaster assistance may not cover complex recovery needs. For example, a single mother may need to re-build close to her source of employment among kin who help with child care. An elderly couple may require a ramp or elevators in areas where building codes require that homes be elevated above storm surge levels. A parent caring for a child with a disability may need bathroom adapta-tions. An African American neighborhood may need its pastor back to provide spiritual care. A Vietnamese American community may shy away from outside organizations, having been hurt previously by a lack of cultural sensitivity. Understanding such needs often falls to faith-based and voluntary organizations sensitized by experience and belief systems. To illustrate, MDS altered housing construction practices to save a tree in more than one Native American community. Though small in contrast to the damage of Katrina, such an effort supports concerns raised by culturally marginalized residents in a context of environmental degra-dation (Bolin 2006). Faith-based organizations appear to offer the flexibil-ity needed to rebuild not only homes but the spirit of survival and the opportunity to return to meaningful ways of life.

HOUSING RECOVERY

Most people just want to go home after a disaster, to familiar locations, valuable social networks, and jobs. Doing so was not easy after the 2005 storms, and organizations that faced helping hundreds of thousands of displaced residents soon realized "this one is different." The catastrophic impact of Katrina, coupled with Rita, meant that those assisting had to organize disaster housing recovery at a scale previously not experienced. In 2006, the Federal Coordinator for Gulf Coast Recovery released num-bers based primarily on financial cost and graded into the categories of minor (less than $5,200), major (up to $30,000) and severe (over $30,000) for Hurricanes Katrina and Rita. Table 2.1 summarizes those data to illus-trate the magnitude of the task facing homeowners, elected and ap-pointed officials, and voluntary organizations as they looked across an affected area the size of the United Kingdom. When hurricane Ike came three years later, the state of Texas lost over 8,000 housing units for a total of $3.4 billion in losses (Texas Division of Emergency Management 2008).

But government reports conceal important issues. Federal numbers count only those who have applied for assistance, and they do not in-clude applicants who give up in the face of bureaucratic paperwork, personal life complications, or language barriers. Federal counts also in-clude only those places where federal agencies have inspected damage. Inspectors may refuse to enter an area over concerns of personal safety, as has been the case in some bayou communities, the majority of which are populated by racial and ethnic minorities and recent immigrants. Numbers also obscure who is affected. According to the National Low

Table 2.1.   Housing Damage[i] from Hurricanes Katrina and Rita

	Louisiana [ii]	Mississippi [iii]	Texas [iv]	Alabama [v]
Minor damage in 100 year floodplain	15,675	624	108	824
Major damage in 100 year floodplain	50,566	7,854	52	1,347
Severe damage in 100 year floodplain	80,566	6,666		147
Minor damage outside 100 year floodplain	6,809	3,984	581	1,270
Major damage outside 100 year floodplain	15,749	21,183	479	952
Severe damage outside 100 year floodplain	22,033	5,407	54	65
Minor wind damage	288,028	154,390	127,118	51,593
Major wind damage	31,771	16,739	9,992	937
Severe wind damage	4,153	3,537	1,526	236
Population	1,656,053	1,046,434	7,393,354	1,737,080
Percentage of state population affected	31%	21%	2%	3%

i Minor damage is less than $5,200; major damage runs from $5,201 to $30,000; severe damage exceeds $30,000.
ii Louisiana includes damage from Katrina and Rita.
iii Mississippi includes damage from Katrina.
iv Texas includes damage from Rita.
v Alabama includes damage from Katrina.
Source: Cumulated from the Office of the Federal Coordinator for Gulf Coast Rebuilding. 2006. *Current Housing Units Damage Estimates Hurricanes Katrina, Rita and Wilma.* Washington, DC: Department of Homeland Security. This report also offers county and parish breakdowns of housing damages across affected areas.

Income Housing Coalitions (2005), of the 302,000 housing units destroyed or damaged by Katrina, approximately 216,000 units represented "affordable to low income housing." Thus, Katrina destroyed or damaged 71 percent of the housing categorized as affordable to low-income and 30 percent of affordable to very-low-income. In New Orleans alone, 142,000 units sustained damage with 79 percent (112,000 units) in the affordable to low-income range and 40 percent (57,000) of the units at affordable to very-low-income levels. In short, people who were poor fared badly with Katrina. Similar results occurred for hurricanes Rita and Ike.

Recovery begins with survivors searching for resources to rebuild their lives, homes, jobs, and communities. In the U.S., we use the "limited intervention model" of recovery assistance where individuals rely on personal resources such as savings and insurance with some help from government (Comerio 1998, 1997). What kind of assistance does the government provide? Dismayed survivors realize that federal assistance comes with limits. First, officials in the damaged areas must conduct a preliminary damage assessment and then submit a request for assistance through the state's governor to the Federal Emergency Management Agency (FEMA). Next, FEMA makes a recommendation to the President of the United States, who may release funds through a Presidential Disaster Declaration and subject to the Stafford Act (as amended). Many disaster survivors should be able to secure low-interest loans through the Small Business Administration. Those denied loans, usually low-income households, may qualify for a grant through FEMA's Individual Assistance programs. Legislation allows FEMA to provide grants for temporary housing, eligible repairs, or reconstruction. Applicants must qualify by income levels and can only receive a specified and limited amount of funding. After Katrina, the maximum allowable grant provided $26,200. To secure that grant, applicants needed to submit their claim to FEMA, wait for an inspection of their property, and hope they would be approved. Denials could be appealed but some homeowners gave up trying to survive the paperwork and waiting period to re-process the claim.

FEMA grants, combined with an insurance payout, might be enough to rebuild a small home but homeowners may need additional funds. After Katrina, many homeowners found themselves without the safety net they thought insurance premiums provided when insurance companies balked at paying for wind or flooding damage. Some homeowners realized their payouts would not cover specific costs like debris removal. Lower-income homeowners may have reduced or even dropped their insurance coverage, or realized they could not afford a high deductible. The limited-intervention model thus "tends to favor creditworthy home owners over poor or financially strapped home owners" (Comerio 1998, p. 127). To meet the needs for funding, organizations and states wrote grants, solicited donations, and funded special programs. But even for these programs, some homeowners failed to qualify or gave up trying. The Road Home program in Louisiana, for instance, provided additional dollars but was criticized for red tape and long waits for approval. Survivors thus end up battling for scarce resources that diminish as the years pass (Peacock and Ragsdale 1997). Voluntary organizations, especially within the faith-based community, may step into the gap people experience because of the limited intervention model. One such effort by Louisiana's Southern Mutual Help Association (SMHA) provided funds to qualified applicants and partnered with other voluntary organizations. By 2010, SMHA had sent 4,432 volunteers to rebuild or repair hurricane damaged homes, primarily in low-income, rural areas. Of those volunteers, 2,029 came from Mennonite Disaster Service.

STANDING IN THE GAP

When outsiders look at a community destroyed by an event, they focus on human elements—the pain and suffering, families separated perhaps forever, and the loss of housing. Altruistic values shared across most communities inspire outsiders to help by aiding those affected to pick up the pieces of their homes and lives. Without such help, many people would never return home again, especially those made vulnerable through low incomes, medical or disability conditions, or other circumstances. Given the limited intervention model, many people fall through the gap between government assistance and personal resources. Volunteers bridge that chasm.

Imagine, for example, the plight of an elderly woman who has lost her home. She provides care for a husband, who must visit health care facilities weekly. It is not easy to maneuver his wheelchair into and out of a home that does not have a ramp or a car without a lift. The couple's combined resources from Social Security and Medicare Part D drug coverage falls short every month. To make do, they stretch out their food budget by reducing the amount of protein in their diet, which is needed to keep them strong and healthy. Over time, they reduce their insurance coverage hoping that the home they lived in for decades, close to church, children, and neighbors, will survive the next storm. Then, Katrina hits. They are lucky, as their children move in quickly to evacuate with them to a public shelter. But they have never been in such a place and feel uncomfortable among thousands of strangers. Though there is adequate food, it is unfamiliar and at times hard to digest. A volunteer comes by and encourages them to get on the Internet (something they have never done) to view the damage. As they watch the maps zoom in, they realize with dismay that water has claimed their home. She leans over, exhausted, and he hangs his head in disbelief. For the first time, they acquire an email address to be able to file a FEMA application on the Internet. Yet, even with insurance and FEMA funds, they do not have enough to rebuild. Anxiety increases and before they even leave the shelter, he is taken by ambulance to the hospital, and then transferred to a nursing home. But they are the lucky ones. A local city employee who attends their church knows their story. Because the city employee serves on the long-term recovery committee, she invites them to apply for housing assistance. With the help of a case worker, who herself is displaced by the storm, they develop a plan for recovery. Through a combination of insurance, federal funds, and donations to the community, the couple's local recovery committee brings in a volunteer team to clear debris, gut the house, and start repairs. The gap between recovery and permanent displacement narrows, because volunteers cut the costs through contributing personal labor.

Long-term recovery committees, often organized by the FEMA VAL with support from external, experienced disaster partners, form the backbone of such local recovery efforts. With support from the National or State Voluntary Organizations Active in Disaster (VOAD), locals form partnerships with outsiders and learn who to trust to walk alongside, face the damage, and rebuild. Most of the local partners have never done this kind of work before. While rebuilding their own homes, local long-term recovery committees help their neighbors, moving into long hours of public service that often go unnoticed by the majority of the community. Typically, committees hold long and frequent meetings, listening to needs assessment presentations by Christian World Relief, and then to case managers trained by the United Methodist Committee on Relief as they describe client needs. They sort through financial analyses vis-à-vis available funds and work out a plan with funds from Catholic Charities to put in a ramp or elevator, household donations managed by Seventh Day Adventists, roofing supplies from Lutheran Disaster Response, paint from a local Baptist organization, and voluntary labor from Mennonite Disaster Service or Presbyterian Disaster Assistance.

Though federal funds and insurance provide at least a partial means to fund rebuilding, many people need additional assistance. After hurricane Ike, which damaged numerous homes of elderly residents, Texas reported that "nongovernmental organizations (NGO) and governmental agencies are joining together to locate these individuals and assist in the cleaning and restoration of their homes" (Texas Division of Emergency Management 2008, p. 19). Without this behind-the-scenes community of government and non-government organizations, many people would fall through the cracks and never get home. Katrina, Rita and Ike, unequaled in their disastrous impacts, also produced record volunteer turnout across the Gulf Coast.

Why Do People Volunteer?

People volunteer for several reasons. American culture socializes people to serve. Having been raised to be altruistic, people give their "time, money and energy" to those in need (Dynes 1994; see also Fritz and Mathewson 1956). Disasters also generate what researchers call situational altruism. When potential volunteers see a disaster area and hear the plight of those affected, they assume that newly desperate people need help.

After the Johnstown flood in 1889, for example, the American Red Cross responded to Pennsylvanians in need of food and water, medical care, and shelter (McCullough 1987; FEMA, no date). The same is true today. People who become aware of disaster-caused devastation assume that personal savings and government budgets do not afford sufficient means to recover—and that people need help. Unexpected numbers of volunteers converge quickly on disaster scenes and unsolicited donations (usually used clothing and canned goods) overwhelm distributing organizations (Piliavin and Charng 1990). Social psychologists explain this behavior as a result of learning pro-social values from our family, peers, and faith traditions In addition, individual characteristics like gender, race, age, and religion influence volunteer turnout (Lam 2002; Ruiter and DeGraaf 2006).

For example, women volunteer more than men, particularly in the U.S. though less so in Europe (Ruiter and DeGraaf 2006). Gender roles also influence volunteer assignments as women may be "steered toward women's work, more of the caring, person-to-person tasks and fewer of the public, political activities and they are less likely to be found in leadership positions" (Wilson 2000, p. 228). Women's place in the life cycle also contributes to age-influenced volunteerism, with younger women more likely to volunteer than women with small children or in the workforce.

Indeed, volunteering tends to be highest among younger and older people, dropping off in the middle years for both men and women as they raise families and work longer hours. Furthermore, parents who volunteer socialize their children to do so. And volunteering early on indicates they may do so later in life. McAdam (1990) looked up volunteers who participated in Freedom Summer, the major civil rights movement events of 1964. Decades later, participants were still dedicated to volunteerism, a trend particularly noticeable among women. There may also be a related "cohort" effect, meaning that the age cohort we are born into may influence higher volunteerism (Ruiter and DeGraaf 2006). Being a baby boomer, for example, appears to be associated with increased rates of volunteerism.

Several researchers have looked at race and volunteering, initially finding differences across races. However, when studies control for education, income, occupation, and neighborhood conditions, racial and ethnic differences diminish (Wilson 2000, p. 228). Still, studies also show that "much volunteer recruitment is intraracial" (Musick, Wilson and Bynum 2000, p. 1560). Churches appear to serve as a mobilizing location for volunteerism, and in faith-based settings, "blacks are more influenced by their church than are whites" (Wilson 2000, p. 228; Musick, Wilson and Bynum 2000).

Certainly, religion functions as one of the most critical of all social institutions. Religious institutions organize rituals that move us gently and supportively through life transitions. Faith frames social celebrations of births and marriages, provides a means to build relationships and community solidarity, explains sudden bereavement, and offers meaning in the face of confusion, chaos, and loss (Durkheim 1912). Religious beliefs also guide people in searching for meaning and purpose (Smith, Pargament, Brant and Oliver 2000; Spence, Lachlan and Burke 2007; Ahler and Tamney 1964). Religious beliefs offer a "broader rationale for service" that moves people to look beyond themselves (Becker and Dhingra 2001, p. 332). Worship attendance is also associated with volunteerism. The more frequently people attend worship services, the more likely they are to volunteer (Ruiter and DeGraaf 2006). However, just sitting and listening to an inspiring sermon is not the only influence that sends people out to serve: the relationships that form through regular attendance embed us in social networks that recruit, motivate, and reinforce volunteerism (Becker and Dhingra 2001). The type of congregation matters as well. For example, the "family" congregation, where parishioners experience close social relationships, is more likely to encourage participation in group missions (Becker 1999).

People living in more devout societies (such as the U.S.) also volunteer at higher rates than people in more secular societies (Ruiter and DeGraaf 2006). In terms of faith traditions, conservative Protestants volunteer at higher rates than either Catholics or Jews (Ruiter and Degraaf 2006). Not surprisingly, religious affiliation creates a spillover effect into secular service, with Catholics volunteering at a higher rate than Protestants (Ruiter and DeGraaf 2006). Liberals tend to see volunteerism as their civic duty while conservatives view volunteering as a spiritual act to express their belief systems (Becker and Dhingra 2001). Clearly, though, faith serves as a motivational force in compelling people to serve. Most faith traditions also see their role in attending to those affected by tragedy and have developed faith-based organizations to do so. Surprisingly, though, we do not know much about why people, particularly people of faith, volunteer in one of the most trying of circumstances: disaster. Yet thousands of volunteers feel compelled to leave their work and families, donate vacation time and personal funds, and travel into the lives of complete strangers to heal those wounded by disaster. The most effective volunteers work through experienced, disaster-focused organizations.

The Role and Value of Faith-Based Disaster Organizations

In terms of disasters, most studies have noted the arrival of spontaneous, unannounced volunteers or "SUV's" who converge on a disaster scene (Fritz and Mathewson 1956; NVOAD, n.d.). Such volunteers usually arrive without a disaster-affiliated organization to support them but eager to clean up, repair, and rebuild. Yet immediately after a disaster, hazardous conditions still exist and most local residents and officials have yet to determine when, how, and where they will pick up and rebuild, let alone where to put the debris. Many SUV's go un-used because they lack training, credentials, or experience (Neal 1993, 1994). Volunteers may leave feeling unappreciated, not realizing that their labor will be needed months-to-years down the road, after the long work of recovery commences.

In contrast, volunteers affiliated with experienced organizations usually have a useful skill or learn under supervision that enables them to make a meaningful contribution (Britton 1991). In the long-term recovery faced by Katrina, Rita, and Ike survivors, the contributions of affiliated volunteers embedded in experienced disaster organizations proved invaluable for efforts from reconstruction to rebuilding lives.

Religion provides an organized structure, such as traditional mission teams, through which people can serve. For many Louisiana congregations, the level of disaster response after Katrina was significant. Churches, mosques, and other places of worship opened their doors to shelter thousands of displaced residents. In a study of 157 Baton Rouge area churches, 69.4 percent used donations to provide food, clothing, and financial assistance (Cain and Barthelemy 2008). A full 75 percent of churches in the Baton Rouge study tried to connect evacuees with external resources such as FEMA. Close to one-half assisted families with reuniting by linking evacuees through databases, telephones, and the Internet. When people realized they would not be going home any time soon, congregations collected funds, found temporary housing, helped evacuees search for jobs, reunited separated families, and held funeral services (Phillips and Jenkins 2009; Jenkins 2012). Indeed, organizational adaptation has proven valuable in meeting needs after other major disasters, such as when religious organizations modified internally to meet needs generated after September 11th (Sutton 2003).

Many denominations support faith-based organizations (FBOs) such as Southern Baptist Convention Disaster Relief, NECHAMA-Jewish Response to Disaster, Presbyterian Disaster Assistance, Lutheran Disaster Response, and Mennonite Disaster Service. Typically, faith-based organizations send volunteers during three post-disaster phases: immediately after impact, during short-term recovery and for the long days of rebuilding homes and lives. FBOs that respond to disasters have become more specialized over time. Baptist men, for example, move in large, mobile kitchens to feed thousands of survivors, first responders, and fellow aid organizers. Their mobile showers represent a particularly appreciated service when homes have been destroyed and infrastructure disrupted. The Church of the Brethren provides credentialed and trained child care workers capable of offering multicultural and therapeutic activities (Peek, Sutton and Gump 2008). The Seventh Day Adventists work with community and faith-based groups to sort and distribute massive quantities of unsolicited donations.

And when media attention wanes and the public moves on to its next concern, many FBOs remain. Now is when the real work of recovery begins for socially vulnerable populations. The faith-based sector, in concert with local leadership, works quietly behind the scenes to catch those who would otherwise fall through the cracks of available assistance. The key to making their efforts successful is an effective long-term recovery framework coupled with appropriate and sustained case management. In such cases, outside organizations like the United Methodist Committee on Relief (UMCOR) may guide locals through what has worked elsewhere. Though such a process should be in place to do this type of work, the reality is that most communities never plan for recovery. Local recovery work thus usually emerges as an ad hoc process, and without the support of experienced, external organizations, may very well fail.

Outside organizations arrive with not only expertise but an array of resources. Depending on a local needs assessment, their contributions may range from rebuilding assistance to economic development and opportunities as well as support for temporary housing, education, counseling, and health care. For rebuilding, the focus of this volume, these organizations bring in expertise, material resources, building plans, funds and—most importantly—volunteer labor. The contributions they make are profound and number in the thousands of hours—yet there are intangible benefits as well.

The Consequences of Volunteering

Common wisdom and personal experience suggest that we get more than we give from volunteering. We feel good about ourselves and the work that we have done. Studies have found that benefits from volunteering fall into several categories: generating social capital, promoting physical and mental health, and improving occupational skills (Wilson and Musick 1999).

"Social capital" is produced when we engage in volunteer activities that provide intangible benefits to both individuals and the broader society. Social capital also accumulates when people work toward a common goal and generate trust among participants and beneficiaries. Though not all voluntary associations generate trust, religious organizations are among the ones that do (Wilson and Musick 1999). The camaraderie that volunteers experience gets carried back to our social networks, which in turn brings more volunteers and spills over to civic society through an increase in local volunteerism.

Volunteers also experience physical and mental health benefits. The link is probably indirect in that volunteering builds strong social networks that reduce stress and related diseases. These health consequences seem to be particularly beneficial for women, including longevity (Wilson and Musick 1999). Physical health benefits also seem more robust for people who volunteer through religious organizations—again, by embedding volunteers in a social network that promotes healthy relationships and behaviors (Rogers 1996). Most studies use self-assessments of mental health from volunteers rather than more objective measures (Wilson and Musick 1999). Those self-assessments do reveal that volunteering makes people feel better. This does not mean we should rush out and dedicate ourselves continually to volunteering, as doing so may result in role strain and mental health issues (Wilson and Musick 1999). Though we are not sure why, "volunteering in a religious context is especially good for mental health" (Wilson and Musick 1999, p. 161) although the effects may be more influential for white women than for Black women (McIntosh and Danigelis 1995).

Occupational gains may accrue as well. Through volunteering, we learn to work as a team and may develop leadership skills transferable to other places, volunteer efforts, or work settings. Women may be the biggest beneficiaries occupationally, as volunteerism seems to be associated with job prestige later in life. Volunteering also appears to increase self-confidence, which may contribute to promotions in the workplace (Wilson and Musick 1999).

To date, though, studies have focused on benefits of volunteering for volunteers. Researchers have not investigated the intangible effects that volunteers have on beneficiaries. Organizations typically enumerate the hours spent, debris cleaned up, and houses rebuilt but share only anecdotal evidence of the effects on beneficiaries. The findings in this volume shed light on the benefits experienced by clients and local community partners who collaborated with one Anabaptist organization, Mennonite Disaster Service.

MENNONITE DISASTER SERVICE

Emergency managers and researchers know that faith-based organizations (FBOs) play a crucial role in housing recovery, with a particular focus on helping those who would otherwise fall through the cracks of federal, state, and local recovery funding and programs. Despite this reality, researchers have rarely examined the role of community and/or faith-based organizations in disaster recovery. Among those FBOs, Mennonite Disaster Service enjoys a reputation as one of the best organizations involved in reconstruction and working with local communities. As described in chapter 3, MDS began in 1950, by focusing on disaster response and relief efforts. Over time, the organization spread rapidly from its Kansas origins across the U.S. and into Canada. Embedded in faith-based notions of service to one's neighbor, the grass-roots organization has turned out many thousands of volunteers for decades of relief and recovery efforts.

Major disasters have produced record numbers of MDS volunteers. In 1972, hurricane Agnes brought 8,200 volunteers who worked a total of 37,000 days in Pennsylvania and New York. In 1992, unique programs and eager volunteers stunned by damage from Hurricane Andrew in Florida and Louisiana served 42,000 work days. The five-year period between 1995 and 2000 saw MDS rebuild 139 homes including efforts for the historic Red River Valley flooding of 1997 that left 50,000 people homeless in North Dakota and Canada. For each event, MDS received funding sufficient to conduct meaningful work and then quietly moved on to the next disaster. Over time, its reputation for quality construction and effective interaction with local communities became well known within the disaster management sector. For most communities, though, their first experience with MDS comes in the turmoil of the days immediately following a disaster. Over time, they begin to understand Anabaptist beliefs and why people come from so far away. Or, as one respondent for this study put it, "God sent them."

The Gulf Coast storms proved to be Mennonite Disaster Service's biggest challenge, with more donations, volunteers, and projects than ever. Between 2005 and 2010, MDS managed the biggest volunteer turnout for a single effort in their history. For the Gulf Coast storms alone, a total of 15,115 volunteers arrived to help after Katrina and Rita. Volunteers worked 112,582 days for Katrina and Rita and 12,803 for Ike (and hurricane Gustav, which occurred within weeks of Ike). In addition to these storms, MDS dispatched volunteer crews to wildfires, tornadoes, floods, and other disasters in the U.S. and Canada. This is their story.

THREE

Mennonite Disaster Service

Why do I do this? To follow Jesus.
—MDS Volunteer, New Orleans, 2009

In late August, a Kansas Mennonite Disaster Service (MDS) volunteer proclaimed to a reporter: "It was terrible. I've never seen anything like it . . . it looked worse than the worst tornado I'd ever seen. When you got down to the real bad parts, there was just nothing left." A Hesston, Kansas man said: "Some barges were washed inland a couple of blocks, and a lot of ships'll have to be destroyed. There were terrible lots of homes wrecked. We went through the poorer sections and they said they didn't know how they were going to clean up."[1] "The mess is indescribable. You read about it, but it's humanly impossible to comprehend the destruction unless you see for yourself," wrote a married couple.[2] Winds nearing 200 miles per hour had battered the area, pushing a 25-foot storm surge through Pass Christian and nearby coastal communities. Local residents buried 134 neighbors and awaited the fate of 23 still missing. With 5,000 homes destroyed and another 36,000 badly damaged, they faced personal and financial devastation. Massive losses to the economic sector made people wonder how they would ever earn a living again.

A local Mennonite pastor described the early days of recovery: "You start this kind of looking around and going to the people you know and seeing if people are ok, trying to get through the maze of debris that blocks the way . . . Highway 90 that was the beach front road, four lane highway, was just crumbled up, just washed out. Most of those beach front buildings, shopping centers, you saw steel girders and everything else was washed out. The eye went through Pass Christian."[3]

Help arrived two days later when an MDS investigator walked off the first plane to land in Gulfport, just ten miles from the "Pass." On the fourth day, a National Guard plane full of Kansas MDS volunteers landed noisily because an engine had failed. Through the following months, volunteers came from nineteen U.S. states as well as Canada. Mennonite students from Goshen and North Manchester Colleges (IN), Hesston and Bethel Colleges (KS), Eastern Mennonite College (VA), Christopher Dock High School (PA), Conrad Grebel University College (Canada), Bluffton College[4] and Archbold High School (OH). Working in hot and humid conditions, they salvaged or burned damaged furniture. Other volunteers conducted emergency repairs and launched home repairs and reconstruction. By February, MDS had sent 1,793 people to Mississippi, contributing 8,955 volunteer days or 62,685 hours of time. Volunteers had completed 690 jobs with 15 new homes well underway. Donors, primarily Anabaptists, contributed $20,488 for projects. Working efficiently and conservatively, MDS still had $6,116 left by February.

But this disaster occurred in late August of 1969 and MDS was responding to people hurt by hurricane Camille (Haines, date unknown; Graber 1970). When MDS arrived, local Mennonite pastor Harold Regier said the volunteers "took on a lot of initiative. You just have to give MDS a lot of credit for knowing how to impact an area, come in and make contacts . . . made a real impact on the initial cleanup work . . . we were in a very very oppressed Black neighborhood. People lost so much in terms of what little they had that the long term work focused there."[5]

MDS's pattern of early investigation, rapid response, conservative use of funds, and focusing on those with the greatest need had been set two decades before Camille and would remain in place for Katrina forty years later. The question that begins this chapter is why did Mennonites go to Pass Christian in 1969, and why did they return in 2005? To answer this question, the chapter begins with Mennonites as descendants of and informed by Anabaptist beliefs, then works through connective stories linking MDS origins to Anabaptism. These connective threads emerged from interviews conducted for this book and represent stories meaningful to MDS volunteers and staff. A subsequent section outlines Mennonite Disaster Service history since 1950. Readers are encouraged to look further into the original and secondary sources as the first section is necessarily limited; a reference section includes additional recommended readings. Historical content is based on original sources, the majority of which can be found in archives open to the public. Original sources are identified in the endnotes.

A LEGACY TO BUILD ON

During interviews conducted for this book, clients and organizational partners spoke compellingly about a mindful presence brought into their communities by volunteers. They characterized the demeanor of MDS volunteers as gentle, team-oriented, non-argumentative, faithful, humble

and service-minded. Many clients mentioned the consistency of volunteer behavior: though crews changed weekly, clients were hard-pressed
to find behavioral deviations. As a man in Texas said, "One of the best
groups of people I have ever met. They do what they say. They live what
they preach. Nearly to the man and the woman. They put their life on
hold to help you." A community partner in Louisiana described volunteer demeanor for many interviewees: "They are a kind and gentle people." A client in a remote bayou contrasted willing labor vis-à-vis the
conditions: "I was blown away. I don't know if they choose people to
come out here from cooler climates but they worked in the mud, wet,
bugs, and heat. They smiled every morning and when they left." She
described further the intangible impact the volunteers made: "They were
singing at another house on a very hot day and it carried down the
bayou. It really made my day. I am still in awe."

What clients and community partners sensed, but did not yet know,
was that Mennonite service orientation emerges from Anabaptist history
and beliefs. The next section of this chapter introduces readers to Mennonites. Connective, historic threads of relief work, peacemaking, and
social and economic justice concerns then lay a foundation for exploring
the origins of MDS.

WHO ARE MENNONITES?

Mennonites as well as Amish, Brethren, and Hutterites descend from a
faith tradition called Anabaptism. Though Switzerland is considered by
many to be the "cradle" of Anabaptism, the ideas of Anabaptism caught
fire throughout Europe with descendents today traced to Switzerland,
Germany, Austria, France, and the Netherlands (Kraybill 2010; Weaver
2005).

Anabaptist Origins

Anabaptism emerged around 1525 in the immediate wake of the Protestant Reformation of 1517 (Kraybill 2010). Critical, reflective action de-
marcates Anabaptists from the dominant religion of the time. Rather than
accept beliefs and rituals mandated by the powerful Catholic Church,
early Anabaptists chose to read scripture for themselves. Cognitive disso-
nance over interpretations, and the lack of scriptural support for practices
such as infant baptism, led them to question religious authority. People
who had been baptized as infants in the Catholic Church chose rebaptism
as adults, which set them apart. The term Anabaptist, or rebaptizer, thus
refers to people who choose to be baptized as adults as a result of intentional consideration over scripture. Dominant religions met such choice
as heresy, and responded by imprisoning, torturing, and martyring Ana-

baptists (Dyck 1993). Catholics burned Anabaptists while Protestants used beheading or drowning in an ultimately unsuccessful effort to thwart the dissidents (Murray 2010).

Other beliefs besides adult baptism set Anabaptists apart. What captured early adherents was a "new ecclesiology . . . when people decided that the story of Jesus and of the early church was the norm for Christian faith and Christian behavior" (Weaver 2005, p. 20). One early leader, Menno Simons, came to believe that following Jesus required "nonresistance, nonswearing of oaths, and endurance of suffering to the point of martyrdom" (Weaver 2005, p. 147). Out of their beliefs and experiences arose consistent "concerns for peace and nonviolence" as a means to demonstrate the faithful manner that was characteristic of Jesus (Weaver 2005, p. 162).

Several views of Anabaptism have since evolved. One dominant view situates Anabaptists not only as followers of Jesus, but through separation from the world by practicing love, brotherhood, and nonresistance in all relationships (based on Bender, see Weaver 2005). A second view places Anabaptists squarely among those who originated ideas about the separation of church and state as well as tolerance and freedom of conscience (based on Smith, see Weaver 2005). A final view locates Anabaptists as a counter-cultural alternative to the dominant society (based on Yoder, see Weaver 2005). Anabaptists believe that Jesus challenges his disciples to address issues of justice, poverty, and social isolation. His association with lepers, prostitutes, and outcasts characterizes the direction his disciples should go (Weaver 2005). Contemporary Anabaptist practice accordingly concerns itself with those marginalized by political and economic circumstances and seeks ways to ameliorate such circumstances among those who have been harmed.

Economic issues come to the forefront for many Anabaptists today as they seek ways to live more simply and share their resources (Murray 2010). Yet sharing does not connote charity. Rather, directly helping others is seen as a matter of justice and a way to extend sixteenth century practices of mutual aid (Murray 2010). The principle of mutual aid has been well-established by Anabaptists, who historically have turned out to help each other in crises, such as with Amish barn raisings or "the readiness of Mennonites to go to disaster zones to help personally in addition to sending donations" (Murray 2010, p. 122). Indeed, "followers of Jesus are to share their resources freely with one another" (Murray 2010, p. 153). Following Jesus, for Anabaptists, compels behaviors that reflect "humility, gentleness, peacefulness and commitment to simplicity" (Murray 2010, p. 158).

Discipleship requires actively participating in mission work, in order to be among those that Jesus would have touched with his life. Doing so reflects a commitment to being the hands and feet of Jesus in the world, with a particular emphasis on relationships. Following Jesus means living an ethical life through intentional concern for those made socially vulnerable and powerless: "Those who would follow Jesus adopt his way of being on the side of the victims." Following Jesus thus means "going the second mile" (Weaver 2005, p. 182), serving as the motivation for helping those rendered vulnerable to disaster by social and economic circumstances.

Anabaptists Today

Today, at least 150 Mennonite groups exist in North America alone and adherents and denominations exist worldwide as well (Kraybill 2010; Murray 2010). Mennonites, followers of Menno Simons, represent the largest concentration of Anabaptists, with groups located mostly in North, Central and South America, Africa, and the Caribbean (Kraybill 2010). Groups include Mennonite Church (MC) Canada, Mennonite Church USA and others. Mennonite Church USA is the largest group in the U.S. with 916 congregations across 44 of 50 states. Mennonite Church Canada represents the next largest group with congregations spanning seven of ten provinces. Mennonite congregations are the most racially and ethnically diverse Anabaptist group today although the majority remain Anglo. About 11 percent of Mennonite Church USA members come from racial and ethnic groups, within which 50 percent are African-American, 35 percent are Latino/Hispanic, 9 percent are Asian and 4 percent are Native American. Mennonite Church Canada includes two dozen congregations with Asian and Hispanic membership. Both MC Canada and USA actively promote mission, relief, and service work (Kraybill 2010). The Mennonite World Conference indicates that about 500,000 Mennonites live in Africa, 241,000 in Asia, 155,000 in Central/ South America, 52,000 in Europe and 500,000 in North America for a total of nearly 1.5 million baptized Mennonites.

Three other main groups descended from Anabaptism. The Amish have followed Jakob Ammann since about 1693. Approximately 233,000 Amish populate 27 U.S. states and Ontario, Canada today with the majority in Ohio, Pennsylvania, and Indiana (Kraybill 2010). Alexander Mack Sr. first led the Brethren or Dunkards who baptized adults through dunking or immersion. Though not directly descended from the sixteenth century, Anabaptism influenced their practices and beliefs. About a dozen groups of Brethren live in the U.S., Dominican Republic, Haiti, and Puerto Rico (Kraybill 2010). Hutterites, followers of Jakob Hutter, practice pacifism and live collectively. Their belief in sharing communal goods as a form of mutual aid insured their survival during a time of martyrdom in Moravia (Weaver 2005). The Hutterites have established 480 colonies in Alberta, Manitoba, and Saskatchewan Canada as well as South Dakota and Montana (Kraybill 2010). Additional denominational diversity can be found within each Anabaptist branch.

FOLLOWING JESUS

The notion of separatism characterizes all Anabaptist groups to various degrees. Separation, though, "does not mean disengagement or withdrawal." Separation implies engagement with society by "maintaining an alternative witness" based on core Anabaptist beliefs (Weaver 2005, p. 204). Ultimately, Mennonite Disaster Service volunteerism emerged as a vehicle for that alternative witness in a way that would powerfully affect communities, clients, volunteers, and staff (as described in chapters 4 through 8). The Anabaptist focus on relationships, justice, and mutual aid fueled thousands of volunteers who followed Mennonite Disaster Service as servants of Jesus. Every Anabaptist branch has donated and volunteered to MDS: Amish, Brethren, Hutterite, and Mennonite.

Mennonites often funnel their service work through Mennonite organizations. The Mennonite Central Committee (MCC) began in 1920 to provide relief to those affected by war in Russia. Its activities now span more than fifty nations and encompass refugee assistance, drug rehabilitation, health care, education and more. Furthermore, long-term dedication to affected communities characterizes Mennonite service work. To illustrate, MCC relief work for the Haiti earthquake in 2010 built on a base first established in 1947. Another organization, Mennonite Economic Development Association (MEDA), concentrates on reducing poverty by offering micro-loans and small business consultation. MEDA first began in 1953 to help Mennonites relocated to Paraguay by MCC after World War II. Mennonite Health Services Alliance (MHS) stemmed from conscientious objectors who returned home after World War II to found health care services, nursing homes, and hospitals including help for people with disabilities (Kraybill 2010). Mennonite Disaster Service (MDS) shares the same heritage.

Early Relief Work

Mennonite Disaster Service originated in Kansas (U.S.), with ties to saving those facing crises. Mennonites first arrived in Kansas through diasporic movement. Fleeing persecution, Mennonites needed land to support their families. To survive, many Mennonites immigrated to Russia at the invitation of Catherine the Great. Multiple settlements grew in Russia, reaching a total of 1,200 families in fifty-eight villages by 1835 in the Molotschna area alone. Rapidly growing families further increased the population, reaching 34,500 by 1859 and then 120,000 by World War I (Dyck 1993).

Population growth, coupled with governmental policies regulating the size of plots, meant that immigrants became increasingly pressed to support themselves. Expanding government control over agriculture and education made Russian Mennonites increasingly uneasy and marginalized them into a less powerful, minority group status. Government officials met Mennonite efforts to survive with political marginalization and loss of exemption from military service, a practice critical to pacifists. Russian pressure on Anabaptists to assimilate further imperiled distinctive cultural practices and institutions. Some Mennonite economic successes also threatened the state, especially as the Bolshevik revolution of 1917 neared. Mennonites became "enemies of the state" and suffered robberies, rapes, and murders, yet tenaciously practiced "nonresistance and love" (Dyck 1993, p. 183). In 1920 and 1921, when famine and typhus swept Russia, millions died including 2,200 Mennonites. The newly established Mennonite Central Committee responded, providing food to starving refugees and evacuating 20,000 Mennonites into Canada (Dyck 1993).

Remaining Mennonites in Russia faced continued threats to the practice of their religion and even their survival. The impact of World War II was traumatic: one refugee, Jakob Giesbrecht, wrote down his story (Dyck and Dyck 1991, p. 88):

> The place is our village of Nieder-Chortitza in the Ukraine. The year is 1943, and the time is the beginning of September. On all the fields of the Mennonites there is a beehive of activity . . . the land is again theirs . . . .but now there is talk about the front coming back again . . . we did not have to wait long for an answer. At the end of September, the German commander of our area ordered all inhabitants to get ready to evacuate . . . in all, 614 persons fled from our community.

Jakob Giesbrecht described how survivors pushed on through intense suffering and starvation, their horses and wagons taken by the Germans: "The old people, women with children, and the sick could not escape and were shipped back into the interior of Russia." Forced onto and off of trains, shot at by Germans, and separated permanently from each other, only a few of the original 614 made it to safety. In a refugee camp near Mannheim, Germany, they joined with Dutch refugees and fled to Holland in July 1945. A connective thread to MDS then began to emerge through MCC work in response to Giesbrecht and fellow refugees. MCC workers Peter and Elfrieda Dyck found Jakob Giesbrecht and remaining survivors. As the Dycks learned, these initial refugees (33 in number) "were only the tip of the iceberg" (Dyck and Dyck, 1991, p. 102).

When Mennonite refugee numbers reached 420, Holland closed its doors due to pressure from the Russians who wanted "their" citizens back. Mennonites en route to Holland ended up in refugee camps in Germany. MCC workers, along with refugees, established relief facilities: "We needed a small office, a food storage room that could be locked and a dining room" (Dyck and Dyck 1991, p. 141). They organized a school to keep children busy while refugee nurses opened a makeshift hospital. They held worship services, funerals, and even marriages in a temporary encampment that meant the difference between dying of starvation and survival.

Moving on to more permanent refuge became extremely difficult, requiring negotiations with American, British, and German officials "at many levels" (Dyck and Dyck 1991, p. 161). Canada, which had welcomed over 20,000 Russian Mennonites after World War I, closed the border to new evacuees. MCC did not give up, though, as:

> Mennonites have a long tradition of taking care of refugees. In 1533, North German Mennonites gave asylum to English Calvinists fleeing for safety from their Catholic queen. In the 1660s, Dutch Mennonites sent large contributions to the Hutterian Brethren persecuted in Hungary. In 1710, they organized the Foundation for Foreign Relief in 1710, which helped 400 refugees from Switzerland. (Dyck and Dyck 1991, p. 177)

Peter Dyck, a Mennonite saved by MCC food during the Russian famine of 1921 and living in Canada by 1928, did not give up either. Through long meetings and their strong will, "Operation Mennonite" sent 3,000 refugees from Germany to Paraguay. Elfrieda Dyck, a nurse and fellow Russian evacuee to Canada, accompanied multiple shiploads of refugees to Paraguay, and explained to an official from the International Refugee Organization, "We have no strings, no hidden agendas, no expectations in return. To serve is the agenda. Our people simply attempt to follow Jesus" (Dyck and Dyck 1991, p. 307). In 1950, Peter J. Dyck moved on to serve as the pastor of Eden Mennonite Church in Kansas, where he would influence the development of Mennonite Disaster Service.

Peacemaking

Anabaptists practice nonviolence and pacifism, a choice by faith that has consistently characterized their path since the sixteenth century. As Mennonites immigrated to North America, they have repeatedly faced the issue of military conscription. Mennonites established their first settlement in what would become the U.S. in 1683. Despite the absence of a draft, Mennonites suffered mob violence near their homes in Lancaster County, Pennsylvania when they refused to take up arms during the American Revolution. Conscription during the Civil War in the U.S. meant paying $300 or hiring a substitute to secure an exemption, neither of which was acceptable as Mennonites could not conscientiously send someone else to war. Rather, where possible, they worked in hospitals or cared for freedmen. Mennonites living in Virginia at the time were jailed for their beliefs and suffered harsh consequences from an unsupportive public. World War I brought more severe trauma to Anabaptist conscientious objectors. Five hundred went through court-martial proceedings and 138 spent time in prison for their refusal to take up arms. Two Hutterites died, one at Alcatraz and one at Leavenworth, Kansas and Mennonite churches were burned by arsonists. Rather than being deterred, though, their experiences strengthened them internally and collectively and prepared them for the next conflict (Gingerich 1949).

In the U.S. during World War II, the National Service Board for Religious Objectors operated various Civilian Public Service (CPS) units for those with pacifist convictions. Of the 12,000 conscientious objectors who engaged in alternative service projects, which were managed by various faith-associated organizations including MCC, approximately 4,665 (38 percent) were Mennonites. Conscientious objectors served communities in the U.S. and Canada by working in mental institutions, soil conservation, irrigation, hygiene, agricultural service, juvenile justice camps, and firefighting. Collectively, they provided over two million hours of alternative service (GAMEO, no date; Gingerich 1949).

In Canada, which declared war against Germany in 1939, a group of Anabaptist churches organized into the Conference of Historic Peace Churches. After considerable negotiation with government officials, Canada agreed in 1941 to a program of alternative service for noncombatants or hospital service in the army or civilian work in parks and roads. Mennonites typically chose the latter option, as noncombatant service still implicitly supported violence. To illustrate, a 1,944 report listed 8,932 conscientious objectors. Of these men, 245 went into the military, 122 served as noncombatants in medical and dental military care, 3,188 went into agricultural work, and 1,295 served in other areas. About 60 percent of the 9,000 total conscientious objectors in Canada were Mennonites. Manitoba, "the home of thousands of Russian Mennonites and Doukhobors,[6] furnished the largest number of conscientious objectors of all of the Canadian provinces" (Gingerich 1949, p. 420).

Mennonites in alternative service worked in a variety of emergency response capacities, such as when a tornado in 1942 damaged portions of Marietta, Ohio near a U.S. CPS camp: "A group of Mennonite young men doing Alternative Service in a nearby Civilian Public Service Camp [probably CPS Camp #8] for conscientious objectors volunteered to help in the clean-up aftermath of the storm" (Waltner and Walter, no date). Six CPS camps were established to fight fires, create firebreaks, reduce fire hazards, and pre-suppress fire hazards. Firefighting alone accounted for 169,493 man-days. Camp #103 in Missoula, Montana trained 240 "smoke jumpers," placing squads of 8 to 15 men at six strategic points in Montana, Idaho, and Oregon. After rigorous training, they parachuted in to extinguish 31 fires in 1943, 70 in 1944, and 181 in 1945. On September 10, 1944, they successfully battled a 132-acre fire on a high mountain divide between Idaho and Montana. Additional emergency work totaled 11,807 days while emergency farm work to help with drought and storm damage summed to 110,320 days (Gingerich 1949). Related work gave them experience on large diversion dams, levees, dikes, and jetties. They

checked dams, cleaned streams and lake banks, repaired equipment, operated large machines, dug ditches for sewage disposal, laid pipe, and
worked on construction sites. Thus, thousands of men returned home
capable and ready for disaster cleanup and reconstruction work. Survey
data gathered by Gingerich (1949, p. 488) suggest this as well. Among
Anabaptist conscientious objectors[7] surveyed, 58 percent agreed that CPS
work "will be of value to your life vocation" while 11 percent reported
they had changed their life vocation as a consequence of alternative service.

Participating in CPS assignments inspired those returning from alternative service to commit themselves to their communities. Former conscientious objectors established health care and mental health centers and
addressed economic injustice. An interview with an MDS volunteer in
this study revealed deeply held convictions by those active in Mennonite
Disaster Service with a past rooted in alternative service: "The Anabaptist
servanthood mindset is what we cannot lose. Anabaptism is intrinsic to
MDS." He continued, pointing out the connection from past history to
present obligations: "We know from Anabaptist history that was done by
ordinary folks; that our responsibility is to serve humanity. We have to
remind ourselves of the intrinsic stuff that is in our DNA of servant
mindedness."

Entering disaster service ultimately meant confronting issues associated with military service. Threats over national security in the 1950s and
1960s spurred development of civil defense capacities in the U.S. and
Canada. As pacifists, Anabaptists associated with MDS studied the issue
of civil defense thoughtfully. Determining appropriate roles, relationships, and boundaries for their work mattered as both U.S. and Canadian
national and state agencies placed preparedness, response, and recovery
activities within civil defense offices for both natural disasters and nucle-
ar attack. The Anabaptists' concern formally emerged in 1956 when MCC
convened representatives for bi-national organizing and discussions of
the relationship to both the Red Cross and Civil Defense.

The matter strengthened by 1961, when a report presented at the Sixth
Annual MDS meeting confirmed early principles to "refrain from membership in Civil Defense organizations."[8] Guidelines further recommended that MDS should not register services or equipment with Civil
Defense. Recommendations also stipulated not to accept Civil Defense
equipment. Recognizing the need for further study of the issue, those
present at the 1961 meeting identified concerns around civil defense drills
and alerts, people like cooks and firefighters who might be assigned to
civil defense through their occupations, the role of ministers, personal
needs for survival training in case of external attack, and distribution of
Civil Defense materials by teachers. In "A Plan of Action in This Time of
Cold War" meeting, participants recommended that MDS be "the official
Mennonite agency for disaster service in both natural and man-made

disasters in the United States and Canada" and "be recognized by the church as the Mennonite alternative to the Civil Defense program of the government" to be "consistent with our peace witness." MDS Coordinating Committee secretary Harry Martens wrote, "There is no doubt that today our organization is standing at some crossroads with new vision and new horizons before us. This annual meeting may go down in history as being the most important MDS Annual Meeting in the decade of the sixties."[9]

MCC, through its Peace Section, sought recognition for MDS as an alternative service program though ultimately this did not occur due to the small size of MDS units. Meanwhile, MDS encouraged people to be "ready and qualified" to perform should the cold war warrant. MDSers, focused on the Civil Defense issue, urged people to register with MDS and be ready to support a program "conceived, developed, and administered as a positive ministry of healing, of love, and of reconciliation, without any military frame of reference or contribution to military modes of thought." Doing so required additional study on the potential for atomic attacks, and those studying the issue urged Mennonite scientists to share information so all would understand the potential risks and what to do should attack take place. One route was clear, though: should attack or disaster occur, MDS would be willing and able to help survivors, host evacuees, and join in the recovery.

Social and Economic Justice Work

Hurricane Camille, in 1969, was not the first time Anabaptists went to Mississippi. Mennonites knew Mississippi well, having had a presence there since 1922 through a Mennonite settlement in Gulfhaven. Toward the end of World War II, MCC set up Civilian Public Service Camp #141 near Gulfport. The location, originally a Girl Scout site, was named Camp Bernard after a local bayou (Haury 1979). Workers arrived near the end of the war, with some suggesting that MCC saw the camp as a route to establish a national voluntary service program (Haury 1979, p. 4). The goal of Camp Bernard focused on improving human sanitation, particularly establishing privies, killing rats, and eradicating hookworm. The context of severe economic deprivation and social injustice in which the CPS men worked gelled well with Anabaptist principles. By late 1945, MCC had formally approved sending Mennonites as the first MCC Voluntary Service program. These volunteers sought to expand sanitation to include drilling wells, providing home nursing and health education, and offering summer religious programs. Additional efforts centered on community needs, especially housing, schools, and recreation. One report as early as 1947 indicated a local need for a safe place to swim, one that could be used by African Americans in a time when strict racial segregation largely excluded them from Gulf Coast beaches. As CPS work phased out and Voluntary Service increased, the Girl Scouts reclaimed their property and MCC moved to Camp Landon by 1948 with a new director, Orlo Kaufman.[10]

Camp Landon volunteers continued to work on public sanitation by supporting local health department efforts to curtail typhus. They built chairs, tables, and playground equipment for African American churches and schools. Volunteers offered shop and sewing classes and distributed critically needed clothing, food, and holiday gifts. "Camp Landon provided one of the few sources of emergency welfare assistance in Harrison County at this time" (Haury 1979, p. 20). One especially successful effort brought African American children in for Christian education, reaching well over 13,000 children. Camp Landon also established a Christian Community Center for recreation, deemed critical to provide a wholesome atmosphere for local children (Haury 1979, p. 36).

A Voluntary Service member from Eden (Kansas) Mennonite Church, Ethel Jane Krehbiel, worked with young African Americans to create the Good-Deed Club in 1953. Together, they made items which they sold to raise funds for local and international relief work. Tragically, Ethel died in a car accident in 1956. A memorial fund financed her dream for a swimming pool in North Gulfport which the Good Deeds Association, formally organized in 1961, installed by 1965. In light of the brutality experienced by African Americans in Mississippi, recreational facilities might seem frivolous. Yet building a community swimming pool symbolized far more than summer fun and created a lasting legacy in the area. In 2010, at the five year anniversary of hurricane Katrina, a Mississippian interviewed for this study said, "Mennonites are very compassionate and very willing to help regardless of race or creed. They are known for that here. The Mennonites in Gulfport put in a swimming pool in a black neighborhood in the 1960s. They stand for integrity and fairness. *People remember the pool.*"

Intergroup contact emerged as the hallmark of many Camp Landon initiatives. Camp Landon walked a fine line to promote intergroup relationships, dealing with racist whites and even some Mennonites reluctant to integrate, and a local government intent on maintaining segregation (Schwartz 2004, see also Shearer 2010). Harold Regier, a camp administrator and pastor, joined Civil Rights Movement marches. Camp Landon also hosted a workshop for the Council of Federated Organizations, an important umbrella organization for the Civil Rights Movement. In retaliation, those at Camp Landon ended up on a list targeted for action by the Ku Klux Klan. At least one cross burned near their camp. They also individually challenged a local Mennonite congregation unwilling to integrate. Harold Regier later said:

> There was appreciation for what Camp Landon was doing. There was a sense that we didn't understand the South and the way of life there.

There was not really any involvement or participation in the kind of things that we did in the South. When I pastored the Cross Roads church, that was in a time of beginning of change. I said at that time that I would accept some responsibilities there with the understanding that the church would be open. That was a reluctantly accepted request. One member left the church immediately. But most of the Mennonites, the established ones, were beginning to make some movement in terms of acceptance . . . but this area of being exactly on the same wave length when it comes to the advocacy things and the type of involvement in the Black community was something that was difficult to share.[11]

Voluntary Service brought whites into the segregated South, connecting people across racial lines they might otherwise not have crossed so easily. Beginning in 1960, Camp Landon's "Fresh Air" program transported 274 local children over a 15-year period to rural areas in Kansas, South Dakota, and Ohio. The children spent ten days living with a host family, learning about farming and Mennonite faith. Director Kaufman said, "They have often felt rejected and unwanted by white people. . . . Being able to live in a white Christian home could help remove some of the fear," with benefits for whites as well: "It will give the children an opportunity to correct some misunderstandings about Negro people in areas where there is little contact with Negro people" (as quoted in Haury 1979, p. 46). Staff at Camp Landon also rejected local norms by inviting local African-American residents into their homes. Such shared meals served as one of many nonviolent actions that helped to undermine segregation. Camp Landon's outreach efforts brought other positive consequences as well, such as when attendees graduated from Mennonite colleges, benefiting from opportunities that would not have been possible in an otherwise segregated society under impoverished conditions.

Camp Landon represents one of many initiatives that allowed Anabaptists to "follow Jesus." They did so through peaceful means that built meaningful connections across time and made a difference in health care, education, recreation, faith, and economic circumstances. Perhaps the most meaningful component, though, stems not from simply providing programs and funds. It is through the commitment of time, persistent and dedicated, to restructure conditions beyond the control of local residents. In 1969, Mennonite Disaster Service volunteers staged their relief and reconstruction efforts for Hurricane Camille from Camp Landon. They built new homes from a very firm foundation. Pastor Regier saw that connection:

> My sense from observing was that there was a lot of surprise and appreciation about the longevity of people coming in to help. Not just the immediate crisis and the clearing away of things and seeing the disaster but staying on for the long haul . . . so it became a project where you were helping to put families back into a shelter, into a build-

ing and a place where they could live more comfortably. That kind of relationship with the families and seeing that we are not here just for the glitz of the beginning, we're here to help these people get back on their feet. That is something that made an impression, somewhat surprising, but affirming of the way Mennonites work.[12]

MENNONITE DISASTER SERVICE

Intentional disaster-focused service by Mennonites can be dated to at least 1947 in the U.S. when the "Church of God in Christ Mennonites did cleanup work after the Woodward, Oklahoma tornado."[13] By oral tradition and from written documents, MDS origins date back to a picnic held in May, 1950, when a group of young couples from Pennsylvania Mennonite Church (located in Kansas) held a picnic in Newton, Kansas. A number had served in Civilian Public Service during World War II and sought additional avenues for continued contributions. They did so out of a conviction that they were "professed peacemakers" who looked for opportunities to "follow the Prince of Peace." Back from national service, they wanted to "seek opportunities to be engaged in peaceful, helpful activity in our own and surrounding communities." Immediate actions secured financial donations to help with mission work and to support an international student. Yet "discharging these obligations worked no hardship." Unsatisfied, they appointed a committee and sent a memo to Mennonite Central Committee and the Mennonite Relief Committee of the Mennonite Board of Missions and Charities.[14]

By August, nothing had been heard back and though "the initial enthusiasm had somewhat subsided," committee members remained determined and created the Mennonite Service Organization (MSO).[15] A first response in the U.S. took MSO members into McPherson County, Kansas after a tornado on June 8, 1950. Because they lacked credentials, the National Guard and Kansas Highway Patrol stopped their entry. They realized quickly they needed to be far more organized and credentialed to be of service.[16]

Mennonite Service Organization

Kansas Mennonites crafted an MSO constitution in April, 1951. Echoing a devotion to servanthood and peacemaking, the MSO set out a fourfold purpose:

1. To promote the Christian ideals of peace and service.
2. To promote a corporate group for mutual inspiration and stimulation.
3. To activate the principles of peace and service in a constant program when and where needed.

4. To provide for personnel, equipment and provisions on short notice in any disaster whether by force of nature or by war.[17]

The first and third purposes, to focus on peace and be of service, resonated clearly from Anabaptist principles. Their second purpose suggested that working as a collective and unified body would help disaster survivors and benefit volunteers. A fourth purpose focused them mindfully on being of assistance to their neighbors in need.

Wanting to bring new people into service, and concerned that transitions undermined organizational stability, the MSO chose to elect officers in overlapping years and without the possibility of re-election. A Service Auxiliary for MSO opened doors for women's involvement, albeit a role that emerged gradually. At the time, the male MSO tasked the Women's Service Auxiliary with cataloguing personnel and equipment as well as providing and distributing food, clothing, and other resources. Membership was open to "any Christian."[18]

A scriptural basis underlay the MSO and infused its notion of service as "motivated by the Love of God." Those in service did so from a commitment that "love to our brethren is not an optional thing for a Christian. It is a direct command of our Lord. It is our duty to those about us." MSO members viewed their efforts as moving beyond the traditional help offered when a barn burned or a neighbor suffered: "I'm glad for Mutual Aid and other types of Church Aid, but we have much room for improvement in application of the teachings of the Word of God in relation to service to our fellow men."[19] Devotions held at the establishment of the MSO ended with Matthew 25:34–36:

> Then the King will say to those on his right, 'Come, you who are blessed by my Father, inherit the kingdom prepared for you from the foundation of the world. For I was hungry and you gave me food, I was thirsty and you gave me drink, I was a stranger and you welcomed me, I was naked and you clothed me, I was sick and you visited me, I was in prison and you came to me.'

Even before formally organizing, volunteers had eagerly reached out to the South Central Mennonite Conference and the Red Cross. Yet, "for a full year no opportunities presented themselves, or they were not recognized . . . [and] . . . inactivity brought the enthusiasm to a rather low ebb at times."[20] And then it began to rain in Kansas.

First Disaster Relief Efforts in the U.S.

In May 1951, just after MSO members passed their constitution, heavy rains deluged Kansas:

> Then came rain, and more rain. The 5:45 p.m. News Broadcast from a Wichita radio station on May 17 requested all available men to report to the river for sandbag duty. Wichita is 35 miles south of us. The river

was expected to overflow. City employees had already worked all day, some for 24 hours. At six o-clock the chairman of our Service Committee left for Wichita. At the same time the Vice President and Coordinator began calling men to ask whether they would be willing to help and to have themselves ready to leave immediately if needed. About seven o'clock our report from Wichita came. We had promised to send fifteen men and a couple of trucks before eight o-clock the first men were on their way. By eleven 45 men were in Wichita with four trucks.

MSO volunteers began sandbagging weak dikes along the Little Arkansas River near Wichita, "being only periodically relieved by sandwiches and coffee from the Salvation Army. About 6 in the morning we were released and we went wearily on our way home to face another day's work." The Wichita experience confirmed that need existed and could be met by broadly based Anabaptist help:

> At this point we discovered that Old Mennonites were not the only Christians interested in this type of service. Our Holdeman brethren, Church of God in Christ Mennonites were there and working with us. The following day, with the help of the Eden General Conference Church we were able to send 35 more men to help maintain the dikes until the water receeded.[21]

One week later, another community facing flooding called and "two carloads went out to help. . . . I am not alone in believing that our greatest aid was given at Great Bend. . . . We carried sand bags here through mud almost a foot deep to the dikes a couple hundred feet away." In Salina, MSO workers rescued people via boats, gathered up cots and bedding for the evacuees, and then returned home to work another full shift on their farms. Both women and men went to Florence, Kansas, to clean houses: "You can scarcely imagine the trail of filth, silt and destruction left by the floods."[22] "Weary men dragging home after many hours of rescue work or sandbagging certainly belied the fact that MSO was just a social function."[23] Given their start in flood relief, members joked that "MSO" really stood for Midnight Service Organization or Mighty Soaked Outfit. But finally, they were fulfilling their mission, with "a feeling that we have given a hand where a need has been presented, and above all a feeling that our service has been in the name of Christ."[24]

MSO members, through experience, realized that even more organization would help. They needed a contact person "to present proper credentials to the Authority in the affected area. We have contacted mayors, State Highway Patrol, Red Cross officials, and the Civilian Defense Chairman, telling them about our organization. We have become known and recognized in some areas with our MSO arm bands."[25] The contact person would use a list of personnel, equipment, and specialties to decide who should be dispatched to a particular disaster. On receiving a call, the contact leader would have to organize a group quickly and efficiently, and "make important decisions at a moment's notice." Yet, this same person would also have to "stay at home and serve by sitting at the telephone."[26] MSO decided on John Diller to fill the contact slot, which he did ably from a wheelchair after suffering a farm-related accident.

Using their contact person and pre-established relationships, the MSO sent 150 men to Topeka, Kansas to help with flooding in the fall of 1951. Volunteers worked through intra and inter-organizational partnerships to find meaningful work, lodging, and meals. MSO men and women worked under the familiar MCC's Voluntary Service Section to rebuild damaged homes with supplies provided by the American Red Cross. The YMCA and YWCA of Topeka provided lodging at $1.25 per night and a Mennonite Service Center offered meals for $1.55 per day, though the American Red Cross provided room and board for longer-serving volunteers.[27] Reconstruction Unit Leader Esley E. Schmidt encouraged longer-term service, noting "since it takes several days to get into the spirit of the work, workers should plan on being on the project for more than one day—preferably for a week."[28] Women went typically for one day of service to hang wallpaper and paint. Often, women provided labor on the family farm so their husbands could serve longer.

Service work in Topeka continued into 1952, with strong representation from "Old Mennonites, the Church of God in Christ Mennonites, and the General Conference Mennonites."[29] A report from the North Topeka Reconstruction Project observed that people came from twenty congregations, and for the first time outside of Kansas as Nebraska Mennonites arrived to help.[30] A total of 5,120 hours of labor poured into affected areas including homes for African Americans and the locally damaged St. Parks A.M.E. Church.[31]

The Temporary Disaster Committee

After serving during the floods in Kansas, MSO volunteers realized they could involve a broader Anabaptist constituency. In the spring of 1952, storm damage in Arkansas caught their attention. White County, Arkansas and the small town of Judsonia, population 1,122, had experienced 39 deaths. John Diller, now the Topeka area coordinator, sent out a call dated March 28, 1952: "We have all worked together in the North Topeka Reconstruction Project as Mennonites. We have enjoyed working, we have enjoyed the fellowship, and we have left a Christian Testimony in that area." Building on the spirit of involvement experienced in Kansas, Diller called on Anabaptists: "Our neighbors in the States to the southeast of us have experienced a severe disaster. The storm that swept that area several days ago left a trail of destruction. Families are homeless, have lost their clothing, bedding and most of their earthly possessions."

The spring storms served to rally those interested in disaster service. Diller advised that interested volunteers could

> pool our resources and work as a unit rather than to work as individuals. It is entirely possible that a major disaster will strike much closer before the year is past. Would it not be well for us to organize and be ready to step right into a disaster area and go to work as a unit, rather than to go in as small groups, independent of each other, yet all under the name Mennonite?

Diller invited those interested to meet on the Hesston College campus in Hesston, Kansas. He added that a local pastor from Eden Mennonite Church in Moundridge, Rev. Peter J. Dyck, would lead the meeting indicating that he "has had several years' experience in relief work."[32]

On March 31, 1952, eighty men and a few women from twenty-eight congregations—all within forty miles of Hesston, Kansas—converged to "unite under one organization so that they could work more effectively, with less time and money being put into administration and more into service."[33] They created a Temporary Disaster Committee (TDC), choosing representatives based on each branch of MCC Constituent Churches and electing officers. One who was present later summarized his thoughts: "It is significant to note the wisdom of this first pattern of organization. It has served the organization well and is still the organizational pattern, practically without amendment." Representation across the denominations and deliberative consultation emerged as central processes that would guide them as they developed the new organization. Philosophically and spiritually, they drew on Hebrews 11 and James 2, saying they had all been taught, "for as the body without the spirit is dead, so faith without works is dead also."[34] They continued to expand across Anabaptist groups, drawing 37 congregations from 5 branches in a subsequent meeting on May 18.[35]

Serving in Arkansas transformed the MSO. A pattern of using investigators (a named role that remains 60 years later) to "immediately investigate the need and avenues for service and report to each local organization"[36] was established. Volunteers learned quickly to arrive self-sufficient, as Rev. Dyck wrote: "You are advised to take along your own sheet, pillow and towel [and] basic carpenters tools. Food will be provided. Your work will be scattered over a large area."[37] The storms generated strong inter-organizational partnerships still present today, particularly with the American Red Cross. In Arkansas, advance investigators (Brother Unruh and Brother Wiens) worked with the Red Cross to identify meaningful work and appropriate clients. Collaboration between the TDC/MSO and Red Cross led them into the lives of people "who are aged, widowed or handicapped."[38]

Again, inter-church service brought out a range of Anabaptists: "When the MSO went to Arkansas, our Holdeman brothers . . . they got there first with more than 50 men for several days work."[39] After responding to a Hebron, Nebraska tornado in 1953, John Diller explained: "We had really discovered the secret of successful work in Hebron, so we told Marvin [who was investigating another disaster] that all he has to do is find the mayor of Meeker (Oklahoma) and together they could work out a pattern of work." The county road supervisor provided jobs for the volunteers and Diller noted that "meals for our men were served in, I believe, a Christian Church by the women of the church and community. It was here that the men were invited to the mid-week meeting. They were reluctant to go in their overalls, but were assured that they were welcome."

As future MDS volunteers would discover, they found themselves answering questions about themselves. Diller noted, "In the course of the evening discussion, the local people wanted to know more about these strange people, the Mennonites. Do you believe in God. . . and so on until finally one of the local people suggested 'we believe the same things, why have different denominations?'" Rev. H. B. Schmidt explained the diversity of Anabaptists for the Oklahomans, as described by Diller: "Some people like red apples, some yellow apples, some sweet apples and some, sour apples, but they are all apples. So with churches. Some prefer one, some another. But they are all Christian." As later volunteers would also discover, "This was the beginning of a friendship . . . in which the whole congregations visited each other."[40]

MDS volunteers grew to love what their service generated, a connection to neighbors through:

> the active type of Christian witnessing of all Christians that portrays to all men the love of Christ. This can best be expressed through His followers by their concern for their fellowmen in time of need. Remember, what you and I do because of brotherly love to help those in need we are doing for Christ Himself, for He says in Matthew 25:40b, 'Inasmuch as ye have done it unto one of the least of these my brethren, ye have done it unto me.'[41]

Diller added, "MDS has been good for the people who served. Response from the people who received help has been gratifying. More often than not this response has been deeper than expressions of appreciation for work done. They have been expressions of appreciation for Christian principles and the love of God."[42]

At a discussion in 1954, those present remembered that a variety of additional service options were mentioned as possible service work at the 1950 picnic: mental hospitals, race relationships, emergency services, mission stations, mutual aid (husking bees, barn raising, clean-up), financial aid, material aid, clean-up and church repair and social service to "migrant groups," "Indian reservations," and "Negro settlements."[43] But disaster relief (flood, tornado, forest fire, earthquake, drought, war) captured many as "there is no similar organization in our Church program. We are launching out, feeling our way, preparing ourselves so that when disaster or catastrophe strikes, we can most efficiently step in and be of real service."[44]

Throughout its decade of origin, participants labored diligently to put a sustainable structure into place. Between 1952 and 1954, MSO established a headquarters in Hesston, Kansas, elected Rev. Peter J. Dyck as chair and began to call itself Mennonite Disaster Service.

Parallel Origins in Canada

At chronologically similar times, Canadian Mennonites launched efforts to relieve those affected by disaster. Similar events characterize their journey to becoming disaster servants. As early as 1940, the Conference of Historic Peace Churches formed Christian Fellowship Services as a World War II Alternative Service Program. In 1948, volunteers responded to the first of several Red River Valley flood events in Canada. C. N. Friesen, who later served as an MDS British Columbia provincial director, recalled the sandbagging effort: "I was a young person then, and I was self-employed and I could find time to go and help. As a family we always felt that there was more that we could give than just maybe money, and that we could get involved personally in projects or programs."[45]

By 1950, the *Mennonitische Hilfswerke*, translated as Mennonite Relief Agency or more commonly as Mennonite Disaster Relief, began evacuating families and livestock from even more Red River flooding. C. N. Friesen helped organize the efforts, which required moving cattle off farms owned by Mennonites and non-Mennonites. Syd Reimer, who would eventually chair MDS Canada, recalled, "It all started for me in 1950 when we had the flood in Rosenort . . . I was very involved in sandbagging in Winnipeg and evacuating horses and cattle and chickens in Rosenort." Kansas MDS volunteers came to the aid of Canada too. Syd Reimer added,

> This of course became world news this big flood and we received help from Mead, Kansas. EMC had a church in Mead[e] Kansas original-ly . . . there were at least three Bartell cousins that came to help us, and they married girls from Rosenort. These were the same people who probably were involved with the beginning of MDS. Now MDS started in the east part of Kansas and Mead[e] is quite far west, but as soon as MDS started organizing these guys that helped us to become involved.[46]

Realizing that disaster needs would continue over time, Friesen observed, "We needed to be more prepared." To this end, they created church-based lists of volunteers and sought out other partners. "We started to feel that working together with others, not necessarily of the

Mennonite church . . . like the Salvation Army, Red Cross and other nongovernmental agencies"[47] would foster effective inter-organizational partnerships to strengthen relief work.

Regional and Bi-National Development

In 1954, the General Council of the General Conference's Committee on Church Program Coordination convened in Wayland, Iowa to discuss service programs including disaster work, mental hospitals, race relationships, mutual aid (such as husking bees, barn raising, and refugees), Fresh Air programs, and social services for migrant groups, Native Americans and African Americans. An open discussion on the value of service programs recognized that the "Kansas group found many ways to witness." Representatives concurred that Christ should be the center of service rather than individual recognition, citing Luke 10:20, "Notwithstanding in this rejoice not, that the spirits are subject unto you; but rather rejoice as your names are written in heaven."[48]

Tobe Smucker reported that Indiana CPS men had talked about the need for a disaster unit in Indiana. After a 1953 tornado investigation in Flint, Michigan, Indiana Mennonites sent 25 men per day to rebuild homes. Canadians crossed the border to help as well, bringing with them a broad range of Anabaptists from Old Order Mennonites to less conservative groups. Over fifty years later, the event remains Michigan's worst tornado, with 116 lives lost in the F5 event.[49]

An MCC executive committee meeting in January 1955 created a coordinating committee and established the MDS logo, basing it on the MCC symbol of hands extended over the cross. The inter-organizational connection made sense for several reasons tied to Anabaptist heritage that centered on relief work and peacemaking:

> The impetus for this came from three areas: a desire by Anabaptists to continue community-based alternative service and social contributions post-war, many post-war European immigrants to Canada who had experienced much loss and devastation and relocation assistance from MCC, and church leaders wanting to participate in the Canadian Civil Defense/civil preparedness in some way but separate and autonomously.

Organizational meetings commenced in 1956 and Eddie Barringer was elected to help develop MDS across Ontario. An MDS unit then formed in British Columbia that same year followed three years later by units in Manitoba, Saskatchewan, and Alberta. In 1959, a meeting in Winnipeg "led to the recognition of the value of MDS as an integral part of the church's ministry."[50]

Successful disaster-focused service also spurred coordination. In 1956, the MCC Peace Section and Mennonite Disaster Service called for "national-level" coordination (despite representatives from two nations) and convened a meeting of MDS representatives on March 2 in Chicago, Illinois. Twenty-eight representatives came from thirteen states and Ontario, Canada. Meeting participants associated themselves with MDS Iowa and Missouri, MDS Kansas, California MDS, MDS Franconia Conference, MDS Eastern Ohio, Indiana-Michigan MDS, Western Ohio MDS, Lower Deer Creek MDS, Oklahoma MDS, MDS of the Delmarva Peninsula (Delaware), Lower Deer Creek MDS (Iowa) and Illinois MDS. Just six short years from inception, the MSO had spread into two nations with chapters rapidly assuming the name Mennonite Disaster Service. Supporters then set out a plan for committee coordination with one representative from each of the "constituent groups," which included Mennonite Church, Brethren in Christ, General Conference, Evangelical Mennonite, and Conservative Mennonite.[51] Committee members, reflecting geographic diversity, came from Newton, Kansas; Mount Joy, Pennsylvania; Elkhart, Indiana; Archbold, Ohio; Greenwood, Delaware; and Akron, Pennsylvania.

After Chicago, the Historic Peace Church Council invited 60 national delegates to Winnipeg, further spreading the MDS movement across Canada. Ontario elected Elwen Schantz as the first Ontario chair with Bill Wiebe as the first British Columbia chair. Eddie Barringer stepped up as the MDS national representative. British Columbia then approached and established ties with the British Columbia Red Cross. The Red Cross sent MDS volunteers to work immediately, feeding 6,000 refugees from Hungary. MDS Canada helped with relocating the displaced refugees, an experience that no doubt echoed deeply within the ancestral heritage of MDSers. Within two years, volunteers in British Columbia, Manitoba, and Ontario called their area Region V, while those living west of Ontario referred to themselves as Region VI. Eventually, though, all of Canada merged into one Region.[52] MDS became part of MCC-Canada in 1958 by joining the Peace and Social Concerns Section.

The Historic Peace Church Council of Canada convened MDS leaders with other relief organizations in Winnipeg during late September of 1959. Together, they concluded that MDS was "different" from other benevolent organizations in that its work was "motivated by the redemptive love of Christ." As such, MDS served as an "integral part of the church's ministry" that was "best served by Mennonites working together (inter-denominationally) to meet these challenges with a common service focus."[53]

In 1960 Vernon Wiebe wrote in a new *Handbook for Mennonite Disaster Service Volunteers* that MDS regions, as determined by MCC, usually had a director, an assistant director, and a secretary-treasurer. An Executive Coordinating Committee advised MCC, as the new parent organization, about MDS activities. The MDS coordinator now held office "at the pleasure of the Mennonite Central Committee."[54]

Ten years into its development, MDS had built an established network of congregations, units, and regions tied to an MCC coordinating office that tapped into volunteers across two nations. Congregations now used a "contact man" to forge connections between the congregation and an MDS unit. The unit became defined as "the basic MDS organization of cooperating congregations within a given geographic area, organized to operate in at least one type of disaster situation." Organizers allowed for some differentiation: "In some areas, particularly in the western part of the United States, the unit is organized along state lines. In Canada the organization is along provincial lines. In the central and eastern part of the United States the defined geographic area may be a part of a state or contigios [sic] parts of two or more states." Each unit was tasked with contacting "all related congregations within its outlined area, and it will assume responsibility for exploring major disasters within its area and will investigate need in disaster in neighboring areas as called on by the regional directors." [55]

Most units established an internal division of labor to accomplish their work, with a chairman, vice-chairman, secretary-treasurer, coordinator, and assistant coordinator as well as those tasked with field operations: the investigator, field director and field foreman. MDS, a grass-roots organization, now solidly in place with a clear division of labor and experienced volunteers, included twenty-eight "units encompassing a majority of Mennonite churches." [56]

In 1962, MDS became a formal section of Mennonite Central Committee, dividing the U.S. into four Regions (I, II, III, and IV) representing collections of states and units, with Region V designating all of Canada. [57] Kansas, the original soil on which Anabaptist servants planted the seeds of MDS, became part of Region II. MCC, with U.S. headquarters in Akron, Pennsylvania, made space for MDS "as one of several quasi-related organizations that MCC" helped to develop such as "Menno Travel Service, Mennonite Economic Development Associates, Mennonite Mental Health Services, [and] Ten Thousand Villages." [58] To incubate MDS, MCC hired a full-time staff member and provided office space, organizational support, a budget of $8000, and other resources. In the 1970s and 1980s, MCC established separate organizations in the U.S. and Canada. Despite this division, "the strong grassroots ties between MDS on both sides of the border determined that MDS would stay a single bi-national entity." [59]

MDS volunteers continued to serve in anticipated ways for decades, providing cleanup and reconstruction work mostly in the U.S. but overseas as well. Kansas author Katie Funk Wiebe (1976) described the response to hurricane Hattie that struck Belize in 1961. Twenty-eight volunteers from the U.S. helped rebuild homes and churches. Volunteers went to Haiti in 1963 following hurricane Flora. Using work established by MCC in Haiti as their entry point, volunteers from eight states arrived a month after impact. When hurricane Inez again wreaked havoc on Haiti in 1966, President Duvalier personally asked for Mennonite assistance. Twenty-four volunteers spent over two months after an earthquake rumbled through Managua, Nicaragua in 1972. However, the majority of MDS responses occurred in the U.S. and Canada.

MDS director and historian Lowell Detweiler (2000) chronicled MDS' largest projects in his hallmark volume *The Hammer Rings Hope*. Eighteen events surpassed the Udall tornado turnout of 1,100 volunteers and reveal an ever-rising number of volunteers and days worked on disaster sites. However, focusing on an increasing number of volunteers obscures events that remain important historically to MDS. Volunteers assisted with fire and riot recovery projects in Los Angeles, California in the 1990s, supported drought relief during the 1980s, and helped with reconstruction after hate crimes burned African American churches in the U.S. south. Titus Bender, a Mennonite pastor from Meridian, Mississippi described the MDS response after a half dozen churches were burned by arsonists:

> What has MDS done in Mississippi? How does one approach an evaluation of it? I will mention a couple things about MDS which made it so valuable in bridge building—bridge building by church building in Mississippi. I feel MDS was unique in that, more than any other group that got involved (and there were plenty), they recognized that everybody is worth delivering that still has breath in his body. Nobody is a lost cause.

For MDS, action demonstrated faithful commitment that resulted in meaningful relationships:

"In overalls, one says much more than in theory. MDS men made an impression on people. . . . I think one reason it went over big in Mississippi was because MDS emphasized working with people. From the first it was made plain that we had not come to build churches *for* them but *with* them, and we tried to do more of this all of the time."

Pastor Bender continued, "I have to say that I believe that the Mennonite Disaster Service, the Mennonite Church, in fact every Jesus following Anabaptist belongs where the trouble is. . . . Wherever there is trouble, if the Mennonite church with our simple and forthright way of sweating and working side by side with people can't build bridges, I'd like to submit that it can't be done by anybody. So if there is trouble and it fits into the MDS approach, I think by all means we ought to go to the worst places. It worked in Mississippi."[60]

NOTES

1. Paris, No date. Mennonite Disaster Service Archives, Lititz, Pennsylvania.
2. Waltner, No date. Mennonite Disaster service Archives, Lititz, Pennsylvania.

3. Regier, Harold. No date. Interview conducted by Lowell Detweiler. Mennonite Disaster Service Archives, Lititz, Pennsylvania.

4. Eastern Mennonite College and Bluffton College now hold University status.

5. Regier, Harold. November 17, 1998. Interview with Lowell Detweiler. Mennonite Disaster Service archives, Lititz, Pennsylvania.

6. A Christian group that emigrated to Canada from Russia, see http://usccdoukhobors.org/about.htm.

7. The survey included Old Mennonite, Amish Mennonite, General Conference Mennonite, Old Order Amish, Mennonite Brethren, Conservative Amish and Church of God in Christ Mennonite (Holdeman), see Gingerich 1949, p. 478.

8. Mennonite Disaster Service. February 10, 1971. Exhibit 8: Findings adopted by the Sixth Annual Meeting of Mennonite Disaster Service. Denver, Colorado. From the Mennonite Library and Archives, Newton, Kansas.

9. Martens, Harry. February 9 and 10, 1962. Report of 1961 MDS Co-ordinating Committee Planning and Activities, with Suggestions for Consideration at Business Sessions during our 1962 Annual Meeting, Hamilton Hotel, Chicago, Illinois, February 9 and 10.

10. Kaufman served as director from 1947 to 1950 and returned in 1952 to serve for another 23 years.

11. Regier, Harold. November 17, 1998. Interview given to Lowell Detweiler. Mennonite Disaster Service archives, Lititz, Pennsylvania.

12. Regier, Harold. November 17, 1998. Interview given to Lowell Detweiler. Mennonite Disaster Service archives, Lititz, Pennsylvania.

13. Diller, John (most likely). No date. *MDS In the Beginning*. Mennonite Library and Archives, Newton, KS.

14. *Historical Background of Mennonite Service Organization*, no date. Mennonite Library and Archives, Newton, Kansas.

15. *Historical Background of Mennonite Service Organization*, no date. Mennonite Library and Archives, Newton, Kansas.

16. *Mennonite Service Organization*, as described at Christian Business Men's Meeting in Goshen, Indiana on December 1, 1951. Mennonite Library and Archives, Newton, Kansas.

17. Source: (First) *Constitution of Mennonite Service Organization*, dated April, 1951. From the Mennonite Library and Archives, Newton, Kansas.

18. Source: (First) *Constitution of Mennonite Service Organization*, dated April, 1951. From the Mennonite Library and Archives, Newton, Kansas.

19. Source: Biblical Basis for MSO (Devotions). Attached to the Constitution of the Mennonite Service Organization, dated April, 1951. From the Mennonite Library and Archives, Newton, Kansas. Scriptures cited included I John 3:17–18, 3–23, 4:7–8, 4:10–11 and 4:20–21; Galatians 6:10; John 13:34–35 and John 15:12. For those who do not agree, they offered Matthew 5:44–47, Romans 12:14 and 19–21 followed by Matthew 25:34–46.

20. *Historical Background of Mennonite Service Organization*, no date. Mennonite Library and Archives, Newton, Kansas.

21. Diller, John A. February 9, 1954. *Report of the Activities of the Mennonite Service Organizations Kansas Area.* Mennonite Library and Archives, Newton, Kansas. The Holdeman church formed in Ohio in 1859, spreading across the U.S. and Canada through the rest of the century. Distinctive appearance sets them apart with women wearing black scarves and men with beards. Their faith teaches they are the one true church of Christ. There are about 130 congregations with 14,500 members in the U.S. with about 50 congregations hosting 5,000 members in Canada. They are also known as Church of God in Christ, Mennonite. Total membership globally is approximately 22,000 (Kraybill 2010).

22. No Author. No date. *The Service Organization in Action.* Mennonite Library and Archives, Newton, Kansas.

23. The Mennonite Service Organization, April 6, 1952, talk presented at the Conference on Lay Evangelism at Goshen College Union Auditorium, Goshen, Indiana. Mennonite Library and Archives, Newton, Kansas.

24. *Mennonite Service Organization*, December 1, 1951, as described at Christian Business Men's Meeting in Goshen, Indiana. Mennonite Library and Archives, Newton, Kansas.

25. No Author. April 16, 1952. *The Mennonite Service Organization*. Talk presented at the Conference on Lay Evangelism at Goshen College Union Auditorium, Goshen, Indiana. Mennonite Library and Archives, Newton, Kansas.

26. *The Work of the Co-Ordinator of the Mennonite Service Organization*. No date. Mennonite Library and Archives, Newton, Kansas.

27. Correspondence, Esley E. Schmidt Reconstruction Unit Leader, Mennonite Central Committee Voluntary Service Section to Churches of the Mennonite Faith. December 31, 1951. Mennonite Library and Archives, Newton, Kansas.

28. Schmidt, Esley E. December 31, 1951. Letter from MCC Voluntary Service Section Reconstruction Unit Leader (Schmidt), Akron, Pennsylvania. Mennonite Library and Archives, Newton, Kansas.

29. Schmidt, Esley E. December 31, 1951. Letter from MCC Voluntary Service Section Reconstruction Unit Leader (Schmidt), Akron, Pennsylvania. Mennonite Library and Archives, Newton, Kansas.

30. Wiebe, Vernon. 1960. *Mennonites: A brief history of Mennonite Disaster Service*. Mennonite Library and Archives, Newton, Kansas. See also Diller, John A. Report of the North Topeka Reconstruction Project as Related to MSO 1951 and 1952. Mennonite Library and Archives, Newton, Kansas. Congregations present included (spelling as written in original document by Diller): Alexanderwohl Church; Brudertal Church, Hillsboro; Church of God in Christ Mennonite; Eden Church, Moundridge; Emmaus Church, Whitewater; First Mennonite Church, Beatrice, Nebraska; First Mennonite Church, McPherson; First Mennonite Church, Newton; Grace Mennonite Church, Burns; Grace Mennonite Church, Halstead; Hebron Church, Buhler; Hoffnungsau Church, Inman; Lone Tree Church, Galva; Mennonite Brethern [sic] Church, Buhler; Mennonite Brethern Church, Henderson, Nebraska; Meridian Church, Hesston; Spring Valley Church, Canton; Spring Valley, Canton; Tabor Church, Goessel; West Liberty Church, Conway.

31. Additional work in 1952 included responding to damage from a fire and wind that affected local businesses in Hesston, Kansas.

32. Diller, John A. March 28, 1952. Correspondence, Mennonite Service Organization Hesston, Kansas letterhead to MCC Constituent Churches Central Kansas. Mennonite Library and Archives, Newton, Kansas.

33. John Diller later reported that their list of congregations was not complete and suggested that more than 28 had appeared. Source: Diller, John A. February 9, 1954. *Report of the Activities of the Mennonite Service Organizations Kansas Area*. Mennonite Library and Archives, Newton, Kansas.

34. Wiebe, Vernon R. 1960. *Mennonites: Brief History of Mennonite Disaster Service*. Mennonite Library and Archives, Newton, Kansas.

35. No author, possibly John Diller. Possible date 1954. *Report of the Activities of the Mennonite Service Organizations Kansas Area*. Mennonite Library and Archives, Newton, KS.

36. Diller, John A. March 28, 1952. Correspondence, Mennonite Service Organization Hesston, Kansas letterhead to MCC Constituent Churches Central Kansas. Mennonite Library and Archives, Newton, Kansas.

37. Dyck, Peter J. 1952. Eden Mennonite Church, Moundridge, Kansas, Letter to MCC Constituent Churches in Central Kansas. Mennonite Library and Archives, Newton, KS.

38. Dyck, Peter J. and John A. Diller. May 9, 1952. Correspondence from The Temporary Disaster Committee of Central Kansas to MCC Constituent Churches of Central Kansas. Mennonite Library and Archives, Newton, Kansas.

39. No author, possibly John Diller. Possible date 1954. *Report of the Activities of the Mennonite Service Organizations Kansas Area.* Mennonite Library and Archives, Newton, KS.

40. Diller, John. No date, possibly 1954. *MDS "In the Beginning."* Mennonite Library and Archives, Newton, KS.

41. The Mennonite Service Organization, April 6, 1952. Talk presented at the Conference on Lay Evangelism at Goshen College Union Auditorium, Goshen, Indiana. Mennonite Library and Archives, Newton, Kansas.

42. Diller, John. No date, possibly 1954. *MDS "In the Beginning."* Mennonite Library and Archives, Newton, KS.

43. Outline of Discussion at the Study Conference on Local and Area Service Programs. February 12 and 13, 1954. Sponsored by Committee on Church Program Coordination, General Council of General Conference. Wayland, Iowa. Mennonite Library and Archives, Newton, Kansas.

44. *Mennonite Service Organization,* as described at Christian Business Men's Meeting in Goshen, Indiana on December 1, 1951. Mennonite Library and Archives, Newton, Kansas.

45. Friesen, C. N. August 6, 2008. Interview transcript, files of MDS Extension Office, Winnipeg, Canada.

46. Friesen, C. N. August 6, 2008. Interview transcript, files of MDS Extension Office, Winnipeg, Canada.

47. Friesen, C. N. August 6, 2008. Interview transcript, files of MDS Extension Office, Winnipeg, Canada.

48. Committee on Church Program Coordination, General Council of General Conference. February 12 and 13, 1954, "Outline of Discussion at the Study Conference on Local and Area Service programs." Held at Bethel and Sugar Creek Mennonite Churches, Wayland, Iowa. Mennonite Library and Archives, Newton, Kansas.

49. Outline of Discussion at the Study Conference on Local and Area Service Programs. February 12 and 13, 1954. Sponsored by Committee on Church Program Coordination, General Council of General Conference. Wayland, Iowa. Mennonite Library and Archives, Newton, Kansas.

50. Detweiler, Lowell and Lynn Roth with assistance from Gord Friesen and Paul Unruh. June 20, 2006. Appendix I: Background Historical Information Linking Mennonite Disaster Service and Mennonite Central Committee. MDS Extension Office Archive, Winnipeg, Canada.

51. Minutes of First Meeting of Mennonite Disaster Service Representatives. March 2, 1956. Hotel Atlantic, Chicago, Illinois.

52. Information supplied by Mennonite Disaster Extension Office, Winnipeg, Canada.

53. MDS Extension Office. No date. "History of MDS in Canada." MDS Binational Extension Office Archives, Winnipeg, Canada.

54. Wiebe, Vernon R. 1960. *Handbook for Mennonite Disaster Service Volunteers.* Mennonite Library and Archives, Newton, Kansas.

55. Wiebe, Vernon R. 1960. *Handbook for Mennonite Disaster Service Volunteers.* Mennonite Library and Archives, Newton, Kansas.

56. Wiebe, Vernon R. 1960. *Mennonites: Brief History of Mennonite Disaster Service.* Mennonite Library and Archives, Newton, Kansas.

57. Wiebe, Vernon R. 1960. *Mennonites: Brief History of Mennonite Disaster Service.* Mennonite Library and Archives, Newton, Kansas.

58. Detweiler, Lowell and Lynn Roth with assistance from Gord Friesen and Paul Unruh. June 20, 2006. Appendix I: Background Historical Information Linking Mennonite Disaster Service and Mennonite Central Committee. MDS Extension Office Archive, Winnipeg, Canada.

59. Detweiler, Lowell and Lynn Roth with assistance from Gord Friesen and Paul Unruh. June 20, 2006. Appendix I: Background Historical Information Linking Men-

nonite Disaster Service and Mennonite Central Committee. MDS Extension Office Archive, Winnipeg, Canada.

60. Bender, Titus. February 12, 1996. Bridge Building in Mississippi Evaluating MDS 1965 Church Rebuilding. Excerpts from message given in Annual MDS Section Meeting in Chicago. MDS Archives, Lititz, PA.

FOUR

The Quiet in the Land

Anyone is welcome to help. But few are invited to gumbo. [1]
—Louisiana Community Partner

INTRODUCTION

Within the recovery community, voluntary and faith-based organizations are often called "the first to arrive and the last to leave." Collaborating with outside organizations may be the only way some families recover, as a long-term and experienced community partner explained: "The U.S. doesn't do long term recovery, the closest thing to it is what the Mennonites do. Non-profits do not have the resources for it and the government does not [do it]." When disaster strikes, an MDS site investigator enters the damaged area, conducts an assessment and rallies grassroots volunteers. They move in to clean up, muck out, power up chain saws, and help their neighbors. They do so quietly, without fanfare, as an act of discipleship required by faith.

In this chapter, we learn from interviews with community partners about how they experienced the arrival of an outside, unfamiliar organization. They tell us, in their own words, about MDS work in their towns, for their own neighbors. These partners, spanning communities in Texas, Louisiana, Mississippi and Alabama, include 23 recovery committee leaders, elected officials, and city employees (code inspectors, building permit officials, planners) 15 faith-based partners (usually a local church) and 12 Mennonite partners. Data analysis revealed the process of how MDS enters and works with a range of partners when disaster strikes, with clear implications for how other outsiders might make effective entry into unfamiliar communities.

BUILDING A RECOVERY PARTNERSHIP

Recovery work usually starts within some form of a long term recovery committee. Outside organizations may arrive unannounced or with their own media to document arrival and aid processes. However, from the perspective of local community leaders, any outsider is an unfamiliar entity—who are these people? What can they contribute? How long will they stay? How will they work with our committee? How will they take care of our people?

This chapter documents how MDS makes entry and establishes recovery relationships with locals, a process they describe as "walking" with their new partners. Critical steps involve making entry in a manner consistent with Anabaptist beliefs, helping partners understand Mennonites, finding a place to house their volunteers, getting to know new community partners, and selecting clients.

Making Entry

In 1969, the National Guard flew planeloads of volunteers from Kansas into Mississippi, volunteers who then spread out to restore and rebuild areas affected by Camille. In 2005, Angel Flight pilots brought MDS investigators over the same areas, to view the devastation and determine where MDS might be needed the most. Entering a community is a critical step for any organization and for MDS, it reflects an intentional effort to remain "the quiet in the land," a tradition extending centuries back during their own diaspora. Community partners appreciated such an approach as one said, "Other organizations came in and it was like they said 'see us' but MDS was always low key." In a community steamrolled by a storm surge, a Louisiana partner said, "Their (MDS) role was extraordinarily important and impressive—to do a lot of work without fanfare." For Louisianans struggling with the burden of caring for others and often for themselves, that low-key arrival meant a lot: "They entered unobtrusively. They never mentioned their skill levels." Multiple partners expressed surprise: "They did not want publicity; they just came in to do good work."

Mucking Up

Just like after hurricanes Audrey, Camille and Andrew, work after Katrina began as Anabaptists "arrived early and started high-level debris removal" according to a faith-based partner in Alabama. He added, "They set up immediately and brought in many volunteers involved in clean-up and debris removal." Though many perceive MDS as a reconstruction organization, a faith-based partner in Mississippi offered, "We should not underestimate the importance of mucking up." Removing mud, mold, damaged insulation, and rotting furniture while trying to find, clean, and store treasured china, silverware, photos and other personal possessions meant a lot. The Mississippi partner continued, "This work has an exponential positive effect. Seeing the garbage and destruction around you is very depressing." The arrival of MDS volunteers at the early stage initiated a meaningful connection: "Seeing someone stepping in to help with the clean-up results in a significant attitude change, 'I can make it now.' There is a feeling that someone cares about you. No matter what your financial status, the help is a great boost to your depressed spirit." As one summarized the impact of early relief work, "'God loves me; people care about me; I will make it!' Mucking up has great impact!"

Debris removal simultaneously allowed MDS to scope out locations and to identify work areas. A partner who worked across the state of Louisiana observed, "MDS was popping up everywhere . . . Diamond, Cameron Parish, New Iberia, New Orleans . . . we'd see their faces in all these places or [they'd] show up in another place." As MDS volunteers moved in to help, communities slowly discerned more about these strangers.

Meeting Mennonites

For MDS, rebuilding homes starts with establishing new partnerships in unfamiliar locations. Doing so means introducing themselves to people such as one local partner who "had no knowledge of MDS (before the storm)." Another community partner said, "We didn't know that much about MDS before they came here." A third raised eyebrows in wonder when describing how the unfamiliar organization called "and told us that they could assist us with building houses."

But some knew about Mennonites from previous disasters. A faith-based representative from Alabama recalled, "Many clients in this area knew of MDS and their reputation from past help received. It was very comforting for them to know that the Mennonites were involved." In southwestern Louisiana, a community partner affected by Rita said, "People remember that the Mennonites were here in 1957 for Hurricane Audrey. They were dressed differently, in traditional hats and beards, then." A community partner in Mississippi recalled, "MDS was here in 1969 for Camille and we had Mennonites in here then. I remember the black hats." An MDS staff member concurred, "MDS had been to the Gulf Coast before in several places. After Andrew (1992), for example, they had a base in Franklin, Louisiana and worked in the Houma area." Another faith-based partner observed, "MDS history here dates back to 1970. A local MDS unit had been at the table with VOAD since 1979, maintaining an MDS presence in this inter-faith organization. This helped connect local recovery teams to a national body. What was really appreciated was that MDS always kept in touch with us locally. They worked in partnership with us." In 2005, a Louisiana partner added, "MDS was down here quickly and was instrumental in getting our church going in the disaster response. We had daily contact while MDS was here in our community working to clean up."

Local people and organizations met Mennonites in both formal and informal ways. Many locals noticed more conservative MDS volunteers first because of traditional appearances, but learned over time that a diverse set of volunteers shared a deep commitment to Anabaptist beliefs. Others encountered MDS in the course of their own volunteer activities. In Texas, a future partner met MDS when he stopped an MDS early investigation crew driving through the area, and invited them to the first disaster response meeting. He reported, "All the governmental groups were at the first meeting. Their [MDS] representative explained MDS and said 'could you use help' and a county official said, 'Absolutely, please do not leave' and they didn't. On Tuesday they showed up with chain saws and helped us to clean up." Testifying to the long-term commitment MDS made he added, "In January they segued to repairs for two years; then in spring 2009 the last ones left."

Informal meetings often led to new partnerships: "We were looking at available office space, when we noticed a Mennonite examining a much larger damaged wing which was to be bulldozed." After introductions, "Together we rebuilt the condemned building in exchange for free rental for a year. Three months later we had a large building with kitchen, dormitory and meeting space." Another Louisiana community partner said, "We met in the parking lot, a great way to start a partnership" and continued to meet in their cars for some time until flood waters receded.

Initial encounters also occurred in the context of more formal encounters. A Louisiana partner dealing with Rita and then Ike remarked, "We met in joint meetings of disaster response organizations." The FEMA VALs also directed MDS into areas they knew to have unmet needs, including areas that lacked any kind of recovery committee structure. In one such location, MDS facilitated the emergence of a recovery organization, guiding them through the unfamiliar tasks of working across cultural differences, securing funds, and conducting case management to determine clients for MDS work. From chance encounters to meeting in more formal committee structures, preliminary partnerships began to emerge.

Yet, for MDS to stay, as one MDS staff member spelled out, "four pillars" had to be in place: "housing, meaningful work, finances/funding, and volunteers." Although implicitly in place prior to the Gulf Coast storms, explicitly "these pillars were new for Katrina and Rita" and "determined if a site would work out or not." Those initial encounters often arose out of investigators' efforts to find appropriate housing in areas where hurricanes had dramatically limited the possibilities.

Setting Up "Camp"

Faith-based organizations vary in the types of accommodations they may provide, from groups that secure their own lodging to organizations that provide collective settings. For Katrina, the location, amenities, and qualities of such accommodations varied from tent cities in the sweltering heat and humidity of a Louisiana summer to camps where recreational vehicles housed people in air-conditioned comfort (once the power was restored). MDS has been among the more creative organizations in how they have secured volunteer housing.

In 1952, MDS secured lodging in Arkansas through a local Catholic Church that provided "housing for thirty or more men at a time" and directed that "[the] men should take their carpenter tools, including wrecking bars and nail pullers, also sheets and pillows."[2] For Katrina, two stages of volunteer housing occurred, an initial foray to find sites followed by long-term establishment. For the initial weeks, volunteers often stayed in makeshift lodging offered by faith-based partners as they helped with area cleanup. A shift then occurred as MDS found sites that offered places for long-term efforts. Much like the refugee sites Peter and Elfrieda Dyck set up, as the Civilian Public Service workers experienced, and as early MSO/MDSers described, volunteers refer to their housing as "camp."

Setting up camp after Katrina was especially hard given the catastrophic damage. Local communities had lost resources critical to support volunteers such as grocery stores, medical care, vehicle repair, and lumber yards. Buildings large enough to house dozens of volunteers lacked cooking and shower facilities. But local partners frequently said, "MDS did not ask for anything, unlike other voluntary organizations. We were already strapped and MDS understood that." MDS arrived "self-contained" and took care of its own volunteers, which enabled affected communities to focus on other needs.

With experience in doing so, MDS found a variety of low-impact places to encamp volunteers. In East Texas, a faith-based partner allowed use of a church camp where volunteers lived and cooked. For several locations, a new "RV" program brought in retired volunteers with their own recreational vehicles, a popular strategy among those seeking warmer climates during northern winters. In Plaquemines Parish, the first MDS volunteers stayed in a bunkhouse at a local Baptist church, which also provided tools and a boat. Amish volunteers then cleaned out a flooded Catholic church and converted rooms into dorms. Volunteers further transformed the church sanctuary into a dining hall that fed thousands over several years. The parking lot allowed for mobile homes and travel trailers used as offices and long-term volunteer housing. Enough space allowed for mobile shower units. A flood-damaged out-building served as a toolshed and storage facility. In Pass Christian, Mississippi, MDS bought land for its double-wide trailers. In New Orleans, volunteers stayed first in a local convent hosted by Catholic nuns. Katrina donations to MDS then allowed for purchase of a roof-damaged, moldy church near the Lower Ninth Ward. Volunteers converted it to a long-term facility still in use 6 years past the storm. New Iberia partners offered a community center for offices, meeting space, and dining, and paid for the electricity. MDS added trailers for volunteer housing.

Following a long tradition of "making do somehow (MDS)," volunteers readied space for the long work ahead. Partners attributed MDS' ability to move in self-sufficiently to previous experience, as revealed by a Louisiana FBO: "Their strong organization and preparedness allowed them to move quickly. They were able to become familiar and gain knowledge of the area and needs of our local people, faster and more in-depth than even our local organizations." Once in place, MDS built houses by first building effective working partnerships.

Getting to Know Each Other

MDS initiated new partnerships in several ways, by working with the faith community, joining a long term recovery committee, and listening to what locals needed. To start, MDS often made first contact "with our [Mennonite] church members, then expanded to include all the members of our [new] neighborhood." As an MDS staff member explained, "the use of the word 'neighborhood' brings a core Anabaptist belief into play, that those affected by tragedy are not strangers, they are neighbors in need."

MDS also relied on those they knew best from previous experience, forming ties with local faith-based partners. "The churches quickly became the logistical resource for MDS, providing connection to people in need and to people who could be of assistance," according to one Mississippi partner. Faith relationships often served as the backbone of local recovery organizations, with people stepping over from faith service into leadership roles. Faith partners became a crucial conduit into the community, a connectional strategy that worked well across the region: "MDS used our church as their center of operations. We provided MDS with the names and addresses of people and determined the extent of their needs. Basically, we did the case management for MDS, working daily with the project director to help identify the most needy, in some cases providing translation assistance." In Mississippi, a faith-based partner agreed: "We connected MDS with local contacts. Initially, we did the needs assessments to provide the information to MDS about priorities in housing." Faith partners added further value when they provided "worship services. I did a lot of devotions for MDS."

It was challenging, though, to work in devastated areas where prospective partners had lost their own homes, offices, neighbors, and places of worship. Yet many local leaders stepped up when long-term recovery committees began to form. Doing so was a leap of faith for most, as they had limited or no experience in disaster recovery. A Louisiana partner working on Rita recovery said that the local long-term recovery committee received MDS well, in part when other organizations (such as FEMA) said, "MDS can do this." Not familiar with MDS previously, one local leader remained skeptical for a while as "we had promises from other organizations that did not follow through." He changed his mind, as did a faith-based partner in Alabama who remarked, "When we hooked up with the Mennonites, they were most helpful. They had experience in needs assessment, cost estimates, case management, and [they had] construction skills." Unexpected donations and grants allowed MDS to provide start-up funds and gentle advice to emerging LTRCs. One community partner explained, "We needed to get the long term recovery committees going. MDS said here is $5,000 for one and then wrote another check out for another parish. Mennonites have that 'can do' attitude." In Point aux Chenes, Louisiana, MDS facilitated a Tribal Coalition, bringing four local chiefs into their first collaborative LTRC.

Newly formed partnerships, over time, developed into trusted relationships. In one Louisiana parish, a community partner said, "They (MDS) made working with them very comfortable. The project director would meet with us to figure out what was needed; they always gave us plenty of lead time. If something happened to slow things down, they were always gracious about it." In Mississippi, "we worked closely with MDS to help answer questions about the building codes and inspect the buildings. They were very cooperative. They would ask questions about how to do something and then they would go out and do it right." The demeanor of volunteers interacting with locals, the majority of which did not know Mennonites or Anabaptist philosophies, emerged as the basis for meaningful relationships. Together, they would identify those with unmet needs and work collectively to rebuild.

Selecting Clients

Recovery partners "are under tremendous pressure to get clients into the system, get the job done and get out," often due to grant stipulations. Having partners at the recovery table, along with case managers to present client cases, streamlines the process.

MDS sought out areas that felt neglected: "The Mennonites built the very first home that was rebuilt here in Pass Christian. We needed them. We are just invisible over here; Louisiana gets all the attention and New Orleans after the flood there. We really needed them. The Mennonites are the only ones that built here in Pass Christian, the only ones here." A Louisiana partner continued, "They understood development of the person is as important as the house. They 'got' our organization and that you have to build the person not just the house. The house is an asset. They helped to build a community here." Another Louisiana partner agreed, "That is what they did in Grand Bayou; they asked 'How do we help preserve community?'" Selecting clients became a joint venture in rebuilding not just individual homes but in revitalizing neighborhoods and restoring communities.

MDS criteria for clients center on low-income seniors, single parents, and people with disabilities. One long term partner described how they started selecting clients: "Our experience with MDS was really wonderful. It was great to see their contact with social workers and select the neediest cases to help." An Alabama faith partner described what many local organizations experienced with MDS: "We handed over the most difficult, severe cases to the Mennonites. This was the greatest partnership I have ever seen."

Collaboration involved "taking on those with the most significant needs in partnership." In one Mississippi location, "people would sign up at various places to be considered for a house. It was hard to decide who to pick." Local partners did the necessary case work to determine finances, because they often knew who was in need, including people who had not applied or did not trust outsiders. LTRCs, case managers, and local committee members determined who would be eligible, then offered cases to participating faith-based organizations like MDS. Community partners across the region remarked similarly:

> We identified clients for MDS, did their applications. First they had to qualify and then they got extra points if they were disabled or elderly or had nowhere to stay. It was based on need. Many were living in a shack or completely unsafe conditions. One lady had raw wiring running through her house and the rain came in through the roof. She was waiting three years later [after the storm] and MDS did the rebuild.

Community partners concurred that "MDS held firm with serving a targeted population. They wanted case management and to serve those in need: single parents, elderly, and disabled." One long term recovery committee applied criteria beyond financial need: "The client must be a homeowner with a clear title, have a solid healthy attitude toward the helpers, and be able to contribute financially." Another committee said that clients had to be able to pay taxes and insurance on the rebuilt property.

But selecting clients represented just the first step in a long series of challenges these new partners worked through together. In a number of low-income and minority areas, it became problematic to identify clear title. "Here most people pass the house down from generation to generation. There are no wills." Damage to the area also obscured or destroyed visible landmarks demarcating property boundaries and in some areas, flooding destroyed public records. Securing clear title became a challenge and working with partners was necessary to find the clear title that would enable volunteer organizations to secure building permits. Dogged persistence was necessary in some cases. One MDS project worker secured over 120 signatures of potential heirs to allow rebuilding on one property. The diaspora caused by Katrina made it even more difficult to contact absent homeowners. In each case, the newly established local to outsider connection occurred because of financial need when insurance funds and even government aid often proved inadequate to rebuild.

FUNDING THE RECONSTRUCTION

Voluntary and faith-based organizations rarely bring in sufficient donations to build entire homes. Rather, like MDS, they offer volunteer labor. Most volunteer recovery organizations must rely on a multiple sources to fund their rebuilding efforts including homeowner funds (usually insurance), government aid, donations, and foundation grants. Long-term recovery organizations often serve as the repository of those funds. How did local partners secure funding and view the use of those funds they entrusted to an organization they had known only since the storm?

Securing Funding

Funding the homes of those in greatest need was never easy or straightforward. Insurance companies balked, government grants failed to cover all expenses, and homeowners who had lost all their assets had little to give. Local leaders worked tirelessly for years to secure financing and bring their neighbors home again. Securing funding to rebuild was, as one explained: "A new adventure for us. We started with Katrina and raised about $40,000 to $50,000, most of it from local donations. For Rita we raised about $3 million from across the country."

Another Louisiana partner said, "Financing was a mix to pay for the houses. We got donations and grants, some homeowner's insurance, some Road Home money [a state-based recovery program] and some FEMA money." One recovery committee leader described the multiple efforts required to secure funding: "We got grants and paid the majority through those grants. There was little insurance around here. It cost $70,000 just to do the elevations [required due to new building codes in floodplains] and another $50 to $60,000 to build." Still, one Louisiana partner felt overcome by financial donations: "We got over one million from a major foundation. Amazing amounts of money came in. The giving shocked us all: volunteers would come to help and bring a $10,000 check from their church." In Pass Christian, the local Rotary Club led a drive to fund 40 homes with donations from Rotary Clubs across the U.S.

The Rotary Club of Naperville, Illinois donated funds for over half of the homes.

During the first years of projects, community leaders learned "there were lots of grants. We could build a 1,000 square foot, two bedroom home for someone with no mortgage for about $30 to $35,000 if the labor was donated." Some partners controlled costs by using pre-determined house plans—some made by MDS—and specified square footage: "We offered a small house plan, 866 square feet. If a family needed more room, they had to add money."

New codes for elevations in flood-prone areas meant a considerable increase in the cost of rebuilding homes, which low-income households could not afford. In one Louisiana parish, "we put the homes up 16 feet in the air in some places. That costs $75,000 just to put them on the pillars and then you have to pay for the house. Some homes can cost $200,000." Such costs meant that many seniors and people with disabilities faced significant barriers to coming home. "Houses cost $50 to 70,000 depending on extras like wheelchair ramps. There are no elevators on houses here; they are too expensive," said a Louisiana partner. A Mississippi partner explained further: "Elevators, the metal cage kind, cost about $2,000. We put in two but the homeowners had to pay for it." In some cases, the LTRC relied on partners like Catholic Charities to pay for elevators or ramps. MDS helped by installing ramps yet, "it was tricky putting a wheelchair ramp up on those elevations." In one location, MDS wrapped the ramp around the entire house to make it right.

Partners also worked local relationships to get good prices for projects. "We caught some breaks." A national chain with a local store "gave us things they had left that had not sold like doors and hardware or anything on the floor too long." Local leaders often said: "We got some breaks on trusses and foundations because we used local people and could pay less so they got business." In Texas, "We had to put together multiple grants. We negotiated to get good prices locally." Other local companies donated materials, including the expensive work required to elevate homes.

Yet the battle to find funding beyond the first years wearied local leaders. Some communities felt completely forgotten in the catastrophic impact of multiple storms over three years. "It was hard to get FEMA to turn it around. Most people here got $10,000. Some had a little insurance. Some are still waiting for insurance. It was hard to find people with enough money to build a house. Storms have ravaged homes here." State government did not work out well either; "Some people got their Road Home money (from Louisiana) in 2010. It's five years later." Battles over insurance took years as well. "Cajuns are resilient but how many times can you do it? It is a very long process to get insurance claims. Some people are just getting settled and it's five years later."

Trusting Outsiders with the Money

Given local concerns about outside organizations, what would local partners make of outsiders' use of their hard-won funds? Project directors, construction supervisors, and crew leaders may generate bills for construction needs that need to be charged either to a homeowner's account or to MDS. To insure financial stewardship, volunteer office managers receive training from MDS, updated for Katrina, which includes internal accounting practices with standardized, computerized forms and oversight by paid staff. But what would it be like for local partners to work directly with volunteers, including office managers, who rotate in every 2 to 6 months? To local partners, the transitions felt fairly smooth: "We would train the new person and they would pick it up right away." One Louisiana partner said, "Accounting was very well done, very accurate. Someone came in from MDS weekly, sat down with us and paid the bills. We worked together with the vendors. There was never a surprise with MDS." Another added, "we did the accounting together every morning."

In most locations, partners set up an account for an individual client and placed money into it from combined sources. MDS would then purchase needed items charging against the account or collecting invoices and "they would tell me the account was low and I would add money to it." In one case, MDS "set up the accounts and brought invoices to me. The invoices and accounting were meticulous and efficient." In a recurring theme throughout the interviews, partners compared experiences: "They always had the receipts. We had no worries. They are honest people. We had tales of terror with other contractors, people having their money taken and jobs not finished." In short, all interviewees expressed confidence in the accountability of Mennonite volunteers to safeguard and apply their limited funds, in a promise that built trusting partnerships within increasingly long-term relationships.

REBUILDING TOGETHER

With a long-term recovery committee in place and funding coming in, the rebuilding effort could commence. As the years unfolded, the rebuilding relationships generated rich meaning in the lives of volunteers, both those who served their neighbors locally and those who came from "outside."

Meaningful Relationships

A concerned faith-based partner in Louisiana said, "We had anticipated that there might be frictional relationships developing between two different cultures. However, the MDS volunteers coming in were simply

amazing and responded well to our members, resulting in close relationships being established." Partners across the affected areas consistently
stated that they had a positive experience with the relatively homogene-
ous MDS volunteers, often older, predominantly white, and not familiar
with the local way of life.

Outsiders arriving to help can sometimes, even unintentionally, carry
ethnocentric beliefs into local interactions. However, rather than judging
local cultures from their own perspective, though, local partners reported
that most volunteers interacted from a stance of cultural relativism, or
wanting to understand and appreciate local cultures from the local perspective. Interview data show that the most commonly used phrase
across community partners regarding MDS was "they just fit in." One
partner described the abilities of MDS volunteers to blend in to a diverse
culture: "It is like a patchwork quilt here with people being open and
trusting—this is Louisiana."

Several strategies facilitated the emergence of meaningful relationships. First, MDS fit in by going to local churches for worship; in Mississippi a partner said, "At our church, the Father would get up and say 'we
have some great people with us, they are *our* Mennonites.'" Attending
local events also mattered: "They also came to our events like Carnival;
they enjoyed themselves!"

In an area hit by Rita, one partner said, "MDS did a great job participating in local culture. They went to local churches, they shopped locally,
bought local products." MDS also invited locals to their camp, "which
was a wonderful way to build relationships. In this location, southern
hospitality is very important and MDS was very well accepted because
they extended hospitality as well." What mattered especially to community partners was how outsiders treated local residents. A community
partner in Louisiana dealing with Ike said, "They get it about people."

Another Louisiana parish partner described how that happened after
Rita: "They did not push relationships. This is an area where Baptists and
Catholics are strong—the MDS volunteers would invite others to prayer
at lunch. They were not judgmental about why people wanted to stay
here, to live here, to want to build back. They never questioned why."
She added, "They felt for our people. They understood our love for our
community and tried to help us get it back. They would say, 'what can
we do to get you back on your porch?'" As a Louisiana partner observed,
"It is just their way of walking in, like they have always been in your
community. It was like they walked in and they were family."

Community partners often added, "They bonded with the homeowners. I saw loving relationships every day" in Mississippi. One community
partner in Louisiana watched as volunteers slowly involved an elderly,
devastated homeowner in rebuilding: "He would not talk to them at first.
An MDS person sat down next to him and gently patted him on the arm.
He came back the next day and spoke to him. The man finally spoke

back. Within a while, the old man began to get up, to hand MDS a hammer, to interact . . . it is heartwarming, remarkable, the MDS process of connecting with people." Another in Mississippi saw volunteers going above and beyond the usual: "Some Mennonites even bought furniture for homeowners; that was very nice." She continued, "They did that on their own—you had to go outside here to buy things and bring them back."

In addition to watchful local leaders, government officials also kept an eye on outsiders. Yet the most common response they gave could be summarized by one Mississippi leader: "There were no problems with the community; they [MDS volunteers] were respectful." Another elected official described MDS as "good neighbors and good stewards to the community. We did not have any police calls to come out to their camp. It was a good marriage."

When asked about cross-cultural interactions, one Louisiana respondent became visibly upset at the question and insisted, "There are no problems. They were here to serve and presented themselves well. Mennonites would come and work . . . we never had any issues. Those lines went away. Some individuals had to be taught better or asked to leave, but never with MDS." A partner in Louisiana agreed, "They were fine with the diversity in this community; there was not one discourteous or rude person and never any complaining or cursing. They were all just respectable in all manners and that is very important in this community." A Mississippi partner affirmed the cross-cultural ties that formed: "We had a good fit here, those Canadians; we had to teach them to say y'all!" "He's an adopted, honorary Cajun," one partner remarked of an MDS representative. A resident in Louisiana concurred, giving a firm indicator of the relationship: "They were well accepted. We loved getting to know the Mennonites and how they operate. We sing 'Oh Canada!' now." Community partners, who truly appreciated the manner in which an Anabaptist-centered organization moved into and interacted with their neighbors, showed their deep appreciation in the hospitality they extended to the volunteers. One Louisiana partner summed it up for many: "Anyone is welcome to help. But few are invited to gumbo."

Communication

Communication is a critical aspect of working together. All partners commented positively on their communication with MDS, noting only minor concerns. Analysis of the data revealed two clear themes. The most frequent comments concerned how Mennonite volunteers interacted with locals followed by the frequency of contact.

In the southern U.S., being polite, inquiring about family and attending to the concerns of those talking to you, represent paramount cultural norms. Behind those behaviors lies the deeply held value of southern hospitality. One can imagine that locals who saw outsiders coming to help wondered: "How would they fit in here?" In terms of culturally appropriate behavior, partners affirmed that this external organization blended in quite well. One Louisiana partner said "MDS was always nice and polite; they don't make you feel stupid." Reflecting a broader coastal reaction, a Texas partner said, "They listened and offered suggestions from what had worked in other locations like New Orleans and Mississippi."

Reflecting a common theme from the interviews, a Texas community partner contrasted MDS with government agencies: "When we had questions, no problem getting them." In Louisiana, a community partner dealing with Rita agreed: "They were open and honest. The government promised so much and it always fell through." Another partner said, "You call them and they are at your home right away. They went out of their way to solve problems. They would leave their site to go and accommodate a person." Partners truly appreciated the straightforward and amenable approach brought by Mennonite volunteers. As one code inspector said, "Of all the groups, they tended to be sufficiently communicative and compliant. If they were told to do something, they did it. No whining. They would explain if there was an issue and why it was a problem. If more were direct like that, there would have been fewer problems."

Both clients and community partners observed a lack of internal conflict on project sites as well, where they observed both short-term (weekly) and long-term (multiple monthly) volunteers. Only one partner reported he "heard one disagreement and it was over how to improve something." He added, "None of the volunteers knew each other and to get that many to work together was impressive. They didn't argue." Clients indicated that when a difference of opinion occurred on the project site, "they would just gather around and work it out." The absence of conflict mattered in a context of trauma. Bickering would only make the situation worse and increase stress. A lack of conflict, especially in an area where locals often felt exasperation or anger toward the government, eased the local burden.

Once projects opened, frequent contact also reassured local partners as they built relationships with strangers. "My communication with MDS was personal meetings, daily, with the project director," a faith-based partner in Mississippi shared. One Texas partner said, though, that "It varied by leader; it was poor with some crew leaders and sometimes between the crew leaders and the home office" but added that things worked out. Frequency also included promptness, and a faith-based partner in Texas noted a common response: "Communication was efficient and prompt, never more than a day. When you are onsite, they have that 'what can I do' attitude. I can't think of a single instance where I thought the communication was poor."

A rural Louisiana faith-based partner said, "You could get them on the phone; they were always there at the camp and they could get the project director. They always called back." One Louisiana community partner expressed surprise at the same phenomenon: "They usually answered the phone when you called. They were like a phone call away. They were always smiling and easy to work with." One respondent did note that using the phone was an easier way to be in contact with the volunteer crews but that e-mail (easier for the respondent) did not work as well. Though long-term volunteers had access to e-mail in the camp office, the newly acquired "Katrina" cell phones did not offer e-mail features, which probably accounted for the e-mail delay but overall resulted in saving dollars donated to MDS. To compensate, volunteer project directors and office managers checked e-mail regularly, printed out critical communications, and discussed responses regularly throughout the day, with a nightly meeting as well.

At the five-year mark, even on closed projects, many interviewees held out their phones to demonstrate a point. "I still have their cell phone numbers. They still call me on a regular basis, even after they returned to Canada," stressed a Mississippi partner. In Louisiana, a highly appointed community official said, "A lot of times you would like to tell an evaluator [the interviewer] that there is an area to improve but I just can't do that. I have all their cell phone numbers and I can call them any time. They always answer or call back. They are awesome. I trust them."

Partners also expressed surprise that MDS would build homes from the ground up: "Most groups won't work from dirt; most don't have time or capacity to rebuild the entire house. MDS comes in with pre-existing plans; they are ready and it doesn't scare them away." Partners came to rely on the dependability of MDS, observing "They have picked up jobs dropped by other organizations." Partners also appreciated the quality of the work. As a Louisiana official said, "MDS never takes on more than they can handle. Some organizations will bring in 150 to build 10 houses in a week. And they don't do that good of a job. MDS does one or two at a time and they are well supported, about 26 people, and they are well supervised. They have a timetable. They go and get it done." In one Mississippi community, "The Mennonites got the cases from the case manager and they would start on the houses. They worked as a team, they were ready to go!" Many local partners concurred, "They are so well organized. They came in and cranked up. They were good partners."

MDS's Reputation

As part of the study, interviewees responded to the question: "What is the reputation of MDS in your community?" Analysis of those responses yielded three main themes. The first concerned the quality of the construction and the second reflected partner's perceptions of MDS' ability to meet local building codes. The third and most frequently occurring theme centered on the ability of MDS volunteers and staff to work with each other. Although the praise from the interviews may be uncomfortable to Anabaptists who practice being the quiet in the land, it demonstrates the value of such consistent work. Also important to MDSers, local partners said MDS volunteers clearly worked hard to "get it right."

Partners typically responded to the question by saying "MDS was new to us and we did not know them in this area" followed by multiple examples of how pleased they were to discover the quality of MDS' efforts. They often contrasted that quality vis-à-vis the arrival of unskilled labor, a matter that concerned some: how would volunteer labor build houses up to code and resistant to future storms? Interviewees concurred with this Texan: "Excellent workmanship!" A Louisiana partner used the same word, "Excellent, sturdy, and in a short amount of time." Concern over unskilled labor disappeared in Texas: "The quality is good, only minor repairs, the kind you would have with any construction, probably less. The quality is better than what could have been done by any professional. They should survive another hurricane. We have nothing to complain about." In Louisiana, "These are solid, well-built houses." A Mississippi partner raised his eyebrows as he contrasted volunteer labor with construction quality: "They rotated in a lot of volunteers, they did good work, built good houses;" a work colleague agreed, "They do wonderful work. I was amazed." An elected official in one community used a word offered by many: "The *craftmanship* is second to none. I don't know anybody that is better than the Mennonites."

MDS' success in building solid homes occurred in the context of several challenges. In Grand Bayou, Louisiana, for example, homes perched precariously on land eroding away from bayou streams. Initial efforts required sending volunteers into the muck, insects, and debris left by Katrina to clear building sites. Soil samples had to be taken and elevations of 18 feet had to be approved in a process that took years. Permission for special sewage systems had to be secured. Before construction could begin, docks and movable storage units had to be built so that volunteers could come in by boat. Volunteers would have to set, square, and brace twenty-four poles per home deep into the ground. Every construction tool, piece of sheetrock, lumber, plumbing, septic tank, and bucket of paint had to go in via small boats, an effort that required multiple trips daily. Yet in 2011, residents, partners, and volunteers celebrated the tenth home finished on the bayou. A local partner said, "The houses built by Mennonites were the best post-Katrina construction in the parish. MDS has a solid reputation; there is quality work with them."

Partners contrasted the quality of MDS work against the "volume other groups like to maintain," suggesting that "it is not about speed, it is about quality work." A Louisiana partner said, "The recipients were never dissatisfied and I would have heard from them if they were." In Mississippi, a partner said, "The quality is key. You can pick out the Mennonite houses when you drive by them. Just look at the foundations; they went past the minimum." She added, "They surpass anything here that was rebuilt. The craftsmanship is superb. They are skilled craftspeople. We never worried. They were strict on the volunteers. We never heard a single complaint." She added, "They were flawless and meticulous. They would clean up after they were done with something, very neat and clean. You can spot a window that a Mennonite put in."

Partners also appraised the internal organization that generated homes faster than they expected. "The Mennonites brought labor. You did not have to wait on someone to come in to lay brick or to hire a contractor." In Texas, a partner said, "The most amazing thing was that when they came, the houses went up immediately. This was different from many of our experiences where money flowed in but nothing was accomplished." Another suggested that quality stemmed from overall management, which was handled on-site by long-term volunteers: "They have a defined process and program and they have done it well. They know how to get it done. They know what assets they need to get it done." Across all states, partners concurred with a Mississippi official: "People came like clockwork when they were needed, the right number of people to do the foundation, roof, and painting." In some locations, projects did close down for the hot summer months, which caused anxiety among partners—will they come back? They learned to trust that MDS would return to finish a home still under construction. In some locations, such as New Orleans and Plaquemines Parish, MDS sought volunteers to keep coming despite summer heat, to inspire confidence and encourage those still homeless after four or five years. They did so with particular dedication after the BP oil spill so that communities would have hope. Volunteers labored diligently even as the heat index, starting in the 80s, rose steadily to 110 during the day.

Gulf Coast Building Codes

Recovery partners might be happy, but what about local building experts? After most disasters, government officials, planners, and building code inspectors work diligently to find ways to improve structural resistance to local hazards. After the Gulf Coast storms, the most common structural improvement concerned elevations. Because of the widespread damage, most elevation requirements meant completely rebuilding the home. As the years went on after Katrina and Rita, codes continued to change, meaning that contractors had to change as well. Given that volunteer crews, long-term and short-term, moved in and out constantly, conveying codes and changes could prove challenging.

Yet a Mississippi partner said, "They [MDS] were anxious to learn our way of building. Not all contractors would do that. Our codes are different here." One Mississippi partner said, "They put on hurricane clips. That was new to them, but they put them on here to take a 130 mph wind." An elected official said, "The houses are well built and meet every code. They are above code. These houses have integrity; they look good." A Louisiana code official said, "They [the clients] were built beautiful houses. I was real worried. I had seen houses that other organizations built and they did not meet code. So I went every day to check and did daily inspections. The MDS houses met or exceeded all international, city, and state codes." A Mississippi partner agreed: "MDS was told the depth of the elevation and they went another extra foot to make sure. These houses might be the only ones left standing if a storm comes; they are up to code." A Louisiana engineer agreed: "They did a great job."

Codes continued to change in many communities, yet "MDS went to a higher grade on a lot of things. We would require a half inch bolt; they went to 5/8 because they knew we would be going to it eventually. If they knew it [a change] was coming they would go ahead and do the expected code because it was the right thing to do." In one case, an inspection failed due to a misunderstanding over the new code, yet "there were no gripes from MDS; they just redid it." Two Louisiana partners shared, "Their end product was exceptional; you couldn't find a flaw in the end product. It was well, well done," and "I am a big fan of MDS. They were here with us from the start." Partners contrasted MDS with other contractors who "griped about having to do our code but not the Mennonites. And they worked from sun-up to sun-down. Their reputation here is for first class work without any problems. I never saw a bad thing with any of their work."

Collective relief at the quality of the work stemmed from communities and clients who had experienced harsh lessons as "bad contractors stole money from people or left work undone" in Texas, Louisiana, and Mississippi. A Louisiana code inspector shared a sentiment commonly found across community partners: "I had a lot of problems with contractors taking shortcuts and complaining when I did not approve them. I never, ever found any code violations with the Mennonites." In a few cases, inspectors found some concerns which project directors and crew leaders always addressed rapidly. One problem stemmed from an elevation that was measured by a local company. Although the house had been completed, the elevation fell short, yet "You never heard one ill word or assigned no blame" from MDS. "They took the house apart and rebuilt it to the higher elevation."

Working well with others prompted one New Orleans partner to observe, "They have had a huge impact on the city and in their connection to other faith groups working for recovery." Another Mississippi partner went on, "In a recovery as large as this, there is also a responsibility. They could have asked for anything and would get it but they never did and never abused it. Other organizations did." Some communities described end-runs around code enforcement ("Others would push their weight around."), lobbying of local officials, and unscrupulous practices. But, "the Mennonites never took advantage." One summed up the experience for most: "They are not like government. They are well loved in the community. They went out of their way constantly."

An organization that stays the course, builds strong houses, and can be trusted creates a positive and lasting impression. Code enforcement, building inspectors, engineers, elected officials, and community partners would likely concur with the statement of one in Mississippi: "These houses are built to last. They have not yet been tested, but they will last." A Mississippi partner explained the quality of the work as emanating from how "MDS was devoted to their mission and that is why we were so pleased with them." A Texas partner added, "It is their ability to work with people and get things done." A Louisianan showed astonishment: "There were times when snow prevented volunteers from coming, so the people already here would arrange to stay another week. No idea how they managed to put their lives on hold to do that!" A Louisiana partner summarized, "Those houses on Grand Bayou are built like Fort Knox. Knowing that volunteers did it, the quality is incredible. To see what they can do—we should praise their accuracy. And the volunteers gain too, especially in how to do something new and carry it into the next project." One partner summed it up for all interviewed: "They have a really good reputation on this coast."

CONCLUSION

Why would community partners express such consistently positive responses along the entire coast regardless of the size, location, or demographic makeup of the community? The answer lies in Anabaptist beliefs that value service, an outward expression of the peace-centered nature of their faith. From the conscientious objectors who volunteer to help rather than to hurt, efforts to save refugees in makeshift camps, and dedication to social justice, the core values of a Mennonite organization reflect identities socialized into place over centuries. Service represents a shared heritage, a common commitment, and a binding tie situated in religion. As an MDS staff member explained, "Those are the roots of Anabaptism. We are a peace church focused on missions as a direct result. One of the arms of mission is extension of peace to our neighbors. We reach out to those in need."

For a faith tradition within which some denominations practice separatism, the notion that people leave their homes and go to serve those in need might seem inconsistent. But theologically, Anabaptists are compelled to be in the world, though "striving always not to be 'of it'" (Neufeld 2007). Given the positive witness provided by community partners across Texas, Louisiana, Mississippi and Alabama, MDS appears to attract people who consistently behave in accordance with their faith, to follow Jesus in demeanor and action. Neufeld, who writes on the need for a Mennonite theology of conscientious engagement, offers "being known as a people with behaviours and reflexes that can be counted on as predictable is at the core of the church's corporate witness" (Neufeld 2007, p. 176). As local partners affirmed, disaster service clearly offers a means to be theologically engaged and bear corporate witness of a faith tradition.

Profoundly meaningful interactions resulted. "It's like they got adopted into the family. MDS was accepted. After 2 years here you would hear people say, 'We love the Mennonites.' They slip in and stay put, even when they are gone, they are still here." The long-term commitment, in a context of catastrophic recovery that would surpass anything in U.S. history, meant a great deal in communities that felt forgotten: "The only concerted, long term, sustainable help was MDS. Period." A Louisiana community partner that provided funding for multiple communities agreed: "The Gulf Coast would not have been rebuilt without the help of the Mennonites." And, "here in Plaquemines Parish, their mission was for the indigenous population in Grand Bayou. They did a magnificent job. Nobody else could have done it."

In Louisiana, a grateful community partner remarked at the five-year anniversary of Katrina, "On a personal level, these people have been my soul brothers and sisters, a way to spiritually connect. These people know what they are doing and they start and end at the right place. People's lives were transformed." It wasn't just the house, it was being a neighbor: "They maintain a presence [at their camp]. Being there is so reassuring to people like me. It says 'you are not alone.' We helped treat your ulcers." A Mississippi partner used a phrase common to several: "They were a breath of fresh air." She continued, "They just love you. We got attached; they are good people. They cried when they left. We did too. It is not just the physical rebuilding, it is that they wanted to do so much for us. In five years out, they helped more than we ever expected. They don't even know us."

NOTES

1. A delicious stew made with okra, shrimp, spices and more.
2. Correspondence. Dyck, Peter J. and John A. Diller. May 9, 1952. Letter from the Temporary Disaster Committee, Central Kansas to MCC Constituent Churches, Central Kansas. Mennonite Library and Archives.

FIVE

Homeowners

People would scream when we told them they were going to get a house.
—Louisiana Long Term Committee Recovery Partner

INTRODUCTION

Without the help of outside volunteers, disasters would permanently displace and financially devastate many low-income households. As one community partner explained about MDS in Louisiana, "They built houses of elderly, single parents, and disabled. They wanted to help people who were literally homeless. MDS is an action group. Several other groups promised to give something but they did not come through, including government." And in Mississippi another community partner concurred:

> Our organization identified 37 people in need. They [MDS] were able to find 14 ready to go that owned their homes outright. Here, most people pass down the house from generation to generation; there are no wills. Of those 14, they could not do all, as they did not have enough money to do all 14. They identified those with medical needs first, especially those at risk because of mold or dust or if they had children living in a cramped FEMA trailer. They also asked neighbors to help find those in need.

For the Gulf Coast storms, client selection again reflected MDS' consistent history. During a tornado response to Arkansas in 1952, the Temporary Disaster Committee (a precursor of MDS) identified and approved eight projects. Chairman Peter J. Dyck described prospective clients in a letter to MCC Constituent Churches as, "people who are aged, widowed or handicapped." MDS's consistent approach over sixty years has provided organizational stability and a clear focus on its mission—to serve those in greatest need—a contribution desperately needed after the storms.

However, an event of the magnitude, scope, and impact of Katrina, followed quickly by Rita and later Ike, threatened the existence of entire communities and led MDS eventually to an expanded focus. In Plaquemines Parish, Louisiana, a community partner said:

> The Mennonites held firm with serving a targeted population. They wanted case management and to serve those in need: single parents, elderly and disabled. They also loosened up some later and said we need to look at not just poverty but also at the community. That is what they did in Grand Bayou, to save the community. They asked how do we help preserve community?

In instances that fall outside a focus on individual households of seniors, people with disabilities and single parents, MDS leaders consult with their community partners, the case managers for the clients, and their own constituency. There are often good reasons for deviations. As one Louisiana community partner explained, "They also picked young families in need. This was essential for our community to survive. Given the economy and the two storms, they [young families] did not have the money to rebuild."

A combined focus on low-income households coupled with a concern for community meant survivors could return from the diaspora generated by the storms to meaningful places and valued relationships. Such social networks have been and remain critical to post-disaster recovery (Weber and Peek 2012; Norris et al. 2002a and 2002b). Being chosen for assistance offered those affected with their first sense of optimism after being left homeless by the storm.

BEING SELECTED

Being selected elicited a range of emotional responses. For some, the offer of help was hard to believe, as expressed by a New Orleans client: "I received an application form at the meeting, which I completed. Then rumors surfaced saying that these people would take away everything I got. I went back, got my application and tore it up. Later a lady came to explain the process more fully and I redid my application." An elderly client living elsewhere in Louisiana had the same thought: "I told them I couldn't afford a house; I thought it was a trick." At the other end of the emotional continuum, a Texas single parent said, "I had been on a wait list for 3 years after Rita with another organization. Then I saw an ad in the paper to call [a local organization] so I did. I got a call a while later and was told they are going to build me a house. I screamed! Everyone knew what had happened."

Many clients contrasted being selected with the long heartbreak that came from losing everything: "The groundbreaking was one of hope and blessing. You could see God's hand moving in this. We loved being part of it." The loss of home, neighbors, jobs and familiar places had been a personal and collective ordeal that lingered. As one client said at the five year mark in 2010, "There's a lot still aching to come home and live in the bayou." Many had been in limbo for years, had moved multiple times, and had lived dependently on family, friends, or the government. Being selected defined a turning point that enabled clients to put the storm behind and move forward at last. For the Gulf Coast storms, two main routes to client selection emerged: collaboration with community partners and connections to social networks.

The Role of Community Partners

In the early Arkansas response of the 1950s, Temporary Disaster Committee members established a partnership with the American Red Cross. These new partners had first addressed the needs of Mrs. Jennings, a middle-aged widow whose only income came from rent and who had tragically lost her sister to the storm. MDS provided volunteer labor to tear down Mrs. Jennings' damaged home and even salvaged the lumber. The Red Cross then funded construction of a duplex for residential and rental unit purposes. As newly connected partners, MDS and the Red Cross provided a home where Mrs. Jennings could earn an income and raise her sister's surviving child. MDS then went to the home of 73-year-old Mr. McFadden who had "a very meager income and [was] bothered with a stiff leg." MDS reconstructed a hen house and a combination wash and well house while the Red Cross worked on the home.[1] The pattern of client selection by working with local partners that MDS established in Arkansas continues to the present day.

Local partners prove valuable in introducing MDS to their neighbors. A Louisiana couple said, "We did not know of the Mennonites. [The long term recovery committee chair] contacted us and asked if we wanted a house. We said we have no money for that. Then she said the Mennonites would build it [the house] for us and it would not cost us anything. She would find the money. Then the [MDS] project director came and talked to us." In Mississippi, a similar pattern emerged: "We heard through the local caseworker. I saw them working on another house here. She explained it and it just took off. The Mennonites came and I met them on the property. They said they would start in a couple of weeks and they did." A New Orleans man "first heard of MDS through the Salvation Army."

In Mississippi, a local community partner further explained the value of locals to an outsider organization: "It was important to do the casework locally because they [the local residents] know the real circumstances of the applicants and how much money they have and can contribute." LTRC-linked case managers walk client files through an application and rebuilding process. Faith-based organizations (FBOs) attend the LTRC meetings where they select clients appropriate to their missions and resources.

Extensive damage across Louisiana involved MDS and other faith-based organizations with multiple, newly established LTRCs. As one example, the Southern Mutual Help Association (SMHA) offered money and case management services. Between 2005 and 2010, a total of 4,432 volunteers, of which 2029 came from MDS, worked on SMHA homes (SMHA website, 2010). Many clients viewed the faith-based-LTRC partnership as a route around bureaucratic struggle. After Ike, one client said, "The state effort to get help was worthless, a hassle. [The local organization] and MDS helped me." He remarked with surprise: "It was the first time I heard of the Mennonites. They came out, looked around and that was it." A few months later, he had a new home.

The Role of Social Networks

Social ties routed people to MDS as well. A family affected by Rita said, "A friend helped us to contact a community aid program. Someone called us to check on our needs and told us about the Mennonites. MDS came over and we spoke with their leader." One Texas client said, "I was in the hospital with surgery; my brother did all the contacting. He went to someone and looked after everything that was required." The brother then added, "I heard about how Mennonites were building houses. When I asked about it, the Mennonites came and found me. There were some from Canada! We had never heard of Mennonites before. We didn't know they existed."

Local churches watched out for their parishioners too. In Texas, "A man at our church had heard of projects done by Mennonites not far away. Our pastor was helping many of the church members. He checked into MDS and let us know about them. We called them and they visited and checked things out. They came back the following year." A Louisiana couple remarked, "We knew nothing of Mennonites. Someone from the Catholic Church contacted us. The Mennonites had talked to the churches. The Catholic Church referred us to the Mennonites." And in some cases, clients attributed being selected to a higher power: "I was very frustrated by all our troubles, unable to find support, unable to do repairs. I walked off my frustrations and one day a car pulled up, the driver asking for directions to a job site. The driver was from MDS, who immediately came over to our house, looked at it, and suggested MDS might be able to help. Three days later she showed up saying that MDS would provide free labor and make the necessary repairs. It was an accidental—providential?—meeting." What would homeowners think of the free labor?

REBUILDING WITH VOLUNTEER LABOR

Within minutes of being asked about their rebuilding experience with MDS, most clients became emotional with, as one client explained, "happy tears." As clients told their stories, moving relationships emerged that spanned state lines and national boundaries, cultures, faith denominations, racial and ethnic differences, and geographic distance. In this section, that process of building relationships is revealed starting with clients meeting Mennonites for the first time followed by strategies that fostered cherished connections.

Meeting Mennonites

What happens when people from a historically farming and rural tradition enter urban areas like New Orleans or rural bayou communities like Grand Bayou? Throughout its history, MDS has been concerned with and listened to issues about being a predominantly white organization. Would outsiders carry prejudice or harmful attitudes into a Native American, Vietnamese American, Cajun French, or African American community? When asked whether outsiders coming into the urban neighborhoods, small towns, and bayou communities along the Gulf Coast brought harmful attitudes, homeowner clients responded with an emphatic "no!" Rather than experiencing separation and distance, clients report that meaningful relationships developed. Those relationships often began with tentative questioning about each other's lives, faiths, and cultures.

Some Anabaptist volunteers were more noticeable than others because of their distinctive clothing and culture. A Mississippi woman said the Amish "walked everywhere," while a neighbor man told of an Amish woman who "appeared rather stern and sober." When they first met, he asked if he could give her a hug per local custom. She hesitantly agreed and subsequently "became more friendly and didn't mind the hugs" with which he customarily greeted people. The same client recalled Amish girls asking him, again hesitantly, if they could ask a personal question. He assured them it was all right and freely invited questions. The Amish girls asked about racial interactions in the area and about skin color. The client said that exchange resulted in an "open discussion" which he appreciated, as they were "eager for knowledge."

He observed a similar reticence among other Mississippi residents toward the Amish volunteers: "We were a little concerned at first to ask them about themselves. But they were open to talk and find common ground among us. I really liked the many different nationalities that came into our community. We had Pennsylvanians, Canadians, Germans and Africans here—all in one week. It was great for our grandchildren to see all this." Food proved invaluable to those initial exchanges. Interactions between Mississippi residents and Amish evolved into crawfish dinners, a local meal new to the volunteers, who "gobbled up everything!" Homeowner clients further broadened cultural ties through local cuisine: "Even the conservative Mennonites connected with us—they really liked our food."

As one Mississippi client summed it up for many interviewed, "Color is not an issue with the Mennonites. I grew up when it was hard being black. I wish everyone could experience the love and caring I experienced from Katrina. Everyone thought their lives were over and it would have [been]except through the help of the Lord and the Mennonites." A woman in Louisiana added,

> It is strange, the people on that side of this street are a little confused by all the white people coming down to visit, and suspicious about them. The people on this side of the street where Mennonites had several projects are so delighted and happy to see white people in our community. I really like the idea of a quilt—all the pieces coming together to make a larger and larger community all connected together.

A Louisiana woman who lived close to the Mississippi River said, "The elders were fascinated by the Amish girls, they were so different. They got very excited by each ship that went past; they would leave their tools and jobs and race up to the top of the levee to watch it go by. This helped us appreciate even more what we had. This was something we were used to and had never given it a second thought."

Local residents felt strongly about their communities, and the way in which a faith-based organization approached these places mattered. A Native American said, "MDS left only compassion, gentleness, and the quality of their work. They [volunteers] were responsible environmentally. They were interested in our life and asked questions and appreciated this environment that we are privileged to be part of. That helped when they came here—it was respect for this place and the life we wanted to reclaim."

A Louisiana couple whose property was damaged by Rita said, "They [MDS workers] were very interested in us and how we lived, our culture. They were down-to-earth people; they liked finding out about us and our food, like oysters. They had a different culture and were happy to explain their religion and culture to us." A Texas client said, "It was a learning experience for them and for us. Even though we were different people with different religions, different beliefs, different cultures, it was just wonderful getting to know each other. People from all over, even from Canada. We shared recipes. I will never forget the experience." And a client from a Louisiana community damaged by Ike said, "It was a thrill to meet people from so many places and learn about their lives." Alabama clients made turnip greens to share with the volunteers. Sharing food led to exchanging recipes and "some of them also made me whoopie pie. I had never heard of it; it was good!" Another Ike client pointed out, "We educated each other and we are lifelong friends."

People connected through more than food. In February 2010, the New Orleans Saints football team won the XLIV World Championship. Just short of the five-year mark since Katrina, the victory represented far more than a football title. Joyful pandemonium broke out in the streets of New Orleans, as the event planted Katrina firmly in the past. Winning reclaimed and redeemed the Superdome from horrific memories as the city's shelter of last refuge. One Louisiana client used her love of the Saints to illustrate cross-cultural connections:

> Quite a few Canadians came to work here. This was something new to most of the community. At first the community and the volunteers were a little shy, but that changed quickly as we saw what the Canadians were doing and how they connected to us. They were all supporters of the New Orleans Saints—our football team! We invented a new expression which the whole community and the Canadians enjoyed. Everyone here knew it. It was "Who-dat Eh!" combining our separate identities.

Clients shared similar sentiments across the coast. In May of 2010, when MDS closed the camp in Mississippi, one said: "Their last day in Pass Christian, *everyone* came."

Shared Meals

The MDS tradition of establishing camps provides opportunities to invite clients over, an interaction mentioned independently[2] by many clients. An especially meaningful interaction occurs on Wednesday nights, when clients share their story with weekly volunteer crews. A woman in Louisiana who survived Katrina and Rita but lost her home to the storm surge from Ike enjoyed those visits where "you come together in awful circumstances, yet you come together and wonderful things happen." She visited the camp and "gave my testimony." Another Ike survivor proclaimed, "They invite me to supper, and they come pick me up. I cannot forget them for the rest of my life. I am always telling everyone about my experience with the Mennonites."

Clients thoroughly enjoyed visiting camp: "They had some good cooks out there!" A Mississippi resident "prayed with them several times at their camp. That was real nice, that singing." Visiting camp also allowed for intercultural exchanges to continue, as when a Louisiana family used the campsite to boil crabs and crawfish. As they cooked and ate together, they learned that crawfish were called mudbugs in Pennsylvania and that the volunteers called supper "dinner," which sounded strange to local ears. Families took their children to play games with the volunteers and felt comfortable enough to let their teenagers visit alone for an evening. Sharing meals promotes community, a practice that resonates from the earliest days of Anabaptism (Murray 2010) and is reminiscent of MCC camps established to feed starving war refugees (Dyck and Dyck 2001).

For clients able to be on their construction sites, lunchtime afforded a way to pay back. Clients from all project sites reported they offered the volunteers "food, coffee, tea; they were really grateful. It was very bonding; they talk to you over tea and coffee." Homeonwers across all the Gulf States also offered jambalaya, cakes, and "daily treats, cookies, cupcakes, Cajun food and took it to all the houses they worked on here, not just mine." An Alabama client kept track of the 35 pounds of coffee that she brewed for the Mennonites. Her husband jokingly referred to a dessert she made as "possum pie," which caused some hesitance among the first volunteer taste-testers. Subsequent crews came in asking for it as word spread through the weekly volunteer teams.

At a broader level, communities collectively returned the volunteer effort with local hospitality. In Pass Christian, a local client said, "I went out for the Wednesday meals at the Baptist Church. MDS would be there too. They sing and pray. They were there every time." In Texas, a client couple joined in the construction and "I cooked for them every day even though they said I didn't have to. But the whole community was so excited that we were getting a house that all the ladies brought food and we cooked together. The whole community participated. I just loved it. It was a labor of love for us!" She laughed, and added, "I think they heard about our cooking so they all wanted to come here—that is why we know so many volunteers."

Shared Outings

Invitational and intentional outings to learn about local culture also helped build connections. Because MDS worked in a number of communities along or in bayou areas, many volunteers went on boat trips. A Louisiana couple said, "A highlight each week for each group of volunteers was taking them out on my boat to watch the porpoises and feed the gulls. We would often end the day with a dinner from our area—they especially enjoyed the Vietnamese dinners. The community really enjoyed sharing their local customs with the volunteers." An east Louisiana couple shared their livelihood: "We gave them a tour of the business. They had not seen that before."

Another Louisiana family took the volunteers out oystering. The family observed the potential social and cultural distances but noted the new relationship: "We gave them oysters. They learned about our way of life. Not one word that would make you feel bad." When one artistic volunteer thanked the family by sending a painting of the trip, it was "the first thing we put up on the wall" in their new house.

Deeply felt connections emerged as shared outings revealed common ground. A fishing family from a Louisiana bayou felt warmed by the non-judgmental approach of outsiders who understood why locals stayed in a disaster-prone location. They saw a tie between their way of life and the rural Anabaptists who came. "God ordained all of these people to come here, to share our differences and our ways of life. Farmers and fishers have a common cause; they have to stay where they are and so do we. And we are now lifelong friends."

"Like Family"

Homeowners clearly stated that volunteers transitioned from unfamiliar strangers to chosen kin. The phrase "family" resonated across client interviews. One woman from an isolated Louisiana community said, "They did a wonderful job, really great! We did not see them often while they were working but when they left they were like family." Indeed, a majority of clients independently used the word "family" to describe the strong, intense, and enduring relationships they experienced with volunteers. An Alabama couple commented, "They were great workers, very friendly. They became like family to us in just a week. We love them to death." A Mississippi man concurred, "They treated me like family and I treated them like family." From a client in Plaquemines Parish, Louisiana: "In spite of living away, I formed a very close connection with the program directors. They were like family and we were frequently in contact by phone." Another client, located in Pass Christian, Mississippi, shared, "MDS became part of our family." A client affected by Rita in Cameron Parish, Louisiana leaned forward to stress the same sentiment: "Very good people, very nice. They became part of *our family*."

A client, in Franklin, Louisiana, proudly showed photos of all of her volunteers. She knew many of them by name, saying: "We was family." In Terrebonne Parish, Louisiana, Native American clients let volunteers stay on the property in RVs and built bonfires for them. The clients also cooked for them: "We all became a family. We still talk and stay in touch. Some of them have come for a visit." At an even deeper level, volunteerism represented a means to bring clients' own families back together. As a Louisiana woman began to cry, she made deliberate eye contact and said, "It was a very rewarding experience. I have grandchildren [in another town]. They can visit now." By making it possible to reunite families split by disaster, MDS volunteers became family members too, and remain welcome in the bayous, small towns and urban neighborhoods across Texas, Louisiana, Mississippi, and Alabama. Shared meals and outings served as the key social means used by MDS to connect with clients. Nor were meals and outings the only way that homeowners and volunteers connected. They also joined together, when and where possible, in rebuilding homes.

Homeowner Participation in Rebuilding

MDS does not require homeowners to contribute sweat equity toward their home. Further, many MDS clients face insurmountable challenges to contributing sweat equity.

Some volunteers deter homeowners from participating, assuming (sometimes correctly) that the homeowners have already borne enough pain or may not be able to participate physically. Concern also exists that a homeowner could be injured during construction. Yet homeowners longed to contribute and often found ways to pay back. Client interviews revealed nine barriers against and three facilitators for homeowner contributions. Decision-making emerged as the primary way through which MDS could involve the majority of their clients.

Barriers to Homeowner Participation

Nine types of barriers to client participation included medical conditions, jobs, being dislocated, a lack of construction knowledge, depression, family obligations, age, grief, and being denied an opportunity to help.

Given the client selection criteria, it is not surprising that medical conditions emerged as the leading reason why clients could not participate in their own home construction. An Alabama husband reported, "I had surgery so the Doctor told me not to work. The Mennonites put a chair in the middle of the place and told me I could be the boss." His wife added, "I made food for them sometimes, which they really enjoyed." During reconstruction, another couple who lost their home to Ike dealt with the wife's surgery and a terminal medical condition for her husband. In Texas, one client worked full-time to support her family adding, "When my husband was home from the hospital, he helped a bit." A New Orleans client had back problems that prohibited helping. A Mississippi couple faced his declining health throughout rebuilding, while a man in Louisiana said, "I was in the hospital when they started, then lived nearby with family until I got a FEMA trailer on site." The majority of clients simply could not provide sweat equity due to medical conditions.

Jobs, the second most common barrier, meant that many clients could not be on site during the day. Several complicating conditions made the job situation difficult to fit with construction times. For example, those employed in common coastal industries like tourism, restaurants, and fishing worked hours at odds with those rebuilding their homes. The storms also took local jobs, requiring clients to travel considerable distances to and from work. In a typical situation, one Louisiana client commented, "My husband was away most of the time at work but able to be around at least one day each week."

A third barrier occurred when the storms dislocated people, from hundreds to thousands of miles away from home. A couple in an area devastated by a 40–foot storm surge said, "We were split up in different locations" and while he was able to be on site during some of the construction, her medical condition required that she remain with distant family. One older woman was typical: "I was living in Memphis," while another lived "in Houston." Clients were "living quite far away" as a Texas woman explained, but "we did drive over to our place a few times when they were building." Despite the distance, social networks helped them stay in touch during construction. One Louisiana woman said, "I was living about 35 miles north. One day I got a call from a neighbor who said 'they planted your pilings!' I was off-the-chart happy."

A fourth barrier stemmed from lack of knowledge about the construction process. Few had built their own homes. A number of single parents and elderly said they just did not know how to do some of the tasks. One woman who tried, "put my foot through a piece of sheetrock!" The damage brought her to tears but to her surprise, "They took that sheetrock and used it around a window!" Clients who learned new skills felt comfortable by the manner in which they learned: "Yes, they taught me how to paint and I really appreciated that. They started me on a bathroom so I could learn and I was slow but I did it with volunteers telling me how to correct something."

Several clients described facing sadness, a feeling not surprising given the magnitude and scope of the disasters. One client spoke of how it felt to return home: "One of the most depressing sights was to see the beautiful green bayou with all its birds completely empty. All the plants were black and burnt by the sea water. The whole picture was very dismal." However, the rebuilding also offered some relief from depression. A client, who had faced serious depression prior to the disaster said that the reconstruction process brought him out of deep despair as volunteers suggested things he could do. A Texas woman reported that near-immobility ceased when her home began to come together.

Family obligations also prevented clients from participating. Several had to care for loved ones with disabilities, ranging from family members who were relatively independent to those requiring extensive support. The majority of clients with disabilities faced mobility challenges. Those in caregiver roles often managed mobility challenges for spouses or cognitive disabilities experienced by their children. Many elderly clients also served as caregivers for children, grandchildren, or a partner. A Mississippi client took care of grandchildren during the day and often at night as their parents sought income to support multiple generations. Many elderly, particularly women, cared for ailing spouses. In many of the working-age households, one parent had to care for children while the other spouse worked. For parents who worked an evening or overnight shift, such as fishing, caring for children during the day meant struggling with personal exhaustion as well.

Age also prevented some from participating. Coupled with medical conditions or caring for a partner, being older often meant that little time could be devoted to social interactions and contributions. A Mississippi woman spoke of caring for her husband, who was "too sick to go to the camp." Local social workers expressed concern that the impact of the disaster had caused so much stress that seniors deteriorated. In Mississippi, social workers reported "going to a lot more funerals" after Katrina. Caring for seniors with medical issues also led to grief in several cases. One client said she was "still in the grieving stage" having just lost her husband. Interviewees reported that the loss of their spouses impaired their abilities to focus and make decisions. Losing a spouse also made it more difficult to unpack and put things up on the walls. The circumstances, though, were tempered by believing that the lost partner had died knowing the surviving spouse would have a home. A most compelling indicator came from a Louisiana widow. She said that, close to his death, her husband began to talk to people he thought he saw. As he called out their names, she realized they were MDS volunteers who had worked on their home.

In a few instances, clients felt disappointed in not being allowed to help on their site. For a Louisiana client, "This was a sore point. I was a professional carpenter. They would not let me do anything." A community partner expanded, "MDS is very self-sufficient and brings enough people. But homeowners would like to be involved even if it is a little thing."

Facilitators for Homeowner Contributions

Client interviews revealed three conditions that facilitated homeowner involvement: proximity to the job site, knowledge or ability, and involving clients in decision making. The condition that facilitated homeowner participation best arose out of proximity or nearness to the construction site. Because of the wide dislocation experienced after the storms, such proximity came via the presence of nearby temporary housing. One client said, "We were around, we lived in a FEMA trailer on the property. We helped although they told us we didn't have to work, but we wanted to." A man in Louisiana "lived in a trailer beside the house and watched the Mennonites." A woman in New Orleans, living in a trailer said, "I got excited seeing my house getting built. The Mennonites opened the door to happiness in my heart." Some homeowners managed marginal conditions to be close enough to help. A client in Louisiana said, "My husband lived in a shed on the property and was on site all the time."

Knowledge of how to participate also facilitated homeowner contributions. A Texas client reported, "We were here every day. My husband is a carpenter and it was hard to hold him back. He joined in the construction." She added, "I cooked for them every day even though they said I didn't have to." A Rita survivor, "I was on the site every day. We were able to help along with the crew. I did jobs that required less expertise and my husband did more complicated tasks in the building." A retired resident used his carpentry skills as well: "I was on site seven days a week, working along with the Mennonites when they were there and continuing working on their day of rest by rebuilding floors and walls."

Many MDS long term volunteers further empower clients by involving them in decisions about their homes. Yet, few homeowners had actually built their homes or had experience with doing so. Many also lacked confidence in choosing materials, often telling the project director, "You decide." For a few, the gift of a house overwhelmed their expectation to provide input: "We were so appreciative we did not ask too many questions." Another client agreed: "You don't look a gift horse in the mouth." Yet clients expressed trust in project volunteers. A Texas woman's trust arose from religious beliefs: "The Lord sent you here and I have confidence in you that you will build me an adequate home." Even so, she said, "They always asked me. I did pick out the shingles." Another Texas couple let the project director select the bathroom mirrors and to their surprise, "We thought it would just be a mirror and it was a nice three-way mirror in a medicine cabinet." A Mississippi client positioned her response vis-à-vis affordability: "I would say 'whatever you want is fine' but they urged me to pick out the colors I wanted. I would ask 'which is cheapest?'"

For those distant from the project site due to storm displacement, medical conditions, job responsibilities, or family obligations that limited involvement, clients remarked on the effective communication they had with project management. A Mississippi client commented, "I was very busy with work and family. I received progress reports regularly but I told the director to do what he thought was best. I am very pleased with what they did. My house is well built."

MDS offered floor plan options to most of their clients. A woman in Cameron Parish, Louisiana explained, "They showed us a basic plan and what they could and would do. They asked us if there were any changes we wanted (within the basic plan). They honored our wishes." An Alabama couple had a similar experience: "The Mennonites came with 4 house plans from which we could select. They adapted the plan to suit us. There was a big picture window in our bedroom and a small one in the living room. We asked them to exchange the two" and MDS did so.

The couple continued, "They moved the door to a side wall. There was one wall in the kitchen which they replaced . . . They were most accommodating."

The degree to which MDS allowed clients to take part in decision-making including alterations to the building plan appears to be unusual among rebuilding organizations. Several factors limited alterations such as the amount of funding available: "They told me at the start that they would build it the way I wanted it but they didn't do that exactly. The size of the house was determined by how much money became available." Limitations also happened when other organizations partnered, as a Louisiana client observed: "MDS made an agreement with another organization . . . to use their plan for building houses. Ours was the first of these." Even in this case, though, the client reported: "We did however have the ability to change the floor plan. I immediately asked if I could flip the kitchen and the living room around." In response, the project director "told me to study the plan, sit on it, imagine your life in this house, stake out the walls and walk around it. I marked off the plan with string. I asked for several changes and they accommodated me. They flipped the two rooms which I had earlier requested." She continued, with appreciation for the financial impact on her budget: "This did not cost extra."

MDS even resituated new houses for reasons important to the clients. One Texas woman wanted to save a front porch that held important memories, with family names carved into the steps. In an environment badly maimed by Katrina where severe coastal erosion had ruined environmental resources, and where Ike took down beloved trees, local residents took a strong stand to save what remained. In Louisiana, a family declined rebuilding until MDS turned the floor plan to save oak trees planted by the family years earlier. MDS did the same for a family in Texas, saving a tree by moving the house further back on the lot.

In a few instances, clients expressed amusement over geographic differences during the construction process. A Louisiana woman laughed when describing a requested change with a project director from the colder climate of Canada: "The other change was the removal of a closet designated as parka storage. Why would I need to store parkas? I will never own one!" In Mississippi, a client shook his head and smiled as he explained how the project director agreed to remove the coat closet to increase living room wall space. In each case, clients chuckled at Canadian concern over coat closets. "It's just something we don't need down here!" For several, eliminating the coat closet extended a laundry area, bedroom, or bathroom or afforded space for the water heater.

The portion of reconstruction in which most clients took part came toward the end, with selection of paint colors, cabinetry, and flooring. Again, physical ability to be present and funding influenced options. One client, unable to be onsite, stayed in touch via telephone. One day, the office manager called and realized the client was discouraged and feeling down. A group of MDS women drove to the client's location and took her to pick out colors and cabinet stains to cheer her up. Project directors empowered and encouraged clients to make decisions, with powerful results beyond construction choices. In a context where storms had stripped them of all they had owned; torn them away from family, church, and community; and made them dependent on others, decision-making lifted them emotionally: "I felt like a kid in a candy store to pick it out, it was like a time of recreation." She contrasted the trip with how she felt after the storm: "It felt like the government took us over. I got food stamps for the first time. I felt like I lost myself. I didn't feel independent. Picking out was the fun part especially when you are not used to living off the state. I didn't even know how to use a laundromat."

Involving clients in store trips transformed and empowered clients marginalized by storm effects: "We got a choice of house plans. Oh yes, to us it was wonderful. We had nothing. They asked me what colors I wanted. They would ask me if I could come over the next day to look at something and I always said sure." This Mississippi woman especially enjoyed the tangible consequences of shopping for her own home, "We went with the project director to look for countertops; that was so fun. I put my hand right on what I wanted." For many, store trips allowed them to personalize their homes as this Louisiana woman discovered: "We had fun shopping! We got to sit down at a computer [in a construction store] and it created exactly what we wanted with our choices and we got a printout. This helped us to put in some really helpful things including a lazy susan and a larger cupboard for big pans."

Involving clients in making decisions proved empowering: "They asked me about everything. What kind of wood, paint, hinges, doorknobs. I would go to Home Depot and we would check the list and find what we needed. It was amazing to go up and down the aisles." Clients expressed joy at being able to create a home that, for them, ended a personal nightmare. As if they had been watching decorating shows for years, they took the opportunity to live in the house of their dreams. One Texas woman described her delight: "I got to pick the colors inside and outside. I was very careful to have it all match, the blue specks in the counters look real nice with the vinyl." She also enjoyed new features on her rebuilt home: "The project director suggested a French door leading off the kitchen, I had never heard of that kind of door before."

Providing opportunities to make decisions gives dignity to clients. For the impoverished, for those who had lost everything, and for those who had to rely on others to survive, being involved in decision-making provided positive psychological and emotional benefits. A Mississippi community partner understood the value of personalizing a home: "They did change up the interiors to make it fit people's personalities a little more." In Louisiana, someone moving back into her community said, "They gave us choices so we are not just cookie cutters. We are individuals and they tried to address that. Because we live here, we could choose to imprint something of ourselves on the house."

A national-level, faith-based partner contrasted the MDS approach to decision-making with that of other organizations: "They were even able to allow people to make some changes to the housing plans. That is very unusual. I am impressed with their program. Their reputation with the clients is above and beyond the norm." The partner further explained how MDS accomplished such a feat: "They work with the homeowner, will even say 'we can try that' when someone wants a modification. It does not cost more; they just use their skills to enhance what the housing plan calls for and the client needs." Local partners appreciated such an approach: "Not any voluntary organization could do that; they are a good match to local needs. To me that says they have more than just the homebuilding skills. They care about the homeowner, they are compassionate." Perhaps the best explanation came from a Mississippi client who no longer felt poor or dependent: "You would have thought that I gave them a million dollars to build my house; that is how they treated me."

Disability Accommodations

A challenging area for many rebuilding organizations concerns accommodation of disabilities. Though homes must be constructed to local codes, those codes can vary across jurisdictions. Further, basic housing plans may not anticipate future needs and some funding may not allow for meeting all needs. MDS met or exceeded local codes for disability issues and in many cases added elements to make the home more accessible. MDS also listened to client requests about mobility issues: "The Mennonites were very accommodating. I asked for several changes. Wider doors to accommodate a wheelchair. One large bathroom instead of 2 smaller ones. An open area design instead of rooms with walls. They were very agreeable and made all the changes."

A Native American family, whose husband used a wheelchair, spent two and a half years in temporary housing. MDS workers widened the hallway and put in an accessible bathroom for the wheelchair. They also installed laminate flooring so clients could move the wheelchair more easily. Most requests to add disability-friendly elements were fulfilled. "We requested a handicap ramp be built, a tub instead of a shower, and a different stove for handicapped people," reported a Louisiana family. The project director also installed flat sections on the ramp so that the wheelchair user could rest while negotiating homes that had to be elevated above potential storm surges. But required elevations added considerable expense for residents with disabilities and not all requests could be honored. One Louisiana client described what MDS offered, "They made several accommodations for a wheelchair in the layout. All doors are wider; however no ramp was built. I have high stairs. I am planning to put in an elevator but that has not happened yet."

Though not all clients could be accommodated as completely as they desired, MDS clearly went to some effort to enhance accessibility in most homes, even changing the height of kitchen and bathroom counters. A Louisiana man said, "Katrina took away everything I had. MDS built a new house for me behind the concrete pad on which my business used to stand. They modified the house plan and built in a wheelchair ramp to my back door. Later another group extended the porch so I had access to the ramp from the front door." One individual praised crews that built raised garden beds accessible from his wheelchair. A Texas family benefited from a project director who realized that accessibility would be a future need. Two years after MDS finished their home, the client said, "The project director thought of everything, a handicapped tub and commode."

Accommodating disabilities meant independence: "We both were sick or handicapped. I didn't think I would ever walk again, so they built us a ramp for my wheelchair. They also put in a handicapped shower." Accessibility also meant couples could stay together. "My husband was quite sick. MDS put in an elevator for us. We didn't know they were going to do that, it was a surprise, but thank God they did that; we couldn't get over it." A community partner in New Orleans confirmed the impact: "MDS had a role in the major disaster after Katrina to assist the elderly, disabled, and homeless who had no resources of their own. They have done that job well."

People with disabilities spent longer times in public shelters because the bulk of temporary housing did not offer accessibility. Required home elevations had the potential to displace them permanently and in several locations, individuals with disabilities felt compelled to enter assisted living facilities (National Council on Disability 2009). Simple metal cage elevators cost around $2,000, which fell outside the usually approved uses of grants. Many ramps and elevators were funded by faith-based organizations particularly Catholic Charities.

HOUSE DEDICATIONS

Moving into a new or repaired home represented not just the emotional end of an ordeal but an increased sense of capacity. "This was a blessing from the man upstairs. Besides my kids, I never owned anything. When I moved in here I had peace of mind, and when you have that you can cope with anything," said a client in Mississippi. From the perspective of homeowners, the lived experience of a house dedication incorporates much of what they experienced during construction. In Alabama, "they had a prayer of blessing" and in New Orleans, "the house dedication was awesome; the prayer was awesome." Inter-organizational partnerships that characterized the construction effort reappeared at the dedication also: "My priest came and blessed the house." For many, the light at the end of the tunnel appeared despite remaining challenges: "When they finished, we had a house blessing. We still had no electricity, but we managed in our dark house." Homeowners joined in: "I sang a song for them—I really enjoyed singing together with the Mennonites." Excited clients talked about the beautiful music, often raised a Capella. The diversity of volunteers brought in new talents too: "I enjoyed the young people playing the guitars."

A representative service contained a litany to bless a new home:

Reader 1: 1 Peter 4:9–11. Home is not merely a dwelling but a living fellowship. We are together in this place today to ask God's blessing on this home. Phil. 4:4–7.

Reader 2: We dedicate this home to love and understanding. May its joys and sorrows be shared and may the love of Christ be exhibited to all who enter this home.

All: We dedicate this home to work and leisure. May it have happiness and close fellowship, with kindness in its voices and laughter within its walls.

Reader 2: We dedicate this home to a friendly life. May its doors open in hospitality and its windows look out with kindness.

Women: Bless this home to love and kindness, to courage and patience, to courtesy and mutual understanding, to loyalty and close fellowship.

Men: Bless the life of this home to the service of God and all of God's children.

All: Bless all those who enter these doors, family and guests, with the presence, peace and love of God.

Reader 1: Eternal God, we recognize you as the source and giver of the love that draws families together. We pray that you will be present in this home, that your love may enrich its fellowship, your wisdom be its guide, your truth its light, and your peace its benediction, through Jesus Christ our Lord. Amen.

Bless this house, O Lord, we pray. Make it safe by night and day; Bless these walls, so firm and stout, keeping want and trouble out. Bless the roof and chimneys tall, let thy peace lie over all. Bless this door, that it may prove ever open to joy and love.[3]

Social networks, which had carried clients from dislocation to reconstruction, joined in celebrating: "It was a special evening; friends and family were part of the celebration." At least one project director, "made a special trip to the hospital far away to include my husband in the dedication." Tremendous joy showed on survivor's faces as they described that day: "The house dedication was celebrated on the same day as our grandchild's birthday, so it was a doubly good time. The final crew from MDS was from a conservative group. They participated in the dedication along with family, our church members, friends and other organizations." Finishing the house brought family and friends back together in a collective movement forward, by closing the door on a devastated life and opening a new window toward the future: "Now it is like it is supposed to be. My kids are here. The tables are now turned, now *I* can help *them* [her emphasis]. We are together at last with our kids and grandkids."

House dedications serve as community rituals, transition points through which individuals pass from one phase of their lives into another. Volunteers often gave gifts to clients. The most common gift was a book about MDS, *The Hammer Rings Hope* by former MDS director Lowell Detweiler, along with a traditional quilt bed covering or wall hanging. Homeowners still treasure these gifts and lovingly pointed them out during interviews. In many homes, the only items clients had placed on the walls had come from MDS. During interviews, clients told about individual volunteers who, days, months, and sometimes years later arrived to donate furniture, kitchen appliances, gift cards, and more. In talking about "their" volunteers, clients pulled photo albums and lists of volunteer names from nearby drawers. Even those who had to get up to retrieve such items found them quickly—having kept them close, the way you do with personal treasures. One older woman in Louisiana pulled out a pad upon which she had written all the names and contact information of her volunteers. Opening it lovingly, she looked up and said: "*This* is my Bible."

PAYING IT FORWARD

Homeowners spent considerable time during interviews talking about how much the volunteers meant to them. Despite challenging personal circumstances, most tried to repay the kindness they had experienced. Three forms of contributions were common: providing food, helping out, and sharing their faith.

Food

In New Orleans, one man said he "sometimes cooked food for the volunteers, red beans or turkey necks." Often using affordable and local food, clients stretched their budgets and shared. Even the MDS cooks discovered new dishes and recipes to cook, finding that jambalaya "used up quite a bit of our leftovers!" Food provided a way to share recipes handed down for generations. "I cooked them a big dinner when it was done, a family recipe for wings, baked beans, potato salad."

The coastal location and subsistence economy in some project sites brought in meals from the sea. "I fixed food and they loved it, especially seafood. They would fix some for us too." Volunteers new to seafood brought delight to the clients who shared their bounty: "When I offered them [the volunteers] oysters, they tore right at them as if they had never had oysters before. I think they downed a whole gallon of oysters between the two of them."

Food created a fulfilling means to aid cross-cultural exchanges. A client from Mississippi said, "Everybody knows everybody here. The Mennonites fit in. This is a different culture and they accepted us. They were not familiar with the spices in the food but they all liked it. They asked about where to get po'boys and gumbo. They had never heard of etouffe or sauce piquante. There is nothing better than sharing food with somebody and enjoy it. They fit in because they were just themselves and that was enough." A Louisiana woman chuckled describing how volunteers would mix up names like gumbo and etouffe, then smiled remembering, "They loved that crawfish and shrimp." Culturally situated contributions from homeowners became commonplace. A client in an area steamrolled by a massive storm surge rewarded her hardworking volunteers with "chili with beans, soup, chicken and dumplings, chicken and sausage gumbo, and shrimp gumbo." New food sometimes meant learning new skills, as a client explained: "Half of the volunteers didn't know about oysters so we showed them how to shuck them." Others reported: "I taught them how to peel a crab."

Food served as an important way to connect to each other across differences, as noted by multiple clients. A Native American woman living in a Louisiana bayou said, "Yes, the volunteers were open to the local culture and food" while another client added, "They enjoyed our Philippine food." A Louisiana woman proudly linked feeding volunteers to her culture: "I fixed gumbo for them one night and other Cajun cooking, stuff they didn't know. I brought king cakes for Mardi Gras and ran off cards that explained about the baby[4] and gave beads to the volunteers. The Amish women were really fascinated."

One community partner in Louisiana offered a suggestion about southern hospitality: "Be sure to accept the food. Some feelings got hurt when it was declined." Food emerged as a way to give back, a form of social exchange that equalized relationships and empowered recipients. Those who cooked were no longer being served, they were givers as well. Food allowed people to explain who they were and to situate their identities in the land and sea from which many made a living. Food explained who they were to outsiders. The delight that volunteers expressed in learning about and enjoying the new food meant a great deal to the clients: it meant *acceptance*.

Helping Out

A second form of homeowner contribution came from helping with the construction where able. Because many clients were unable to do so, something as simple as "even picking up a hammer to hand to a volunteer is a big thing for some homeowners," according to one community partner. Some homeowners who could not participate in the construction loaned tools to the workers. Particularly important for men who had previous work in construction, carpentry, or similar jobs, the loan of a tool represented an extension of the owner's identity. For those who had lost many of their tools in the storm, a hammer that could be used by a volunteer might symbolize what remained to build on. An Alabama family, for example, offered the tools they had been able to salvage from what remained of their shed after the storm.

A related contribution was by homeowners who would come "home" from work to sweep or clean up after the volunteers. Keeping the floors clean, picking up nails, and stacking lumber were tasks that many could do. By making sure that no one stepped on a nail, a single mother could contribute to the safety of her volunteer crew. Through stacking the lumber, clients readied the site for the next day. Though the tasks might have taken only a short time, homeowners expressed pride in being able to contribute. "We did go over every night to pick up and sweep up the sawdust," noted a Louisiana couple. An elderly client with damage from Rita saw his effort as providing respite to the hard-working work crews: "It was my job—they didn't ask this of me—to clean up the tools at the end of the day, so they could have some more time in the evening for themselves."

Other family members, friends or neighbors sometimes helped also. A Texas family said, "Some relatives helped when they could" by bringing food and building a fire people could use when it got cold. A Louisiana family "helped out on the floors." A medically fragile couple in Texas involved their son: "Our son helped a lot," though "I cooked for them."

Sharing and Reaffirming Faith

Many homeowners held deep religious convictions, and expressed sureness that God had sent Mennonites to them. One New Orleans client, unable to be onsite during the day, would visit her house to pray for the volunteers. Her efforts were echoed by an African American woman from Mississippi: "I prayed for them and thanked God for them every day. They have a spirit in their heart to come here and do work on the coast. I prayed to God every day for help. He was true to His Word. They were a fantastic group. Every week we would have a new group. I couldn't believe it. They were so friendly, hard working. College kids, elderly, all ages. They came from everywhere, Oregon, North Carolina, Utah—several states and Canada."

Because Mennonites were new to most people and communities, it is not unexpected that suspicion arose about why they came: "The community elders were very concerned about this new religion. They were sure MDS was out to proselytize and that their real motives would eventually be revealed. After 5 years they are still helping because of the goodness of their hearts and have not started proselytizing." She appraised the MDS approach, "The work of MDS has spoken volumes to the community. There is great appreciation. MDS has done a fabulous job—an amazing thing for this community. People in this community have been keeping a close eye on MDS. They are the only organization to stay in the community and keep helping. It would be very unfortunate if MDS did pull out at this time."

Locals also contrasted MDS volunteers with those of other organizations in which they had lost confidence. A faith-based partner affected by Rita explained MDS as, "A disaster organization, but it is a strong arm of the body of Christ. It is spreading the word in a unique way." She contrasted MDS with other organizations that left a month after the storm: "It is transformative what MDS does. It is more than a house. There are a lot fewer Mennonites than (my faith) but their accomplishments far outweigh their numbers." A Mennonite partner organization observed, "Faith is a very important part of poor communities. People there have more trust in the church than in government or in stand-alone organizations that are not church connected."

Numerous clients intently affirmed their faith during interviews and believed their devotion had led MDS to them. The most common statement they made about volunteers centered on their strong conviction that "God sent them." Clients in every state affected by every hurricane said independently that MDS volunteers were "doing God's work. The time they gave to us was meaningful." Clients believed that God sent the volunteers in answer to prayers. A Louisiana man averred, "God just set up that organization to help people. God knew I needed to get in and sometimes I had sixteen volunteers working on my house." A widowed single parent affected by Ike confirmed, "I got the Good Lord on my side." Belief in a higher power that guided volunteers to meet their need felt overwhelming to tearful, grateful clients, "I must have done something right (she points to heaven). I prayed for this since 1995. I prayed so hard that God heard my prayers and told me in a dream they would be answered."

THERAPEUTIC HEALING

In Mississippi, one client described the overwhelming images as they tried to return home after Katrina: "The military had to cut their way down Highway 49 to Pass Christian. The National Guard sealed off the town. Houses were in the middle of the street." People returned to the devastation to see bulldozers clearing piles of debris, their former homes, furnishings, and family mementos. They struggled to help children understand: "My daughter would say 'Could you just get my slippers? They were right by my bed,' I couldn't explain it." The conditions some clients endured while waiting to return home were also horrific. One Texas couple lived in a tent without heat or air conditioning for two years after Ike took their home and precious family mementoes. Native Americans from a single Louisiana community splintered into multiple states after Katrina, with dozens still not home five years later. Overcoming the loss of a home, coupled with the loss of social networks that provided support, child care, family ties, shared food, and heritage felt staggering.

One bayou family sat quietly as they shared that Katrina "was one of the lowest times in our life." Clients spoke of depression that put them "in a fog for a long, long time after the storm" and of children still traumatized by incoming storms. The volunteers who just listened touched them deeply: "At dinner they would listen to our Katrina experience. They hugged us, they felt sympathy. Everyone in Pass Christian lost their homes. The water covered everything. It is just amazing that people can see your sorrow and hurt. They treated me like a queen. I am very happy and pleased. I can't stop shouting the joys. Everyone will tell you here, they are God-filled, Spirit-filled people."

A client dealt with not just rebuilding but supporting her spouse: "My husband was suffering from depression. Their presence left a real feeling of calmness for my husband and me. Everything seemed so much more pleasant when they were around. Their working with him, allowing him to be part of their crew, was very calming for him." Survivors of other hurricanes felt similarly, as shown by a man affected by Ike: "Sometimes life is very difficult. When things are not going well, I look around me and think how lucky I am to have all this [he points around his rebuilt home]. That is a tremendous boost to my spirits." Others agreed that the influx of faith-based volunteers turned things around: "They took the worry and what we had to endure away."

Volunteers helped heal those wounded by the storms, by perceptions of neglect, and by the marginalization caused by poverty, stereotypes, and exclusion: "No one has ever done this kind of thing for me before. I didn't think it could happen. I have sometimes read of miracles happening to other people but I didn't expect this would ever happen to me [in Texas]." Another said, "It was like God dropped a miracle here [in Louisiana]." Community and faith-based partners concurred with clients about the healing impact of the volunteers: "The infusion of volunteers is like a breath of fresh air. The battle to get back in a house is wearying." They described the arrival of volunteers as "an uplifting emotional and spiritual experience, a second wind. You can't quantify that."

A community partner explained further: "Every week the homeowners are on the verge of giving up. We have over 600 still in FEMA trailers at the five year anniversary. They keep wondering every week 'can I keep going?'" Being with the volunteers renewed survivors, who "would walk in a house being gutted by volunteers. The volunteers would pray with the kids before school. That made such a big difference." A resident of Pass Christian agreed: "This work has an exponential positive effect. Seeing the garbage and destruction around you is very depressing. Seeing someone stepping in to help with the clean-up results in a significant attitude change—'I can make it now.'" Recipients of volunteerism experienced "a feeling that someone cares about you" and realized: "God loves me; people care about me; I will make it!"

One Louisiana client drew upon scripture, comparing MDS volunteers to the ants of Proverbs 30: "The people that came were so uplifting, not just in building the house. They were an inspiration and renewed our determination. They did not stop. They pulled together and kept going, like ants." The volunteers kept the momentum going: "The next group came in and picked it up and carried it along. They even cleaned out under the house." She continued, describing benefits beyond her own home: "We are getting there as a community. One day we will be whole."

Indeed, continual streams of volunteers made it possible to feel whole again: "They came and they have not left. They are a blessing indeed." Because volunteers served, people displaced from neglected neighborhoods, isolated bayous, devastated small towns, and impoverished rural communities finally got to come home. One client said: "I could never repay them for how it feels to have my home and life given back to me." Then, speaking from her modest bayou home rebuilt by volunteers, she added: "But when we get to heaven I am going to tell God they deserve the best mansions there."

NOTES

1. Correspondence. Dyck, Peter J. and John A. Diller. May 9, 1952. Letter from the Temporary Disaster Committee, Central Kansas to MCC Constituent Churches, Central Kansas. Mennonite Library and Archives.

2. The word "independently" refers to clients who brought up these observations outside of the context of the interview guide. They thus serve as words that interviewees felt especially relevant to share.

3. McCoy, Esther, as printed by Mennonite Disaster Service. No date. *Hands and Feet: Devotions and Prayers for Project Sites*. Lititz, PA: Mennonite Disaster Service.

4. King cakes arrive around Mardi Gras time. A tiny "baby" is baked into the cake and, as tradition has it, whoever finds the baby buys the next cake.

SIX

Serving Neighbors, Serving Jesus

We are an organization of doers, not bureaucrats.
—MDS Volunteer

INTRODUCTION

How can we explain the consistently positive experiences of community partners and clients? This chapter explores MDS work through the perspectives of long-term and short-term volunteers. Qualitative data include interviews with 15 project directors; focus groups with three different kinds of long-term volunteers: project directors (N = 59), office managers (N = 9) and cooks (N = 5); participant observation at multiple project sites and visits to MDS offices in Winnipeg, Canada and Akron, Pennsylvania; visual data including hundreds of photographs at project sites; thousands of documents and photographs in various archives[1]; and MDS internal records. Quantitative data include surveys from 852 volunteers representing a diverse set of Anabaptist denominations across the U.S. and Canada.

Training Disaster Servants

Training is an important first step in preparing people to serve. Even in the early years, MDS noted a problem not unknown to other organizations, and one that would be re-experienced when Katrina, Rita and Ike generated needs for additional long-term labor. A letter written from the Temporary Disaster Committee in 1952 stated: "One of our problems is that of continued leadership. We simply must have someone there who can stay for at least a month. If any of you men know of someone who has leadership ability, who could act not only as foreman for our volunteers but be contact man for the Red Cross and other officials, and of course a man who could stay for at least a month, we would appreciate to know about it."[2] Long-term volunteers required knowledge of effective procedures and Kansas initiated training for field volunteers early in the 1950s. Efforts paid off in May of 1955 when a deadly tornado struck close to where MDS originated. Udall, Kansas, with a population of 610, lost 88 citizens to the massive twister, approximately the width of the entire town.[3] Whole families perished, with three-fourths of the victims under the age of 18 or over 60. Debris extended for nearly fifty miles (NOAA 2010a). Over 1,100 Mennonites arrived to clean up, their largest effort to date.

Training has always emanated from Scripture, emphasizing disaster service as mission work. At the Fourth Training School in 1958, leaders invited trainees to "memorize the Sermon on the Mount so it is hid in the heart and head" and challenged them: "How ready are you to put MDS on your priority list?" Training was based on a belief that disasters provided an opportunity for an "ordinary layman" to share the gospel. Disaster servants would "alleviate human need, lift the fallen, get under the load of our neighbors burden." Trainers profiled MDS work as offering self-growth for volunteers, as "many who have gone have seen a new Christ." They expressed belief that the impact would reveal "goodwill and understanding to our fellow men of other faiths" and "bring about a greater revival in our own church." And trainers encouraged those present to extend MDS work to those most vulnerable in disaster: "What can MDS do in Texas, Alabama, Arkansas—across the racial barrier— when disaster strikes? Nothing will talk louder than an expression of Christian love, to anyone in need." Training sessions also recognized the "need to take our young people into consideration in disaster service. Take them along and let them work under the supervision of adults. The reason for serving should be made plain." Older people could go as well, "listening to the grief of those affected, baby sitting and taking care of things at home."[4]

In 1958, self-sufficiency began to characterize Kansas Area MDS work as leaders saw the need to enter with "our own food canteen so as not to impose upon Red Cross or other groups."[5] Kansas MDS modified a Chevrolet bus they had bought in 1956 for $350, adding first aid kits, work stations, communications equipment, and tool bays. They next made a recruitment film about the cleanup work in El Dorado, Kansas, a community badly damaged by a 1958 tornado.[6]

By 1959, participants at the Fifth Annual Training School in Kansas had worked out well-defined titles and roles in a carefully crafted division of labor and had devoted time to a seven-step Disaster Plan, to be put into operation should a major disaster strike. Kansas MDS then scoped out differences across the disaster phases of rescue, relief, and rehabilitation, breaking them down by time, personnel, duties, training, supplies, and agency partners. Within its first decade, MDS had created an organizational structure, identified and resolved barriers to entry and work issues, built key partnerships (e.g., with the Red Cross), and created a training model based on Scripture and designed to enable volunteers to make a difference.

Today, volunteer teams formally consist of two groups: long-termers, who typically stay from two weeks to six months, and short-termers, who usually come in their own group for about one week. Long-term crews have varying configurations but, at a minimum, include a project director, an office manager, and cook(s). Some teams also include construction supervisors, crew team leaders and hostesses. The first section of this chapter reveals the experiences of long-term volunteers, followed by how an analysis of survey data that explain how both long-term and short-term volunteers encountered and found meaning in their disaster work.

PROJECT DIRECTORS

This section describes the project director job (using interview data and focus group content). The most prevalent themes project directors talked about during interviews (in order beginning with the strongest) included partnership work with local committees, faith, financial stewardship, clients, blessings received, teamwork, building matters, volunteer matters, and the impact of Katrina. One way to measure of the importance of a theme stems from how many directors commented on it; all of the interviewees spoke at length on partnerships and faith followed by 14 of 15 commenting extensively on financial stewardship, clients, blessings received, and teamwork. Additional themes emerged (e.g., working with youth) but clearly project directors experience their work as faith-driven, relationship-oriented teamwork. To organize their perspectives and to permit comparison with perspectives found in previous chapters, this section proceeds chronologically from first setting up the project site through managing the thousands of volunteers that may arrive.

Setting Up the Project Site

As one director said, "Every disaster has its own personality. Katrina and Rita had their own." Even for an experienced project director, "It was hard to imagine the destruction from Katrina. Two hundred and fifty miles of the Gulf in a 25 mile swath were totaled." This director ended up with "a sick pit" in his stomach: "How can they ever be normal again?" Early site investigators and the first directors in felt the most impact: "Those first days, there was mud on the sides of the road, furniture to be picked up. Graders were out taking mud out; it was hard to drive in."

Project directors all agreed: "Roads were blocked, street signs missing; it was difficult to scope out the sites."

Katrina made investigating new project sites especially hard: "One challenge was that there was no community nearby" making it difficult to set up, find local businesses to support the project, and use time wisely. Focus group participants noted a "lack of infrastructure . . . widespread lack of materials" for cleaning camps, and long waits for power and telephone hook ups, because "the hurricane damage was so broad." The first project directors on the scene found that it was important to "maintain an open mind set; accept what is there and what you get. Be flexible, ready to deal with unknowns." Among long-termers, many observe with a smile that MDS really means "make do somehow" and that setting up in the devastated region meant just that. As directors determined where to establish projects, they managed with "no power or phone service on site. No local services available. [We] transported in building material and used auxiliary power generators." One camp did "without power for the first five months." Similar to homeowners waiting for power, rebuilding volunteers also found that although "a trailer was provided by HQ . . . [it] was not usable without power." At one site, "it took us a month to get the electrical work done in the building and to get the electricity back up." The next step was to "set up a double-wide for kitchen and office," or, in another typical strategy, set up a "temporary trailer park." Many brought their own RVs and used their own resources: "Our little fifth wheel became our office." Others stayed at RV parks away from the project site and drove long distances to establish volunteer housing.

Setting up camp occurred simultaneously with finding "Who is the local long-term recovery person?" Local recovery committees helped the set-up process in many locations: "Upon arrival we were soon welcomed by [name omitted] from the local recovery team. She contacted the RV park owner and he came to help us select a site and hook up." After finding the RV spot, the director and team members (often a spouse) had to find out "where to purchase supplies, [arrange for] power and phone hookup, where the medical facilities are located, a grocery store to purchase food, suppliers for materials, bank location." With "gasoline for vehicles" in short supply or available only at long distances, they spent a lot of time making do and searching for solutions.

Transitioning into more permanent housing occurred in various ways. Again, "we found most of [what we needed] by asking local people. We also got advice from MDS headquarters." In one location, a local thrift store donated "anything we wanted, gratis, because MDS had helped the store manager's family after a previous disaster. They stocked our kitchen with dishes, pots, pans, a sofa." At some sites the telephone company donated phone and internet service. Quite commonly, town officials did not charge for water and the electric company set in poles at no cost.

Many locations provided electricity, water, and utilities through the LTRC. In New Orleans, local partners helped out in what came to be called the "MDS Hilton." Volunteers converted the already-elevated, two-story church into housing for volunteers with dining facilities, air conditioning, multiple rooms for bunk beds, and showers. Once again, MDS benefited from local support as area "kitchen designers donated all the cupboards." Managing it all was daunting, and one project director spoke for many, "Those first few weeks are very stressful." So they coped by digging in: "You need work to do."

Building the Long-Term Volunteer Team

Project directors felt pressure to get things going so that eager volunteers could get to work. That meant bringing in a long-term volunteer team. Traditionally, project directors have recruited their own team but with the size of Katrina—so many sites and frequent rotations—MDS centralized some of the selection process at headquarters. Still, project directors liked to work with their own team, one they had built during previous disasters. Transitioning to a more centralized form caused some confusion within the primarily grass-roots organization. "People will call and say 'you haven't called us! We want to work with you.'" One director commented that the main MDS office "learned that relationships are built with long-termers and it is best to call in those you know." An experienced director said, "I prefer to put my own team together and put key people into place," but he added that after headquarters became involved in the process, someone "checks with me on long-termers for my opinion. I ask 'what are their skills?' Long-term people have to be a contributor and a leader due to their knowledge on the job. . . . I like to call and chat with the person. I like to have a strong second-in-command."

Project directors value friendships made on previous sites and look forward to serving with these friends again. They believe that teamwork is essential because "we are part of a partnership." All agreed that "the relationship between a director and the construction foreman is the most important relationship on site." One explained their partnership: "We were able to connect; it is like we were twins! You don't always have that meshing. We were always able to resolve issues," adding "I would be lost without him. I have seen how much we can do together."

One director encouraged others to "serve as long-term volunteers at least once before accepting the project director role. There is no such manual as 'Project Directing for Dummies.' [You] need to understand the impact on your team" when something [negative] happens, recommended a director. One project director said it was common to "hold weekly meetings with project staff." Experience in all the roles helps, they said. "Spend some time volunteering long-term such as being construction foreman or crew leader before attempting a project director position." In the opinion of one experienced couple, "Past experience in the kitchen or office management is the most helpful." Another director advised others to just "start at the bottom of the ladder and move up as the Spirit moves." But he also saw value in new challenges, adding with encouragement, "It is good to be uncomfortable in unfamiliar territory; God will lead if we let Him."

Daily Routines

Project directors establish the structure and routine of a project site, a daily schedule that varies little from site to site. Remarkable consistency in how the day unfolds for the short-term volunteers focuses activity across project sites. What project directors and their long-term team do behind the scenes to make that possible, though, can vary depending on the abilities and concerns of the project director coupled with the challenges and resources at the sites. "A typical day starts at 4:30. I make lists of activities and put the teams together. Sometimes I do that the night before." Planning the day's events requires coordination with all of the long-term team to use volunteers and their skill levels appropriately. Doing so means reviewing work planned for that day with the construction supervisors and crew leaders. The construction supervisor or the director then creates lists of tools needed for that day's work, determines the appropriate vehicle the team will need, and posts the volunteer assignments in work teams dedicated to a particular house and job. Mornings continue with individual devotions for most. Then directors and office managers check with the rest of the team. Meanwhile, cooks have been busy ensuring that coffee is brewed and numbered containers (linked to the work crew and vehicle) have been set out for beverages and lunches. The director talks with the crew leaders over coffee, reviewing the day's work, safety precautions, and proper construction procedures. Breakfast begins promptly at 7 a.m. following a prayer. A new short-termer leads devotions around 7:25. Around 7:30, the director will "go through the day's assignments" and "check supplies and tools with the long-term volunteers." When temperatures increase, the morning routine begins thirty to sixty minutes earlier.

The volunteers leave by 8 and "then I begin my day." Directors next "visit sites, meet the people, make community connections, and check progress." Despite the structure and routine, directors frequently observed, "My scheduled plan always changes." Most start by swinging by the office manager's desk to check in and make or return phone calls to "partner agencies, suppliers, clients, inspectors" and others. Then, "I review my own to-do list and leave for most of the day." One director's daily list further involved "dropping off needed material already on my truck, bringing forgotten materials and tools to job sites, checking up on all jobs sites every day, stopping at partner agencies for materials or new jobs, meeting building inspectors at job sites, checking out new jobs and getting clear understanding of the job scope, buying and delivering material or ordering material for various job sites, adding more on the to-do list, and visiting with clients." Another said, "I visit with homeowners, especially at the start of a project" and stop by every project site daily at least once to "visit with the crew leader" and "make sure the work is being done correctly." Directors swing back to camp between 4 and 5 p.m., to "greet the volunteers when they come back at the end of the day" and check in again with other long-termers. While volunteers are returning tools and showering, the director continues reviewing the day's issues, returning calls, and discussing the next day's work plan. Supper starts at 6 p.m. preceded by prayer and followed by crew reports after which the project director takes time to "visit with volunteers." Directors then often hold meetings with crew leaders and construction supervisors, meetings which "help to plan the next day, solve problems, and work efficiently." Some may go back out again to buy supplies for the next day's work. They return to the office again "updating the job list, completing job cards." One director "did paper work from 7 to 10 p.m. and worked on relational issues." Late evening work characterizes all project directors, who "basically worked 6 a.m. to 10 p.m., then slept well."

Building Community Relationships

Many project directors saw "connecting with the community, making friends with the clients" as a critical part of their volunteer role. Local partners who knew local people, culture, and circumstances, became "very helpful in sorting out problems and guiding us in making good decisions." Indeed, "building partner relationships" emerged as the dominant theme for project directors: "It is very important to work with the LTRC, and keep well connected with them." Directors report that spending time building relationships "results in a lot of support and assistance" among partners who become "your best allies in working through bureaucracy." "If we work together we can accomplish more." Partners fell along a continuum from completely inexperienced and unorganized to highly functioning committees and experienced disaster organizations. Given that many local volunteers were simultaneously rebuilding their own homes and lives, inexperienced organizations often required assistance: "They are not trained at doing this kind of work. You may have to teach them to help you how to build a house."

In one case, "The LTRC was just starting and not very active. We spent some of our time, assisted by Akron, to help the LTRC in its formation." These efforts paid off, as "later the LTRC became very active in case management and fundraising and started supplying the money for house construction." In another situation, "It took a long time for the

LTRC to become effective. This was something they had never done be-fore." Yet, "eventually they found their place, became comfortable with their role and did a good job." Experienced long-termers gently offered advice, guiding those new to recovery. Though not all directors feel com-fortable in such a role, several believe that "MDS should work closely with the long term recovery" efforts. Project directors take the relation-ship part of their job seriously. One encountered a dysfunctional commit-tee whose members were at odds with each other, so he "had coffee with one of them and that helped somewhat." Another director said: "I per-sonally did not have any issues [with community partners] that could not be resolved by discussing them." At the other end of the continuum, some LTRCs had "everything in place. We never had to worry about things not lined up, ready for us." Directors were able to move right into construction: "We did not have to go to a lot of planning/organizing meetings. They had all their ducks in a row." Project momentum sped up through well-organized LTRCs. "They knew MDS criteria and were able to help us select projects accordingly."

One experienced director said, "It is really important to go to commu-nity meetings, to LTRCs. That is where you connect with people to help you." He emphasized that by doing so, "You feel like a team. You have to realize that MDS is one spoke in a wheel. Everyone needs to carry weight in that wheel." Partnerships yielded meaningful interactions for both long- and short-term volunteers. In Pass Christian, for example, "the Goodwill Missionary Baptist Church fed us a lunch every Wednesday. It was their outreach to assist the larger community and was a great con-necting point for us." Everyone went, from long-termers to short-termers to recovery partners and survivors. "It was a fantastic experience for our volunteers to get involved in the community." Local partners offered two key things so that MDS could build homes: rebuilding resources and case management to select homeowners.

Resources and Funding

Given the overall negative critiques of government it might be sur-prising that MDS long-termers appreciated "FEMA, of course. The mon-ey that homeowners get, we need that money to rebuild and repair the houses. Oftentimes, the FEMA money can make the difference between whether we could go ahead or not." Though some community partners, clients, and even some MDS volunteers felt dismayed at government response, more commonly, long-termers with direct relationships to FEMA observed "They [FEMA staff] are very committed individuals who are trying to work within some very stringent guidelines. They feel for the people but they are bound by the rules." Still, the flexibility offered by non-government organizations like MDS made a difference in a context laden with policy, rules, and regulations. One project director described the value of a more flexible LTRC: "They got jobs through the nearby Lutherans and we worked well together. There were a lot of voluntary organizations coming in and they would go from one place to another." One director was "really impressed with the Methodist church, UMCOR. They were marvelous at funding some of the projects." Another director appreciated "the Baptist church; a lot of spirited volunteers who would do a lot of good work." Catholic Charities and churches also provided funding: "For specific things they would come through nicely and often they were costly items" such as elevators for families with disabilities. Recovery committees also led MDS to critical resources: "Here's where to get sheetrock!"

Being financially accountable called upon strong Mennonite values of frugality: "MDS used the money received very prudently." Still, abundant donations for Katrina meant "it was much easier to provide good meals for our work crews." Even with larger donations, "We used the funds that were available and did not splurge." Project directors exercised careful financial monitoring, knowing they would have to face their own families and friends: "Everything MDS did was done as prudently as possible. We used the money in a manner that made you feel good reporting back to the donors in your church." A project director couple said, "We need to be frugal and practical, both." A long-termer with extensive MDS experience said, "From my standpoint the stewardship is good. The accountability is very good."

Project directors understood the local value of such accountability too as "a lot of the contractors took advantage of homeowners. They took their money but did not do a good job and we had to redo the houses." Another agreed: "There are horror stories about contractors," about homeowners playing "bingo with local contractors" and losing their FEMA money. In light of negative experiences "it was amazing how people trusted us because of the name MDS." Directors repaid that trust by trying to "shop around for best prices" to "do more for less money." MDS also tried to use the money for local impact: "Even though it might be a few cents more to buy gas locally, do it, and the same with groceries."

Some questions did arise among volunteers about some expenses. For the first time, MDS had the financial means to purchase needed resources including increasing rolling stock from several dozen to over 150. A few criticized "the size of our vehicle purchase," but most said, "Tools and vehicles were definitely a good investment. They helped increase safety, kept volunteers happy, and increased productivity." One person shed insider perspective on another area of concern, the use of donated funds to take the long-term volunteers out to a restaurant on weekends. Though on-site observations support the conclusion that most long-termers ate leftovers on the weekends, one project director saw eating in a restaurant as a means to relieve exhausted long-termers: "Give the cook a break and a change of scenery. Some constituents would say, 'why would you go out?' They prefer to use the cook. I do think people need a break."

Working with Clients

Four main themes emerged concerning clients: project locations, the case management process, client selection criteria, and client appreciation. The majority of project directors' comments concerned case management and client selection, not surprising given their managerial focus.

MDS tradition sends volunteers into "areas normally neglected, that are too difficult." Areas came to project directors' notice when "FEMA representatives would point us to underserved areas." A project director explained, "We are a grass roots, rural organization and that is where we should be, in rural areas." Partners also often guided them into areas of need, when funding became available. Still other sites emerged when MDS investigated areas where low-income, elderly and/or racial and ethnic minorities lived historically. One project director said, "MDS does a good job selecting project sites." Finding such places resonated with Anabaptist beliefs to help one's neighbor and those in greatest need. When project directors were involved in determining those locations, they found it a meaningful experience as it allowed them to be "with people in the community."

Case management also emerged as a critical part of the local partnership. "Case workers would meet with the applicants and then present us with a list of clients." Project directors learned to educate case managers, who often were learning on the job. A particular challenge came when case managers inexperienced in construction "sometimes promised things beyond our ability." In some sites, experienced long-termers assisted with case management: "I think when I am doing casework, I have the best job with MDS. I am there and I am bringing hope." The relationship became truly meaningful for those able to work closely with clients: "The connection that I feel for them and the connection they make with me is marvelous."

MDS selects clients with the most meager means to rebuild or, as one director pointed out, "We don't deal with the bourgeoisie." Case management became critical to selecting such clients, and "once the LTRC knew our criteria, it [the case management process] was generally good." Another agreed that "the case workers were generally quite aware of our criteria and the client list usually met our criteria." In a few instances, clients did not appear to meet MDS criteria and "this was very hard to explain to our volunteers." Volunteers "who were sacrificing their time and money" wanted to assist those with the greatest need. Project directors had to explain that appearances could be deceiving and that sometimes individuals with the greatest needs would not have the means (even with LTRC and FEMA help) to rebuild. The majority of clients, however, met MDS criteria. For example, "One couple, he was ninety and she was in her mid-eighties. She still had to go out and work cleaning houses to cover costs of medications for his heart." Another added, "I marvel at our clients in that they get up every day and keep going. I don't know if I could be as positive or as ready to praise the Lord if I was in their shoes." Understanding their clients' acute needs, directors willingly worked long hours to bring them home. One director, recalling the long hours spent working for a particular client, said: "I was so happy for him" when the client finally moved back home.

Directors carried the task of walking people through unfamiliar building processes. Many directors involved clients in decision-making using MDS job cards, "where each detail is discussed with the client, documented, and signed by the client and the MDS PD." The diaspora caused by the storms meant that homeowners might not be present or might have to work during the day and not see volunteers. In some cases, "the homeowners were living out of state and getting job cards signed was near to impossible." Others would have to work during the day. One director said, "We seldom saw the homeowner but every morning we noticed signs that she had been there." One day, he managed to arrive early and "found her at the house praying. She would come to the house every day, early in the morning, to pray for our safety. She would always leave a note of encouragement or a Bible verse for us . . . she was an absolute pleasure to work for." Despite the confusing post-disaster reconstruction environment, difficult clients were "few compared to the number of very humble and grateful clients." More commonly, clients lacked experience in making decisions. Directors also worked with hesitant clients who, when the client was asked by the director "what do *you* think," the director would turn the question around to ask the client: "What do you *need*?" Most frequently, clients would become involved in the final phases: "We would usually invite the homeowner to come with us to the supply center to help select purchases especially for interior finishing." Though doing so could be time-consuming for the director, clients could finally see their home coming together and would step back into the role of homeowner at last.

Despite the daily routine that necessarily limited directors' time with clients, directors thoroughly enjoyed working with clients who they described as "very appreciative, very happy and very grateful for our help." One added, "Some homeowners were amazing," trying to help even if just to encourage us, to talk with us and to provide snacks for the volunteers." Another said, "Most of the homeowners overwhelmed us with their gratitude," and one director chuckled: "Generally this also leads us to do some extras for them with gladness."

Building Houses

Project directors worked closely with construction supervisors and crew leaders to insure quality construction. Even though unskilled labor completes much of the work, directors noted, "The locals thought we all had professional builders doing the work. No, we did not." Project directors and their team took building homes seriously and wanted to do it right and do it well. Again, that effort began with building relationships before building houses. "The building inspector is my first stop on a new project site." "The first and most important thing is to know who the inspector is and introduce oneself." An experienced director said, "You have to have a good relationship with staff and clients and with those in power with codes and permits." Forming strong relationships paid off: "If they can't bend the rules, they will show us a way to work within the rules that is most expedient." "I found that every place I worked that local officials have been great." Directors' own dedication came across to community partners. As one director said, "We believe in quality, not quantity," and, "we made sure we heeded inspection." Another confirmed, "It is hard work to maintain the reputation of MDS. You are being watched."

A lack of codes also made the work challenging. In one community, "there were no standard codes" so that post-disaster, "government organizations had a difficult time coming up with acceptable codes especially as related to elevation." To cope and keep crews moving in, "We generally tried to anticipate and build a little better than what we thought would be called for." In one site, local politics apparently interfered: "The work would be passed by the first inspector but then later a second inspector would come along and deny the permit and we would have to start over." MDS managed fluctuating local codes and inspections by surpassing what was needed: "If a house was not flooded and the roof was gone, we put on six nails per shingle." Construction usually went well on project sites, yet conscientious directors worried about lax oversight. From the point of view of the director, "The inspectors had such a level of trust in MDS that they sometimes passed inspection without actual on-site presence." Another expressed similar concern in some locations with "poor quality of inspection."

Moving projects along was not always easy. "It's all based on planning. Go early to make sure your permits are in place, electrical, plumbing, building permits." And, "make sure you can get what you need locally like special storm windows." Even so, damage and distance limited options. "We were far from other communities. There were no retail facilities. We had to travel 50 miles for all our groceries, gas stations, and building supplies." "Sometimes, building the house is the easy part." One director made 40 trips to get permits for the first houses: "Project directors don't like that part." One especially challenging problem came from "lack of land titles. Many people had family property going back to the French system. Houses were built without title and current occupants had title in the name of land ancestors." Directors relied on community partners, especially the LTRC, to help with titles, which were required before building permits could be issued. Still, "we just had to go ahead a lot of times with verbal consent and hope no law suits happened later!"

The key concern regarding construction quality for program directors—and also for local partners—was the transition from one director to another: "Generally there were no inspection issues if the project director was there long term," but handing over a project could be hard. Some project directors felt acutely high levels of responsibility to finish their jobs and have work lined up for incoming directors. Overlap represented the main strategy for managing transitions. Directors generally spent two to three days with the new person shadowing him, turning over files, introducing clients and partners to the new director, and insuring that orderly paperwork was in place. Transitions also required special care in the area of finances, with some banks requiring a week or more to transition signature authority. One director suggested that "on the first day [the new director], ride along and make a lot of notes and photos. On the second day, drive with the outgoing PD riding along." Maintaining contact with the outgoing director also eased transitions: "Phone calls between the PDs is key, to explain why you did things a certain way." Experienced directors kept client relationships in mind also: "Leave a meticulous job card with clients' choices for colors, sidings. Without that, you can incur hardships and hard feelings with clients."

Directors also worried they would not be able to bring in volunteers for plumbing and electrical work and sometimes hired locals to do the work, though such persons remained in short supply given the devastating local impact. In New Orleans, city officials required that locals be hired for such work, a mandate that often lengthened the time needed to rebuild a home. Timing thus emerged as "the biggest issue. At one house we had to pause for two months before we could continue." Doing so meant that projects often piled up and "we had far too many projects going simultaneously" or, conversely, "we would have volunteers sitting around with no work to do." For an action-oriented organization with a strong work ethic, sitting around is the worst thing that can happen. Volunteers, who had often come from quite a distance, would complain, "We came to work!" Not surprisingly, many directors agreed: "Let's keep the volunteers busy." In the words of one staff member, "We are an organization of doers, not bureaucrats. . . Volunteers don't want to fill out papers; they want to just go out and clean up."

Closing Camp

Shutting down a project becomes the responsibility of the last director along with support from headquarters. MDS keeps careful track of jobs started and completed and the site does not close until the last authorized job ends and headquarters agrees the work is over. Decisions to close a site are hard, knowing that some people have still not come home. Dwindling funding represents the most common reason why sites close, because rebuilding materials must be funded from somewhere. Still, MDS enjoys a reputation for being among the last of the faith-based organizations to close project sites. At one site, the PD was told by the LTRC "to stop work immediately" because money had run out. With volunteers still scheduled to arrive: "We told the group about our dilemma [and] someone suggested we pray. Later that day, as we started to pack up, a man drove up and asked if we would have workers to do a house for someone in need who had money for material but could not find labor." Not surprisingly, "We agreed."

Even temporary summer closures (for heat, hurricanes) were keenly felt, because project directors realized "how much work still needs to be done" and knew that "this is also very difficult for the homeowner." Complete closure involving transferring tools, vehicles, and other resources to the MDS warehouse in Mississippi or to a new project site took time but would "generally go smoothly." When camps are shut down, accounts must be closed and utilities turned off. For long-term volunteer housing, sites must be turned back over to the community, sometimes with resources included such as bunk beds, tools, or cooking items for continued local use. Laptops and files are packed up and shipped to headquarters. Final cleaning of the building and grounds takes place and then the mailbox closes for good.

Given themes resonating from the data on building relationships, it is not surprising that "shutting down a project site is very hard. It takes a big emotional toll out of you." Friends have been made over the years with community partners and especially with clients who still stop by camp, wave hello, and invite you to gumbo. Departures are often characterized by a flurry of last minute home dedications, a final meal at camp and tearful farewells. "Saying goodbye was harder than I thought it would be!" In one community, a project director choked up as he said "We had three house dedications in one day and all the RVs were gone by the late afternoon." Reflecting back over the years spent in one community, a project director felt "many blessings as a result of serving this community and seeing them able to go on."

OFFICE MANAGERS

Office managers, often women, frequently arrive with their spouse, who serves as a project director or construction supervisor. "Yes, it is usually a husband-wife team," remarked a focus group participant. The office manager works to help the entire project run smoothly, serving simultaneously as a central coordinator and support player. In the focus groups, office managers described the daily challenges: "The phone rings and the project director may need something, and you are the 'go-fer.' They may need a tool and you always say yes, so you have to know tools, too, to deliver what they need." One experienced office manager said that "being very well organized was critical. You had to make sure that everyone from cooks to cleaning staff knew exactly what to do at what time." Office managers also described "lots of phone calls" to the Akron office, whose support they appreciated: "It is a blessing to have paid staff" to help, something relatively new after the storms.

The office managers' job required flexibility. "The work varies every day; you don't know what will hit." They added: "Be flexible, ready to pick up jobs as needed like scheduling devotions, clean-up, and so on." Flexibility extends to being prepared to multi-task: "You may be sent [to the camp] as the office manager and end up as a cook." Flexibility also means being ready for seasonal hazards: "We had to evacuate once and it took three days just to get the vehicles back." Another focus group participant agreed, "You must be able to adapt quickly." They also advised, "Maintain good communication . . . so that there is a trust developed should problems get bigger." One explained, "Before breakfast, I would touch base with cooks, and sometimes provide assistance. After breakfast, I helped with kitchen clean-up." Despite the challenges of a dynamic work environment and being part of a team, more than one office manager said: "It is not a hardship."

Office managers also enjoy welcoming the volunteers. Prior to Katrina, volunteers would call the project site directly. Post-Katrina, paid staff members help to coordinate volunteers. Transferring volunteer coordinating to headquarters has given office managers more time: "The call center has cut calls in half." Office managers also work with the headquarters staff to pass information to the project director, hostesses, and cooks so they can be ready to welcome eager volunteers when they pull in from across the U.S. and Canada.

Office manager positions changed significantly in the Katrina/Rita years, when accounting practices transitioned into standardized, online forms so that managers needed to "have some awareness of computers and accounting practices." Though MDS offers computer training with daily support available from headquarters, office managers say the work involves a lot of "on the job training." MDS uses an internally created program to record transactions that requires entering items manually on a computerized ledger and spreadsheet. Overall, escalation in the number of projects after the storms increased managers' workloads too: "We are now handling up to $100,000 on six different projects. There can be multiple funders on a single project." "You will also have six different funders, six different homes, that means 36 total accounts you may have to keep track of." Others agreed, "The paperwork is more detailed, a lot more work, with more funders." "The office manager has to move the money around correctly; it would be terrible to sort it out if you did not have the office manager there," and then office managers must "check in with the LTRC to see if the accounts agree." Acknowledging locally challenging conditions, one office manager said, "Gnats and mosquitoes are a piece of cake. Keeping the ledgers balanced, trying to have a free weekend, that is harder."

Managing new rolling stock after Katrina also increased the workload for office managers. Managers shouldered responsibility for logging miles and maintenance records in a new, online system. If a vehicle breaks down, the office manager often takes it to a shop for repair. Volunteers may also need the office manager to take them to local health care centers, which can take from a few hours to an entire day, especially in New Orleans, where Katrina heavily damaged health care facilities. In short, office managers navigate between technical work with computers and accounts and focusing on the people and making the projects more effective.

Despite being in the office much of the time, office managers may have more extended contact with clients than others. Office managers maintain records and case files on clients, learning about their stories in person, from case managers or over the telephone. "We had clients—Black families displaced from their land, living 1,500 miles away from home—with no connection to even talk to them. So the first thing you have to do is just listen, it's really important" offered one office manager. They felt for those "still living in severely damaged homes, families splintered, surrounded by debris." They saw strength in survivors, "hearing the stories, feeling their pain, admiring their ability to recover again and again after storms." It affected them deeply: "We had to deal with our own sense of helplessness to not add to theirs. After three years, there is still so much destruction." From their own reactions, they also learned to listen to short-termers and let them "talk about their concerns and anxieties."

At some sites, office managers arranged for short-termer social outings, such as visits for coffee and beignets at the Café du Monde in New Orleans, trips to the Avery Island home of Louisiana's famous Tabasco sauce (now a staple on all MDS dining room tables), or out to oil rigs, or swamp tours. Though outings are not a formal part of the office manager's job description, they see value in it. Smiling, one office manager said, "We feel like a tour guide, but the volunteers really enjoyed it. They get an opportunity to buy things to take home to their kids." The end of the short-termer week does not necessarily mean rest for the office manager. Observations on sites suggest that long-termers often use the weekend to get ready for the arrival of more short-termers on Sunday night. Still, office managers encourage fellow long-termers to take some time off. Frequently, long-termers plan meals together, often on Sundays following local worship because, "it binds the group together." A staff member concurred, "eating together is an important part of MDS; it is what gels us, a communal experience."

Long-term crews transition, usually around the two month mark, though sometimes shorter or longer. "There's always someone transitioning and if they are at a new place, they have to find where everything is" from hardware and lumber stores to groceries, pharmacies, hospitals, cell phone stores, permit offices, and more. To facilitate transitions for an incoming office manager, they try to overlap departures and arrivals, leave notes, lists of preferred businesses (as well as ones not to use) and personal phone numbers. Overlap time varies, with a returning manager needing one to two days but new ones requiring longer orientation. The office managers work to smooth that transition because "each site is different. . . . People's notes were helpful."

Serving as an office manager, despite the challenges and long days, brings "joys and blessings that no money could provide." Office managers enjoyed meeting the clients: "I love the first week when we hear stories from the clients, all the energy that is there, the excitement." Connecting with the clients meant the most. "These folks love their way of life. Their livelihood came from fishing, shrimping, oystering. They did not want to leave the bayou." The connection that office managers experienced felt transformative. "We get to interact in each other's homes and we were touched by the personal connection." Such personal connections compelled extraordinary dedication from office managers, who rise early and "spend a lot of late nights on the details." Working with a spouse makes that effort easier. "Being in a couple makes you more efficient. You want that project to run perfectly for the volunteers so they will come back." Keeping things running smoothly matters to the office managers, as "volunteers really appreciate an organized work site, so they know exactly what to expect." "Volunteers like an organized schedule." As one explained her role: "The long-term volunteers help enhance the experience for the short-term volunteers." Office managers focus steadily and over long days, to keep MDS's financial reputation intact, to support the long-term work team, and to attract volunteers to return.

COOKS

Most volunteers never see the behind-the-scenes action that takes place in the kitchen, which easily consumes a fifteen-hour day. For most volunteers, the day starts by clustering around the coffee pot, reading the paper, and checking the daily activities board, all of which is possible because the cook has already been up to prepare coffee and start the meal. Daily routine for the head cook can start as early as 4:30 a.m. during the hot season, preparing for arrival of the work crews to pack their lunches at 6, eat breakfast by 6, 6:30, or 7, and depart to serve by 7:30. Most rise by 5 a.m. and put breakfast in the oven, a meal they often started the day before: "Organization is absolutely key," say the cooks.

An assistant cook sets out lunch items before 6am, arrayed along a table so that volunteers can pack a sack lunch and drop it into numbered coolers taken out by crew leaders to the correct vans and trucks for the right project sites. Miss the numbered cooler and you go hungry—although generous volunteers share their meals and crew leaders, construction supervisors and project directors have been seen donating their meal. Lunches consist of sandwiches with a choice of breads and meats, along with selections of fruit, chips, granola bars, and vegetables. Cooks take care to accommodate vegetarians and dietary restrictions, noted on volunteer arrival forms, and to separate potentially dangerous foods like peanut butter for those with nut allergies. At the end of the table, volunteers can usually find special treats, from packaged candies to homemade cookies. Large containers provide water and sports drinks, particularly important to replenish energies spent in the heat and humidity of the deep south. If sites permit, volunteers may walk or drive back for lunch. With luck, project directors can swing back to camp and enjoy leftovers from the refrigerator at noon with office managers, cooks, hostesses and other long-term volunteers.

Meals start on time, particularly important in the morning, so that crews arrive to the site for a full day of work. Breakfast starts promptly, usually at 7 a.m., following prayer, and concludes with morning devotions. Volunteers then drop their plates, cups, and utensils into vats of soapy water prepared by the cooks and, time willing, help jump start the morning dishwashing. For the Katrina/Rita sites, automatic dishwashers made the job far easier, something considered indispensable by cooks who may serve up to 45 people per meal. It was not unusual to move a dozen or more loads of dishes, pots and pans through the dishwasher during every meal at the Plaquemines Parish site near Grand Bayou, or to use both dishwashers and volunteers at the sink in New Orleans.

"Cooks are important," said one experienced project director, punctuating his comment with intentional eye contact and a head nod. As part of the long-term leadership team, the cook plays a critical role in fueling volunteer energy. Scanning project reports back for 15 years in MDS archives reveals securing a cook as *the* top priority, one that can be quite challenging. Volunteer applications for long-term prospects often reveal the desire to do "anything but cook." One project director said, "You always want a good cook and you want the cook to be happy. You don't want a hot cook and a cold meal." Cooks come from schools, universities, assisted living, workplace, and kin networks. They bring daughters, grand-daughters and siblings in as assistant cooks and pass on a family tradition of service. Couples serve as cooks too, with husband-wife teams working double-shifts together to fill up hungry work crews.

The first long-term volunteer cooks on the site set up the kitchen, which means adapting equipment to available space. Setting up means checking on supplies and asking what else is needed. Katrina/Rita donations made it possible to secure critical items such as commercial mixers, extra baking sheets, and good knives. Yet cooks adapt well to ever-changing kitchens across the project sites. The "dream kitchen" can be found at the New Orleans site, where MDS refurbished a building and transformed a former church sanctuary into a new, spacious kitchen and dining room. Required due to the renovation, an elevator (required for accessibility) and trolley allow cooks to transport massive amounts of groceries up the 18 foot elevated area into the second floor kitchen. But cooks make it work no matter where they land. In Plaquemines Parish, a kitchen area in the long-term volunteer double-wide housing offers backup to the small but well-organized kitchen tucked into a former church sanctuary. Pass Christian offered cooks a double-wide trailer, and in New Iberia, the existing community center afforded a small but workable kitchen, dining area, and pantry.

MDS' advice to cooks begins with "Feed them well." Feeding volunteers well takes considerable effort and time; providing nourishment to volunteers involved in long days on construction sites requires an understanding of their daily needs for energy coupled with adequate rewards for a job well done. A combination of frugality, buying in bulk, experience, careful calculations with advance planning, and home-made items allows cooks to hit the mark nearly every time. Cooks plan things out because, as an MDS staff member explained, "At some of these job sites, it's not like you can just go run to the store for something you forgot." Purchasing food can be challenging, especially for dozens of volunteers in a locale devastated by disaster. Buying local is not always an option, though cooks like to do so. In New Orleans, a large grocery store lies only a mile away but more extensive distances are common due in part to the rural areas, geographically isolated communities, and coastal bayou sites where MDS gravitates. Pass Christian did not re-open a grocery store within 20 miles until 2009; cooks had to take circuitous routes, bypassing damaged roads and bridges, to bring home vans full of supplies. Coolers fill the van on shopping expeditions, keeping food at the right temperatures including ice cream, which is not an optional item on an MDS project site.

To keep costs low, cooks delight in finding good bargains, without compromising food quality. At one site, they found a bread factory that gave out free loaves on Wednesdays. Cooks also "check ads for bargains and link it to the menu." MCC sent beef and turkey from their material resources stores, an effort long in place for sending food to developing countries and, most recently, to Bayou la Batre after Katrina. Cooks say, "We try to be creative. Sometimes we use the leftover meats on pizza for Friday night after the short-term volunteers leave." Local supporters also provide, for example in New Iberia, Louisiana, where they donated several palettes of food. Clients and community members also bring goodies by, from homemade desserts to containers of shrimp and oysters. Local businesses offer discounts and even send pizza, sandwiches, and tacos out to project sites.

"Our cooks work year round to be ready for two months on projects," explained a staff member. "They set their menus in advance at home so that things go like clockwork." Cooks may rely on the MDS project cookbook, which measures recipes to serve twenty at a time but, more likely, use their own recipes familiar from previous projects. Many have spent months planning out their menus and itemizing shopping lists. Best of all, cooks bring food from home: canned fruit for pies, meat from the local butcher or farm, frozen cookies and more they prepared in advance so that volunteers could "have a taste of home." Although they buy bread for lunches, most cooks also bake some kind of bread for the evening meal. A touch of home cooking is very important to cooks, as they have been "told our food is great." A head cook explained, "There is always baking to do, which adds time, so we may have someone dedicated to just that." But despite the extensive planning, "you have to be very flexible." People drop by without notice and the cooks must feed them. "You never know when there will be 40! One day the Salvation Army and Red Cross came; fortunately, I had just baked a bunch of turkeys."

Cooks also embrace local culture as much as their own, "It is important to make meals that pertain to the area, like jambalaya, and it is a good way to use leftovers." "Once a week we had biscuits and gravy," a southern specialty. Cooks also like using local foods, "like strawberries or sweet corn." Yet volunteers earn rewards familiar to them: "Those Canadians must have their baked oatmeal." Few weeks go by without Pennsylvania treats like whoopie pie, shoofly pie, or homemade noodles, usually made with a grandmother's recipe passed down from Russia, Germany, or Switzerland.

Cooks do get a day off on some projects when the project director steps up to grill chicken, sausages, hot dogs or burgers for short-termers. Weekends represent time off, though cooks often spend their free time reorganizing the kitchen, buying groceries, cleaning the refrigerator, and re-checking the next week's meals. Safety concerns also consume cooks' time. "We keep food for four days only, max" marking containers with the day of origin and diligently clearing out the fridge by the time limit. Volunteer forms ask for allergies and food concerns, so cooks participate in the arrival orientation. "Most volunteers say they can handle their own food concerns, diabetics do o.k. on their own. Celiacs usually bring their own food."

Critical to MDS success, cooks agreed that their job "is really time consuming and tiring. It takes two weeks to recover when you get home." Yet the hard work pays off as "we get lots of compliments." Cooks also know the value of feeding the volunteers well: "If you feed them good food and attractive meals, they will work hard and tell others." Cooking long hours while standing on aching feet and legs means that volunteers return and Anabaptist servanthood continues.

WHY DO PEOPLE VOLUNTEER?

Who were these long-term and short-term volunteers, why did they come, and what did they take away? The remainder of this chapter looks at survey data from volunteers who went to the coast. The first section provides an overview of volunteer backgrounds. Subsequent sections emerged from a thematic analysis of an open-ended survey question that asked respondents to describe the highlights of their experience. Analysis revealed six themes that captured 638 different highlights[7]: new awareness, connections with clients, faithful service, blessings received, fellowship, and the MDS experience.

Volunteer Backgrounds

Most studies on volunteers profile people demographically, as a way to quantify those who serve. Consistent with existing research, most short-term volunteers arrive at an MDS site because of their social networks, the majority of which are embedded in church relationships. Long-termers valued how local congregations prepared Anabaptist servants. "It is neat to see how some churches prepare their volunteers ahead of time," such as through mentoring volunteers before their mission trip and giving them "a practical understanding of Anabaptism." Survey respondents also said that MDS was "very important" (20 percent) or "important" (43 percent) to their home congregation, a fairly strong indicator that voluntary service flows from one's personal faith community. Even stronger responses appeared when volunteers answered "how important is MDS to the Anabaptist mission?" With 53.9 percent saying "very important" and 35.5 percent saying "important," close to 9 out of 10 Gulf Coast storm volunteers viewed their service as supporting specific religious beliefs. Seven out of 10 said that MDS was very important or important to living out their faith at a personal level.

Surveys and interviews yield another meaningful and clear finding: that MDS represents a vehicle through which a diverse set of Anabaptists can serve together. A project director explained, "Faith, you live it. With MDS there are [many] different groups. On the job site, we worship and work together. . . . That is one of the biggest rewards; we really get to connect with each other." Noting the diverse Anabaptist presence, one long-termer said: "The majority are Mennonite, but I think virtually every denomination that I know of has been on a site one time or another. That is marvelous. I feel we are enriched by that." Fifteen denominations reported participation[8] with the bulk centered in Mennonite Church USA (27 percent) and Mennonite Church Canada (18.4 percent). Of the Mennonite Church USA and Mennonite Church Canada respondents, nearly 98 percent agreed that MDS is very important/important to the Anabaptist mission. Similar percentages appear for Brethren in Christ (96.5 percent), Mennonite Brethren (91.2 percent), Conservative Conference (100 percent), Amish (88.2 percent), Old Order Mennonite (90.9 percent), EMC (84.6 percent), EMMC (77.8 percent), Sommerfelder (100 percent), Other Mennonite (92.5 percent), and Other Anabaptist (66.6 percent). Clearly, volunteers feel that MDS represents an important vehicle for faith in action. Survey respondents also felt strongly about their work, with 63.8 percent agreeing that they saw MDS volunteers as "missionaries." Still, 34 percent were neutral on the question, perhaps reflecting the non- evangelical approach or perhaps a concentration simply on service. Their Anabaptist focus on serving those most in need came through clearly on the survey, with a remarkable 97.2 percent agreeing that MDS helped those most in need.

Among those surveyed, 37.8 percent were women and 62.2 percent were men. Slight differences appeared between men and women, with women being less likely to volunteer for longer time periods. Of those who served more than five times, for example, 17.5 percent were male and 8.7 percent were female. Women were somewhat more likely to serve one time (42.4 percent) for Katrina, though women emerged as somewhat more likely to serve on Rita sites than men.

Not surprisingly, 97.7 percent reported their race as Caucasian; the next category was 1.2 percent Asian American/Canadian followed by .4 percent African American/Canadian or First Nation/Native American and .3 percent Hispanic. Most volunteers fell into the 60 to 75 year age category, in the time frame when children have left home and free time has increased. Further, one in three volunteers fell into the 40 to 59 year age group, of whom many are also empty nesters and have more mobility. Still, 43.4 percent of volunteers reported that they remained employed full-time. In terms of their education, 12.9 percent have less than nine years of education, a finding consistent with a group influenced by some denominational norms (particularly among the Amish) to complete formal schooling by the age of 16 and the availability of schools when older volunteers were young. Another 7.2 percent have ten to twelve years of school and 20.8 percent have graduated from high school. About one in five have attended college or university with the same number having graduated. About 4 percent have pursued graduate studies with 13.8 percent attaining a graduate or professional degree.

The powerful impact of volunteers' work on clients and community partners might be surprising given relatively low levels of construction skills for most short-termers. Yet, many long-termers felt blessed by the spirit of those arriving: "There are some people who arrive with no carpentry skills but are very teachable and willing to learn."

Those surveyed said that they did learn new skills. Nearly three-fourths indicated they learned how MDS organized sites and said that projects were well-organized. Half learned new construction skills. Perhaps their success came from skilled long-termers who framed the volunteer experience for short-termers. One director said that he would "assign people accordingly so that there is a mix of skilled and unskilled." Another added: "You have to become creative to allow all to be productive and feel productive." Experienced directors knew to always "have some jobs in the wings that require less skill and/or less supervision." Most of the time, volunteer labor worked out well from the perspective of the long-term project directors, who always advised short-termers to "Measure twice, cut once. I am amazed at how good they are at various jobs, carpentry, plastering, whatever." Volunteers reported learning more than construction skills. Given the extraordinarily positive experience reported by clients and community partners, it may not be surprising that close to one-third reported learning new skills in "community rebuilding dynamics."

New Awareness

Survey respondents experienced two new kinds of awareness. The first brought new insights into disaster-generated needs embedded in difficult socioeconomic circumstances. The second generated understanding about communities and people distinctly different from their own.

Seeing the storm damage firsthand brought a deeper understanding of the value of service. Some contrasted the damage with governmental response. "We were in New Orleans and I was very moved by the lack of response that the city has received. It is still very much destroyed and only the tourist parts seem to be functioning at their previous normal levels. . . . I've been praying for the city ever since and telling others that New Orleans still needs much help." Seeing the damage, "I was impacted by the overall devastation suffered by the communities I visited as well as the apparent abandonment a lot of the victims must have felt." One offered, "By seeing all the destruction I gained a better understanding of what happens after a natural disaster and how people must repair their homes and lives after. I was humbled." Respondents were touched by "the experience of leaving [their] comfort and feeling a bit of the pain and suffering of persons affected by Katrina," saying that the highlight came through "opening my world and small community of safety."

Volunteers understood deeply the problem and felt compelled to be involved in "helping those who seemed to fall through the cracks—who really needed help." One watched volunteer service transform people who had fallen into "depression, [an]inability to work, [who] were locked into poverty, become functional, healthy, happy, employed, [able to] participate in rebuilding their own home." The volunteer then added: "They became my friends." Highlights included understanding their role in long-term recovery: "Being able to help where help was needed, helping to bring hope to those who felt there was not hope and hearing the local people who were helped thank us for restoring hope within them. I heard this at several locations."

As the years passed, volunteers witnessed the continuing need: "I was a volunteer in New Orleans, almost two years post Katrina. The devastation was still almost surreal. It really seemed as though the faith-based organizations were the only ones making any rebuilding progress." Another felt stunned about the remaining work: "I will never forget how that the hurricane happened like 5+ years ago, and how there is still sooo much rebuilding that needs to be done." As one summarized for many, the highlight was both insightful and humbling: "Seeing all the destruction and all that needs to be done."

Awareness also included learning more about the people on the Gulf Coast. "I became aware of the lifestyles of the people in the community and how it was different." Many agreed: "The exposure to persons and cultures distinct from my own was also exhilarating." Volunteers came to appreciate new cultures: "I think that was the highlight—the cultural experience, the food, the people—just how different daily life is, how unique the sub-culture in the bayou is, and how much I loved it." Another agreed, "I thoroughly enjoyed the exposure to a whole different culture and way of life as found in the Louisiana bayou country and Gulf Coast." They also appreciated "Seeing how the Louisiana folk live and how they recover from hurricanes." Volunteers learned about injuries people suffered in commercial fishing and oil drilling and how such conditions made disaster recovery even more daunting. Some made deeply meaningful connections across differences, coming away with great concern about their new friends. "I spent half a day with the Native American homeowner checking his trap line. He was a shrimper during the summer so I pray that his entire livelihood is not destroyed by the BP oil leak."

Seeing how people faced challenges, from storms to feeding their families, generated "a great respect for the humility and abilities of these people as well as for their courage and tenacity." Another volunteer contrasted life on their own farm with life along a bayou where people lived in very different homes with "sand, and mosquitoes . . . living on the meager earnings from fishing and crabbing" yet the volunteers understood that "it is their home . . . they brought us meals and sent a bushel of crabs home with us." They learned to enjoy new meals, too, as "eating a shrimp meal cooked by a homeowner" was a highlight for many. Volunteers particularly loved shrimp boat trips: "I could really feel God with us as we were out on the water watching the sun set over the Gulf."

Personal contact enabled them to also find commonalities: "As Christians, our eternal goals were exactly the same." Respondents particularly appreciated faith-based interactions, "the whole-hearted singing, praising God, and praying of the black people. The love they showed us." Volunteers who went to Hackberry, Louisiana enjoyed "the musical gift of entertainment" provided by a local bluegrass gospel group. Another volunteer "was wholeheartedly welcomed by the local Houma Indians to participate in a dance, which ended in a prayer." "Interaction with Christian volunteers from greatly varying backgrounds in a great community experience" was another highlight, for example, "the Baptist church revival service I attended." Sadly, one group arrived in the aftermath of an urban murder. Attending the memorial service, one person said, "It was important for us to stand with those whom we were serving as they traveled into the grieving process. . . . It was also enlightening for the young people in the group, many of whom had never been exposed to inner city life and struggles." Volunteers witnessed other contrasts too: "My highlight was seeing the people of New Orleans come alive and play jazz on the street. Really cool to see how the people of the city are staying strong." Many appreciated "learning to know persons of a different culture and worshiping God together," and marveled "that they still praise God even after all they had been through." And yes, the southern hospitality came through clearly in volunteers' written highlights: "The big smiles, and the southern 'Thank you Maaaam' meant the same" as at home. Volunteers agreed: "The southerners were all very friendly."

Connecting with Clients

Recalling that clients expressed overwhelmingly positive comments about the character of the volunteers, it might be surprising that one in ten volunteers never met the homeowner due to client displacement or work obligations. Over 60 percent reported they met the homeowner but did not spend much time with them; one in four did meet the homeowner and "made a friend."

Connecting with clients meant a great deal. A repeat volunteer said, "I've been on 3 [trips] and each time the highlight has been meeting the homeowner, hearing their story and how much we do is impacting them." Others agreed that the highlight was "the deep appreciation for our help from the homeowners. It was a wonderful feeling to be able to help them." "Every day when we showed up she came out of her FEMA trailer and thanked us, gave us hugs, and told us stories." Making a personal connection for some involved being able "to work side by side with someone I've never met before, get to know them, leaving with the joy of a new relationship."

Volunteers also experienced high points that demonstrated client resiliency against the larger tragedy of the storms: "Hearing the stories of struggles from some of the clients and their appreciation of what we were doing for them." Volunteers identified highlights also in "the optimism of most of the clients we worked for and the appreciation that they expressed." Client appreciation confirmed their time, effort, and expense that went into servanthood: "It is a rewarding experience to know that you have made a difference in someone's life." Indeed, another saw client appreciation as a form of mutual celebration. "Seeing the need firsthand had much more effect on me than hearing about it. I was blessed to see the joy and appreciation that the recipients showed." Yes, said another, "just knowing that what we had done made a difference to someone who had suffered so much loss."

Many volunteers experienced personal affirmation of their labor: "All the sweat, heat, and manual labor was well worth it to see the joy in her face." "It really gave me hope that there were good people capable of doing great things for others in this messed up world." Overwhelmingly, volunteers agreed: "It's unexplainable to others. You have to be there and see and feel it yourself; it will live in me forever." Clearly, the benefits of volunteerism were not one-sided. "The best thing that happened was seeing just how grateful everyone was that we were there to help them . . . and how kind everyone was to us." One volunteer recalled a quiet moment with a client as their highlight: "We spent a week or so completing a wheelchair ramp. The homeowner came out to talk . . . he thanked me profusely and we cried together." One volunteer summed it up for many: "The joy that we brought to the people that we built homes for, that made it all worthwhile."

Seeing the devastation in person brought the value of volunteer work into clear perspective: "The highlight of my experiences with MDS was mostly the thankfulness of the homeowners and the community after many had lost everything. Just knowing someone could now be sheltered and safe in their own home once again was so gratifying!" Volunteers felt affirmed in both action and faith: "We were part of an answer to their prayers when they couldn't have rebuilt themselves."

Faithful Service

Faithful service emerged as the driving normative behavior compelling thousands of people to go to the Gulf Coast: "Helping others is part of our heritage and traditions." Several interviewees stated succinctly: "I do this for God." Volunteering also gave the faithful an opportunity to explain their beliefs. They answered frequent questions about why they came. "It gave us the opportunity to talk about our tradition of helping. Our faith and beliefs came through clearly and strongly in our service work."

The work they did together made them feel "truly engaged with fellow volunteers" as it allowed them to be "the Hands and Feet of Christ and showing His Love in practical ways to those in need." The faith-sharing they did came through action, or as one put it "share the gospel with your hands and if needed use words." They left fairly well convinced that their skills and knowledge made a difference in people's lives.

Volunteers also saw a higher power at work. Clients talked about "how their faith in God grew through the storm and through the fact that others showed up to help in their time of great need." Volunteers also felt affirmed in their broader faith commitment, through "knowing that God called us to do this work." They appreciated "being recognized in a store as one of 'the Mennonites' in a positive way; the trust that we had of the people we worked for." "In each situation, the homeowners regained hope and trust in humanity. That was a great blessing to me." One volunteer described the overall impact of the faith demonstration quite well: "I feel like the Church as a body of people around the globe is much more real to me now and I have a very tangible experience of the Church as the Body of Christ to think of when I need encouragement or faith." As an organization, Mennonite Disaster Service served them well. "I am amazed that our forefathers saw the wisdom in first creating an organization like MDS. I feel a sense of responsibility to help keep it going."

Over and over, volunteers revealed the highlights as "the joy of working together with others to bring hope and joy to people that have had their lives so devastated. It was so fulfilling to me to have had this experience." "Just knowing that we helped good people in a time of real need, and making longtime friends." Yes, said another, "helping to bring hope to people hurting from a disaster was the greatest highlight." "The experience of leaving the work and rat race at home and giving of myself and my time for the benefit of a total stranger, all for nothing, so to speak, although I feel I received something much more valuable than any monetary gains."

Volunteers embedded their work in "a sense of fulfillment and of being helpful to God and to His people—an outlet for my commitment to service." They felt connected through service as a demonstration of their faith, "serving others . . . being Jesus' hands and feet!" and following Scriptural guidance as an "opportunity to be of service (a command of Christ's) to people in need." In short, the highlight was "the experience of giving and receiving through the same act."

Blessings Received

Through client appreciation, volunteers understood the value of their service, "to give and bless others without an expectation of returns—no strings attached—God honors a cheerful giver." Yet even though they saw volunteering as a selfless act, "a chance to help without expecting anything in return," they discovered unexpected benefits: "Being able to help others in their time of need was a wonderful experience; it has opened my eyes to the needs of others after a crisis." From skilled to unskilled, volunteer highlights focused on giving of themselves to others. "This was my first time serving with MDS and as a tradesperson I felt blessed to have my skills developed over 30 years used to help others. I did not expect that. I noted to several people that I am not one to preach a sermon . . . but I was in my element and able to fully contribute." A long-term couple emphasized the non-tangible meaning of their service: "We both feel this call and enjoy our time on projects. I love the fact of being able, in a small way, to bring healing and wholeness to someone." The joy of helping others in person moved them deeply. "It is frustrating to know of such great need and only send money. I felt that I was able to do something to help that was concrete and personal and that felt good." Yes, said one, "volunteerism strengthens relationships and myself personally." And despite the hard work, "physical labor is refreshing." Using whatever skills they brought felt good. "I enjoyed the opportunity to work with my hands and with other people in doing a service to people who had great needs."

The benefits of volunteering also included being able to learn new skills or to put their cooking or carpentry abilities to good use. Some found themselves learning from people younger than themselves or at the direction of older volunteers. Though most arrived unskilled, they learned that "I could go, not knowing too much about a specific type of work, but leaving with a wealth of knowledge." A sense of God's affirmation characterized the experience of many volunteers who thought they went to serve but came away "tremendously blessed!" themselves. They pushed themselves beyond what they thought they could do as well. "I will not forget the total fatigue when I got back to our trailer at evening, and how full and excited and blessed I felt."

A few commented on personal healing they experienced from serving and seeing how disaster survivors moved on. They mentioned the pain of losing a spouse or dealing with loneliness, or medical challenges. Volunteering helped them. "I found it was exactly what I needed, I had a purpose, it wasn't stressful . . . my talents were appreciated and I felt blessed to be able to help someone in need. I will do this again!" Engaging in meaningful service helped another who was experiencing a "difficult time in my life," finding that others, "helped me more than I thought possible." The transition from despair to hope occurred for volunteers through faithful work with others and from meeting "the locals we were helping. . . . They were so awesome and grateful. I have a special place in my heart for the people of the Gulf Coast."

Fellowship

Perhaps the greatest benefit that volunteers received came through interacting with other servants. Data analysis revealed that fellowship benefits included interacting within meaningful social networks, making new friends, and working together with like-minded people.

Analysis confirmed studies that social networks prove important in luring people to volunteer work. "I enjoyed the worksite atmosphere and the opportunity to work closely with friends from my home church. . . . Travelling and working with friends from church was a very positive experience; it brought us closer together." Pre-established relationships became more impactful: "Because I went with a group from church, it was a time of community-building amongst ourselves as we worked together for others benefits." At times, specific groups went, "I went with our youth group. The whole trip was a great experience." When volunteers arrived, they felt connected across generations. "For me the highlight, more than any one event, was the experience of working and eating and socializing with all of the retired couples." The young person explained further, "To be surrounded by people who decided after 30 or so years of marriage to roll up their sleeves and spend time working side by side was really edifying."

Social networks also included personal family ties. Parents brought children, and siblings served together as well. "The highlight of my trip included working alongside my sons." Another agreed that her highlight was "quality time with my sister." The opportunity to "serve with my family" meant a great deal to one spouse who brought along young children, while another said, "I was there with a bunch of my siblings and enjoyed sharing together in this need."

Meeting new friends emerged as a second important category of fellowship. In general, volunteers simply liked "meeting other volunteers." Despite the one-week period that many spent, the work involved them in "the wonderful feeling of meeting new people at the beginning of the week and forming relationships by working together and studying God's word. Definitely a life-changing experience!" One felt nervous on learning she would be split up from the group she came with, only to find "it was a really great idea and it was awesome to meet people from other groups that were also there to serve." Volunteers made friendships within their own denomination and across Anabaptist affiliations as well. "First and foremost I was impressed and awed by the entire Mennonite community. The fellowship, the camaraderie, dedication, commitment to cause, ability to function as a well oiled machine each and every week with a new crew." Some who experienced their first chance to learn about other Anabaptists "fell in love with the Amish young people who came to work one week. . .totally loved the evenings at the end of the day where we all hung out, played games and laughed together." Another encountered "Groffdale girls" and shared time in a group sing on the beach as the sun set. "I still get goosebumps." One summarized the feeling for most: "I enjoyed working with people who had come from all over North America for the same reason that I went. Being part of the global church working together for the good of all mankind has always been a delight for me."

One situated their highlight in a sense of shared faith: "Giving the cup of cold water to needy and appreciative victims of natural disasters in the company of like-minded believers." These new ties, fashioned by common service, lasted: "We still stay in contact" because of "the joy of working with other believers."

The MDS Experience

The way in which MDS manages its work site matters to its volunteers. "The MDS' model of flexible and mobile work units was fascinating—so practical and efficient, worthy of support." Social scientists suggest that faith-based rituals serve as ways to focus people's energies and produce collective meaning. On an MDS site, multiple opportunities exist, both formally and informally, to participate in activities that build relationships and produce meaning for those who serve.

Teamwork emerged as a major theme from respondents' comments on highlights. Short-termers were assigned to crews based on skills and jobs, often crossing denominations, ages, and genders. "It was the team-building we did with the multi-generation aspect of the team I came with" described one volunteer, "working and living in community, having more skilled people teach less skilled people." Another expressed the highlight as "the amount of work that a small, committed team of semi-skilled volunteers can accomplish in one week." They acknowledged the "messy job and hot and humid weather," noting the persistence of volunteers "to get the job done regardless." Teamwork characterized their time together in "working with enthusiastic, Christian construction workers." Crews emerged with "the same goal, to help." They noted that teamwork and fellowship came from the structure MDS provided, "having good accommodations and good devotional periods," which took away their burden so they could serve others.

Volunteers especially enjoyed shared informal times outside of the work week, "the weekly Wednesday time with clients where they would come in and tell us their stories," and the "weekly lunch program" provided in Pass Christian. One interviewee observed that "Anabaptist theology is alive and well in MDS. We noted this in the content of the devotions prepared by volunteers." "Also very meaningful was finding out how we could work and worship together even though there was such a big difference in religious backgrounds." "In MDS there were all types of Mennonites, Amish" and even Presbyterians and Baptists volunteered: "but we experience a unity." Project directors agreed with the value of providing such worship context, as one noted in an interview: "Volunteers should not wonder 'Why am I on the roof in 100 degree weather putting on a shingle? Just why did God put me here?'" Collective worship and reflection allowed volunteers on projects "to talk about the importance of what we are doing and why we are here." Interviewees also saw Anabaptist principles unfold in "relational dynamics, dialogue and discussions over the supper table, love shown to each other, working together as a team."

Those lucky to be present for house dedications enjoyed especially enriching moments. Long-termers set the stage for home dedications much appreciated by all the volunteers: "There was one home in the bayou [where] we didn't spend a lot of money but that couple cried and cried at the dedication." Another project director said: "These were wonderful times. We would invite spiritual caregivers such as pastors, community partners, neighbors and family, the recovery committee." Home dedications were grand celebrations for the volunteers as explained by a project director: "It was an important community event with family, friends, and neighbors. It almost seemed that the people wanted the dedication as an excuse to throw a party!" Office managers organized the programs, during which volunteers "presented the homeowners with a key, a Bible, the occupancy permit, a wall hanging, [and] a copy of *The Hammer Rings Hope*." The celebratory atmosphere also meant something else, noted a long term couple: "A house dedication is a vital part of our Christian witness and becomes an integral part of the volunteer experience." A project director from Canada used the word most common to all interviewed about home dedications, "meaningful."

CONCLUSION

Mennonite Disaster Service relies on its grassroots base to generate volunteers. They come because their faith compels them to serve, but they leave with more than they had expected. New awareness emerges about cultures and denominations distinct from their own, about livelihoods that challenge and people who survive traumatic events. They learn to work in fellowship and as a team across skill levels, ages, denominations, and national borders, finding commonality and purpose. The long hours spent in sometimes unpleasant and arduous conditions pale when reflecting on the meaning of service, their reaffirmed relationship to God, and the connections they make to each other and to coastal residents. They give up vacation time, personal lives, paychecks, and savings to serve their neighbors. And despite the uncertainty that many come with, they leave fulfilled and more confident. As one project director said simply: "I love the work."

Having seen what their hands and feet can do in a short time, many leave feeling as one long-termer: "I wish I could have done more." Many say they will return, most likely through existing social relationships embedded in faith and family networks. And some will come back to work with friends newly made in another week of service or as a new long-termer. As one repeat volunteer shared, "Each time I volunteer I am overwhelmed by power displayed by God and nature's power in destruction and also in that of rebuilding a community both physically and spiritually." They situate their outcomes in a faith experience that shows "how God is in control and when we come together as a community of believers and let Him lead, He can accomplish great things through us."

NOTES

1. Mennonite Church USA Archive, Goshen, Indiana; Mennonite Library and Archives, Newton, KS; Mennonite Central Committee Library, Akron, Pennsylvania; Mennonite Disaster Service archive, Lititz, Pennsylvania.

2. Correspondence, Temporary Disaster Committee (probably written by Peter J. Dyck). April 4, 1952. Eden Mennonite Church letterhead, Moundridge Kansas. Mennonite Library and Archives, Newton, Kansas.

3. Diller, John. No date, possibly 1954. *MDS "In the Beginning."* Mennonite Library and Archives, Newton, KS.

4. Kansas Area MDS. March 22, 1958. Minutes of the Fourth Annual Training School. Held at Hesston Mennonite Church, Hesston, Kansas. Mennonite Library and Archives, Newton, Kansas.

5. Kansas Area MDS. March 22, 1958. Minutes of the Fourth Annual Training School. Held at Hesston Mennonite Church, Hesston, Kansas. Mennonite Library and Archives, Newton, Kansas.

6. Wiebe, Vernon R. 1960. *Mennonites: Brief History of Mennonite Disaster Service.* Mennonite Library and Archives, Newton, Kansas.

7. The survey included a total of 852 respondents. Most responded to the question on highlights. This section includes responses from those who served on the Gulf Coast storms including short-term and long-termers from approximately 15 Anabaptist denominations.

8. Categories possible for responses included Mennonite Church USA, Mennonite Church Canada, Brethren in Christ, Mennonite Brethren, Conservative Conference, Amish (Beachy, New Order, Old Order), Old Order Mennonites (includes Groffdale), EMC, EMMC, Sommerfelder, Other Mennonite, Other Anabaptist, Methodist, Catholic, Presbyterian, Other Protestant, Other Christian, Other Faith.

SEVEN

Behind the Hammer, Behind the Scenes

It was chaos.
—MDS staff member

INTRODUCTION

This chapter outlines the experiences of MDS staff as they managed Gulf Coast storm recovery projects behind a sturdy core of grass-roots volunteers. MDS changed during the "Katrina" years, ramping up from a handful of employees to nineteen staff members in the U.S. and Canada. Their collective narrative originates from individual interviews supplemented by insights from Board members and long-termers, organizational reports, and on-site observations. This chapter opens by describing MDS before Katrina, then segues into how staff adapted internally to support more projects and volunteers than previously in MDS history. Their story reveals how staff navigated significant organizational change during a time of acute stress yet maintained an organizational culture permeated by Anabaptist values. The story begins by situating the staff narrative in MDS offices then describes business as usual in the days before hurricane Katrina.

Akron, Pennsylvania, United States

When disaster disrupts daily routines, MDS usually turns to local volunteer "investigators" to provide information and make recommendations, trusting its grassroots base to fulfill the organizational mission. Behind the scenes, the executive director, administrative assistant, site investigators (paid and volunteer) and communications staff help launch projects. An exception occurred in August, 1992 when hurricane Andrew slammed into southern Florida and parts of Louisiana. Facing unprecedented damage, the MDS executive director traveled to the area, sent back reports and recommendations, raised funds and helped to launch new programs. Within a few years after Andrew, MDS in the U.S. transitioned back to business as usual, supporting volunteers on projects across the U.S. and Canada. As the 1990s unfolded, MDS launched an extension office in Winnipeg. Their experience from Andrew and the addition of the new Canadian office would prove invaluable for Katrina, Rita and Ike.

Many organizations operate formally, with paper being pushed by individuals focused exclusively on a single task. A non-profit association like MDS, though, usually varies from such an impersonal workplace by featuring less formal and more interconnected relationships (Tomeh 1973). Situated in a two-story house in Akron, Pennsylvania,[1] the main MDS office environment feels more like a family workplace where people know each other well, enjoy face-to-face relationships, and care about not only professional work but each other's personal well-being.

MDS moved into its Main Street office in 2000, after renting space from MCC while they legally separated. Such legal separation, though, did not mean division in terms of contacts, resources, and relationships. With less than two blocks between MCC and MDS in Pennsylvania, frequent contact continued. MCC also offered resources for communications and accounting into the early Katrina years. Still, moving the MDS office symbolized organizational independence after more than three decades of being embedded in a larger organization.

Perched on a corner in the small town of Akron, the MDS "house" office featured a wrap-around porch with rocking chairs, plants, and shade trees. Inside, staff used only the first floor as office space and dedicated the second floor to housing guests. A small kitchen always offered the morning paper, coffee, tea, and snacks—often baked goods, pretzels, or chocolate. On special occasions, Pennsylvania treats like whoopie pies or local ice cream appeared as well. MDS operated efficiently with a small staff of 3–4 who did not need additional space. With little employee turnover, MDS staff generated long-term relationships easily. Staff worked diligently to support the grassroots organization, in a normally quiet, comfortable environment.

Winnipeg, Manitoba, Canada

Similar to the situation in the U.S., MDS affiliated with Mennonite Central Committee Canada (MCCC). MDS committees developed across most of the provinces and MCC Canada supported MDS financially into the early 1990s. When MDS and MCC U.S. separated legally in 1992, Canadians followed suit in 1994, which eliminated MDS from the MCCC budget. An MDS Binational Board emerged to represent all five MDS regions in the U.S. and Canada with representation from MCC. That representation changed in 1999 in order to "expand the Anabaptist constituency churches beyond those relating to MCC if appropriate and to cease the automatic appointments of the MCC US and MCCC representatives as Binational Board Secretary and Treasurer but maintaining their representation as Board members."[2] Similar to that in the U.S., their relationship continued "as sister organizations" including disaster response and payroll administration.

MDS established a Canadian office in Winnipeg starting in 2001 with one paid staff member. Not intended as a separation from the U.S., the office opened because fifty percent of MDS volunteers came from Canada (Region V). The MDS board also hoped that a Canadian office would "raise the profile of MDS in Canada" specifically to generate an even stronger volunteer base and "provide a clear practical/applied theology outlet for constituent churches."[3] An administrative coordinator began operating out of a 100 square foot space rented from MCC-Canada and a part-time administrative assistant was added in 2002. As the staff and work expanded, they moved to a 400 square foot space in 2003 with two work stations and a small meeting, lunch, and storage room, an area they maintained with 1.5 full time staff until Katrina. Canadian MDS expansion occurred also in the context of fires in British Columbia. Having a staff resource base in Canada enabled MDS to support reconstruction efforts after the fire. In addition, Region V launched a summer youth project at that time, a program still in place.

Canadian MDS staff dedicated themselves to attracting long-term and new short-term volunteers by promoting MDS across Canada. Their work took them into Mennonite churches to recruit congregational contact persons who would take MDS into the pews of Anabaptists waiting to serve. MDS continued to raise its own money and prior to Katrina "had recently begun fund appeals to Canadian constituents."

Such committed work to recruit and strengthen the grassroots base had considerable payoffs when Katrina occurred, with a ready core of experienced volunteers eager to assist their neighbors to the south. Though small, the knowledgeable staff expanded quickly and effectively to support the largest MDS effort in history, simultaneously the largest documented movement of Canadian volunteers into the U.S. for disaster service.

Being Bi-National

MDS is uniquely bi-national, an intentional organizational structure reflective of Mennonite immigration and dispersion among people who seek to remain tied to each other.

Staff members see value in bi-nationality, as volunteers can help across a mutual border. Other challenges include different work holidays, government rules, and exchange rates. Sometimes, "the US/Canada laws and the paperwork make it so much tougher." Office work varies too, including stationery, fund appeals, graphics, and securing services like printing. Cultural differences also influence how staff and even volunteers approach matters and "the interaction and communication can lead to different conclusions" in each of the two offices. Yet many staff members confirm what one shared, that "a big part would be missing if we were not bi-national." Staff members work diligently at maintaining "internal office communication to keep us informed." One said "We all work very hard to minimize divides and keep the focus on the whole." As one staff member said "we have to be bi-national!" and another added, "We are all MDS . . . it is the mix of different people and cultures, and how similar we really are." One concluded what many embraced, "it is my dream job."

BEFORE THE STORMS

MDS has always enjoyed a reputation within the disaster community of doing quality work. Tucked into modest niches and dated files, MDS has earned an impressive set of plaques and awards, with an equally extensive collection of formal appreciation certificates. In 1970, MDS garnered presidential attention for the first time in recognition of its work post-Camille. President Nixon recognized "that Mennonite volunteers from many states and Canada came to the areas worst hit by the storm . . . several months after the storm had passed, I am told, there were still scores of Mennonite volunteers at work."[4] A few months later, the U.S. Department of Housing and Urban Development presented its Public Service Award to MDS for "outstanding volunteer efforts in helping to provide housing for Hurricane Camille victims in Mississippi and Virginia."[5] The award acknowledged that the American Red Cross provided materials for MDS to build 18 homes and repair 600 dwellings in Mississippi. In Virginia, MDS built 14 new homes and repaired dozens of homes and farm buildings. HUD recognized MDS for helping over 700 families, describing "this act of distinguished public service as a most worthwhile contribution to the development and preservation of our country."

Despite local partners and clients being unfamiliar with MDS, those in the field of emergency management know MDS well, none more so than FEMA directors. James Lee Witt, who served as FEMA director during the Clinton administration, singled out MDS in his book *Stronger in the Broken Places* (2002). Witt acclaimed MDS for rebuilding homes in College Station, Arkansas in a manner that healed generations of inter-racial pain.

Before Katrina, FEMA director Joe Allbaugh publicly stated "faith-based groups at the community level, like the Salvation Army and the Mennonite Disaster Service, play critical roles in disaster relief, as does the American Red Cross. The power of neighbors helping neighbors should never be underestimated. These people make a vital difference without any expectation of thanks or recognition" (FEMA 2002; Dreier 2005). To assess the impact on staff and how they responded to Gulf Coast projects, this chapter starts by looking at numbers of pre- and post-Katrina (Rita, Ike) disaster projects, volunteers, and donations.

Work Before and After the Storms

Numerical totals for MDS volunteers shed additional light into the level of their Katrina effort. And, though the Katrina totals include Rita, Gustav and Ike, the majority of projects resulted from Katrina alone, which demonstrates the expanded scope of work. For example, in 1995, MDS responded to floods, an earthquake, and several tornadoes in Illinois, California, Georgia, Texas, Alabama, and Louisiana. As seen in table 7.1, MDS completed 2,465 total jobs between 1995 and 2000. In comparison, MDS completed 1,655 between 2005 and 2010 for the Gulf Coast storms alone, approximately 67 percent of the total for all disasters combined between 1995 and 2000.

MDS breaks jobs into clean-up, minor repair, major repair, and complete rebuilds. To compare MDS pre- and post-Gulf Coast storms, consider that MDS completed 1,370 between 1995 and 2000 for all disasters compared to 754 cleanup jobs for the more recent storms. The number of minor repairs just for the Gulf Coast storms exceeded the total of minor repairs from 1995 to 2000. The number of completely rebuilt homes for the Gulf Coast storms came close to the total built for all disasters that occurred from 1995 to 2000. It is important to remember that MDS accomplished these Gulf Coast statistics while responding to additional disasters between 2005 and 2010. In short, the Gulf Coast storms alone rivaled all work spent in a previous five-year time period.

Volunteers before and after the Gulf Coast Storms

As a grassroots organization, MDS relies on its volunteer base. Before Katrina, MDS volunteerism demonstrated patterns consistent with research literature (see chapter 2). In 2004, 45 percent of MDS volunteers were under the age of 26, with 40 percent falling between 26 and 64 and 15 percent 65 and over. With the Gulf Coast storms, however, the number of volunteers tripled between 2004 and 2006. Nested within the total volunteer tally is the largest set of MDS volunteers to focus on a single geographic region. The majority served on a single disaster, Katrina. Bearing in mind that the numbers do not include volunteers involved in

Table 7.1.   MDS Jobs Before and After The Gulf Coast Storms[i]

Year	Jobs Completed	Clean Up	Minor Repair	Major Repair	Complete Rebuild
1995	213	58	41	93	22
1996	416	210	72	113	6
1997	1,215	950	118	122	25
1998	172	37	67	44	25
1999	183	24	53	72	34
2000	266	91	83	65	27
Total 1995-2000	*2,465*	*1,370*	*434*	*509*	*139*
Katrina/Rita 2005–2010	1,517	625	656	145	93
Gustav/Ike 2008–2009	138	129	32	64	13
Total Gulf Coast	*1,655*	*754*	*688*	*209*	*106*

[i] Numbers do not include specific efforts such as the Partnership Home Project where volunteers built home sections, shipped them to a site where crews then put them together and do include non-Gulf Coast storm totals. In addition, an Amish group called Storm Aid worked in Mississippi to offer 4 cleanups, 44 minor repairs and 12 major rebuilds for an additional 60 total jobs completed. For 2002, totals include efforts in Princeville, North Carolina where MDS completed 25 homes out of a total of 38 for that year.
Source: Mennonite Disaster Service

some programs (like the Partnership Home Program discussed later in this chapter or localized Emergency Response Teams serving in quick relief work), the numbers of total volunteers for the Gulf Coast exceed those in table 7.2.

Donations Before the Gulf Coast Storms

MDS provides volunteer labor through donated funds, usually operating 3–5 disaster rebuilding projects per year as well as cleanup on even more sites. Before Katrina, MDS secured most of its financing from individual donors in the U.S. and Canada. Internal records show that most MDS funds have come from Anabaptist constituents. Prior to 2003, the majority came from general donations via an MDS donor envelope and an annual fall fund appeal with an average donation of $194.15.

In 2003, though, MDS faced budget shortfalls and decided the organization would respond to a maximum of three disasters at one time,

Table 7.2. Volunteer Numbers to Project Sites, 2002–2010

Year	Total Volunteer Number
2002	1,741
2003	2,878
2004	2,026
2005	3,204
2006	6,103
2007	6,650
2008	4,817
2009	3,856
2010	1,822

Source: Mennonite Disaster Service.

reduce the number of the long-termers to no more than 2–3 couples or individuals and 2–4 support staff. They froze new staff hires and most travel, sold off some vehicles and reduced overall services "till we get our fund balances back to a healthy level." The financial crisis prompted MDS to start new funding efforts similar to other voluntary associations, although some MDSers felt uncomfortable with a direct appeal campaign. In the early 1950s, for example, MDS specifically stated the organization would not solicit funds. The original 1951 constitution of MSO stated, "Money shall be raised by free will offering and grants from various groups as needs are presented." Reconfirming their position, those at a meeting of MCC constituent churches listed a key directive, "They shall not solicite [*sic*] funds. Funds should be contributed through regular church channels and designated either for a definite disaster area or to be held in a fund for use in emergency relief. However, in 2003, MDS was "certain that those days of fundraising are over," mirroring the more common pattern of direct appeals among similar disaster voluntary organizations.

Anticipating hurricanes in Region I or II (U.S. east and Gulf Coast areas), MDS wanted to be ready to respond. For the first time, MDS inserted donor envelopes into its newsletter, *Behind the Hammer*, initiated direct contact with constituents, and began to tell the MDS story more broadly through publications, DVDs, an enhanced website, and traditional and social media. The newsletter-based *Behind the Hammer* appeal brought in critically needed funds, and nearly tripled the internal budget. Disaster events do bump up funding, and MDS experienced modest rises after the 1999 hurricanes in North Carolina and Honduras, September 11th, 2001, and the east coast hurricanes of 2004. Just before Katrina, the average annual donation had increased to $467.19. Though identifying religious affiliation is not always possible, MDS knew that at least 50 percent of the donations came from Anabaptists.

After Katrina, "the percentages shrank to 38 percent because of an increase in non-Anabaptist donors." Indeed, Katrina changed business as usual inside MDS headquarters and for the paid staff. Katrina donations shattered previous amounts and widened a heavily Anabaptist base. Volunteer numbers reached new heights, fueling the largest reconstruction effort in organizational history and generating new programs. Behind the scenes, MDS needed to change as the number of project sites for a single disaster tripled. The organization needed to remain able to respond to additional events—Rita, Wilma, Gustav, Ike—and non-hurricane events outside the Gulf Coast as well.

As one staff member described those pre-Katrina days, "That summer was nice and easy and then Katrina hit. We were all thrown into a nightmare." They relied on experience and on each other: "We all knew our jobs and were competent. None of us were new to our jobs." Continuing, the staff member added, "But we had other issues too. We had a new executive director who came on board in 2004. He took us to new places and had a new style—things were really different." Board changes had also occurred just prior to Katrina with new leadership and, prompted in part by Katrina, new board procedures as well. Echoing the long-termer sentiment that MDS really stands for "Make Do Somehow," the staff member added, "But we adjusted."

HURRICANE KATRINA

MDS represents a well-established type of "expanding organization" (Dynes 1970). This type of organization swells and contracts to meet needs when disaster strikes. However, catastrophic events may compel even more adaptation so that organizations can fulfill their missions (Sutton 2003). The present chapter examines such an evolution from the perspective of MDS staff. The internal changes at the main office in Akron, Pennsylvania included new office arrangements, donations management procedures, resource expansion, staff hires, and procedures and programs; in Canada, MDS moved into larger space, expanded its staff and managed a massive, steady influx of volunteers. Simultaneously, staff engaged in critical external work that included explaining Mennonites, selecting sites, building partnerships, and supporting volunteers. It all began when the phones started to ring.

Katrina Donations

From a strong Anabaptist base, donors and volunteers eager to help called MDS when Katrina hit. During interviews, staff members frequently described those early days in a few words: "It was chaos." Staff reported "a huge increase in the number of donors and the money that came in." Katrina also generated new attention to MDS from outside its traditional constituency: "The most heartwarming part was the large number of people who phoned or came in to donate. Even non-Mennonites were very generous and donated large sums because of our name and the trust they had in us." Even as callers said they believed in MDS, staff members came away "amazed that people would just give their credit card numbers over the phone to a total stranger. I was blown away by the trust."

Tremendously generous donors also arrived in person: "A local farmer walked in. He had just sold his house and wrote out a check for $100,000. He did not want any recognition for it. He just said, 'The Lord has blessed me and I need to give back.'" Still, some new donors checked out the unfamiliar organization before committing their money. "One donor stopped in to make a donation but first wanted to see the operation—and to count how many BMWs there were in the parking lot." Probably surprised by modest cars alongside a hitching post for horse and buggy Anabaptists, "He made the donation."

Bighearted donors supported the staff through the longest hours and work weeks of their lives. "The generosity of the people made me very busy, but also kept me going. The number of new donor files opened was enormous." One recalled, "Our mouths would just fall open at the amounts at the end of the day when we totaled it up." Indeed, donor totals reveal a marked change in September 2005. Donations eventually totaled over $8 million, an unprecedented amount for MDS, with $5 million arriving in the first three months after Katrina. MDS had to adapt quickly.

The first indicator that things would be different came when the local letter carrier stopped delivering mail to the Akron office. Used to the daily drop-off at the office, staff now drove to the main post office daily to pick up multiple flats of donations. Bringing back the mail meant creating a new area and procedures for opening mail: "Sometimes we would get 6 or more flats of mail every day, all of it checks, or we would get faxes with credit card numbers on them."

For the first time in MDS history, staff discovered that the answering machine had a limit for messages. Reflecting the new daily routine, staff kept phone lines open from 8 a.m. to 8 p.m. [in Akron] so that west coast donors and volunteers could call in. By Thursday in the first week after Katrina, "We realized we couldn't keep up with the phones and the checks." To manage, they called trusted friends, former volunteers, and local church secretaries to ask, "Can you volunteer—to open mail, answer phones and enter information on the computers?" And those they asked answered the call for help: "People came from out of the woodwork. I called them my angels. We put them on an angel list and when

they could work." As the angels arrived, staff began moving desks
around. Initially, they created a communications hub so that up to five
phones could be answered simultaneously. Because the Akron "infrastructure was not sufficient to support" the influx of funds and volunteers, staff added computers, tables, and desks throughout the first floor
to process the amounts: "We were running extension lines everywhere
for the computers." Not surprisingly, they quickly "ran out of supplies"
resulting in daily runs to a nearby office supply store for envelopes,
paper, binder clips, and even chairs. On the main floor, "the noise levels
really got high; you heard every conversation. You could not hear." Centered in the communications hub, staff often stood in one place and rotated to answer questions from the expanded workforce.

Winnipeg, with half the staff of Akron, was "severely tested" as well.
Raising over one million dollars from generous Canadians, they hired
additional personnel to manage the inundation and related bookkeeping.
A staff member later observed, "Money just poured in and we did not
have the staff to process the donations and the receipting." And though
"the type of work was the same, there was just so much more of it. Being
organized was most important." Similar to Akron, the challenge quickly
became "getting through every day" as thousands of volunteers sought
assignments and "donors wanted their money into the homeowners as
quickly as possible." Volunteers from MCC also helped out, opening mail
for nearly a month to support Region V as it streamed volunteers and
funds into Gulf Coast recovery.

Acutely challenged, MDS in Akron and Winnipeg managed a newly
dynamic environment with the support of each other and the volunteers
that surrounded them. Paid support staff , including part-timers, dramatically increased their work hours and all of the pre-Katrina staff stepped
into supervisory roles. As one staff member explained, "The overwhelming enormity of Katrina was so exceptional, beyond anything we had
faced till that time. This was an extraordinary event that required an
extraordinary response. There was no question; we had to change, we
had to expand our capacity." When asked how they managed, one remarked, "We just picked up what needed to be done." Another said, "We
looked at each other, made some lists, and dug in."

Strategies to survive the chaos emerged quickly as the phones did not
stop ringing for months. Part-time staff increased their work from 25 to
50 or more hours weekly and everyone "worked night and day." They
arrived and left work in the dark, missed family and church events, and
stepped into new roles. Relying on social networks, they ate when friends
dropped meals by the office or someone walked to a nearby grocery
store. Familiar strategies renewed energies as well. As one staff member
summarized for several: "I prayed a lot. Our lives just became chaotic."
At times, the stress brought some to tears. Laughing upon recalling those
days, another staff member explained a favorite office coping strategy:

"We had a lot of chocolate!" "Yes," said another, "to volunteer here, you had to like chocolate! It became a standing joke." Five years later, one staff member said: "We smile at each other now and say 'We made it.'"

Pre-Katrina staff did not return to normal five-day work weeks until late in November. By then, the pace of daily work had changed permanently. Part-timers did not return to their pre-Katrina work hours until the summer of 2006, when MDS began to hire new staff. By then, MDS had experienced "significant growth due to many new donors," increasing from a pre-Katrina database of 30,000 donors to over 80,000.

Moving Upstairs

Given the scale of the damage, the MDS executive director activated a recently negotiated arrangement with Angel Flights and left for the Gulf Coast immediately. Once there, he realized that the catastrophic nature of the event would require the greatest effort in MDS history. Trusting the staff in Akron and Winnipeg to manage things, he turned attention to finding storm-affected Mennonites, informing the Board, and uncovering unmet needs. Initial places he investigated soon turned into centers of activity, with Mennonites moving in to cut through debris, muck out homes and deliver aid to both Mennonites and non-Mennonites. Arriving in Bayou la Batre, Alabama, he discovered exhausted community leaders without any kind of aid nearly a week after Katrina's storm surge had flooded the area. Within 48 hours, connections to MCC brought trucks of canned meat and blankets into the community, well in advance of other federal assistance. Soon, they would set up a long-term project to build homes there.

With its executive director on the coast, staff members stepped up in Akron and Winnipeg. The first significant internal adaptation occurred with office space. Within weeks the main floor in the Akron office had been transformed. Noise increased daily with phones ringing, copiers processing checks, computers and printers operating, and volunteers moving steadily in and out. In one room alone, "we had six computers . . . at least 15 of us that worked" on the checks and mail that came in. To create a more effective work environment, several staff began to convert the second floor guest rooms to office space. Volunteers moved desks, files, and computers upstairs including that of the executive director "while he was still on the Gulf Coast." Such a move facilitated the organization in several ways. First, it provided space for meetings outside the chaos of mail and phone management. Second, staff could spread out, as several did, placing piles around them on tables, chairs and floor as they drafted plans, returned phone calls, bought resources, and identified project sites. Third, staff could close the door for a telephone call or a moment of respite.

However, being separated split up the family oriented staff in some ways. "That started changing us, not to be together in the same space." In the months that ensued, physical distance meant "you did not hear what [staff] were talking about," and, over time, information flow diminished. In a small organization with a handful of people, face-to-face interaction on the same floor had facilitated communication, but with the move, "we stopped hearing about" volunteers, projects, funding, and other work information. To address the change, MDS increased its communications internally and externally including weekly calls between Akron and Winnipeg involving all of the staff.

In Canada, the MDS office moved into larger facilities in Winnipeg by April, 2006. Over sixty MDS volunteers turned out to gut and renovate a 1,400 square foot area set into a strip shopping mall. Their efforts created a newly functional space with a reception area, four individual offices, a conference room, a small kitchen, and storage space. Winnipeg staff used their space efficiently and quickly doubled the number of Canadian long-termers from 100 to 200 individuals. They exerted effort as well to recruit thousands of short-termers every year, fueling what became the largest and most sustained movement of MDSers into the U.S. from Canada.

Ultimately, moving upstairs in Akron or to a larger space in Winnipeg allowed MDS to fulfill its mission in the aftermath of the worst hurricane in U.S. history. To rebuild on the coast, they also rebuilt themselves.

Expanding the Staff

The MDS executive director walked in after an exhausting week of observing and alleviating suffering along the coast only to stop short and ask, "Where's my desk?" From amid the still ringing phones, someone pointed upstairs. Moving past unfamiliar faces, he found other staff members in temporary rooms, sitting on the floor, answering the phones, and plowing through files, materials, papers, reports, and printouts.

As Katrina unfolded, everyone including the Board of Directors realized that "the system didn't fit the scale of destruction." Numerous challenges revealed themselves: scoping out appropriate and viable project sites; handling increasingly complicated accounting procedures for the array of funding needed to rebuild; training, scheduling, and mentoring long-term volunteers, especially those new to the position; upgrading technology for project use including computers, software, and cell phones; managing newly acquired resources and logistics; and establishing many new procedures and programs.

MDS entrusted an experienced business consultant (and MDS volunteer) to assess its staffing needs with input from the Board of Directors. By the summer of 2006, MDS had hired new staff in critical areas such as communications, reception, finance and accounting, human resources, logistics, and volunteer management. MDS saw the expansion as necessary for "the work ethic, the integrity of the organization."

The bulk of staff expansion took place in Akron. A different hierarchy emerged as people filled newly carved out positions. Staff members began to realize "my job is more focused after Katrina." New desks and cubicles appeared downstairs, organizing both pre- and post-Katrina staff into functional and specialized responsibilities. A receptionist now greeted people and answered the phones as others monitored grants, managed budgets, recruited volunteers, built new databases, and worked on various communications media. Upstairs, formal offices housed staff working on communications, logistics, human resources, volunteer management, and administration. By September 2006, Region V had created a new position called Director of Projects and Region Relations and hired an Administrative Coordinator. In Winnipeg as well, a receptionist greeted people and answered the phones and the conference room hosted planning, training, and coordination meetings.

Additional personnel made it possible for staff to regain a normal personal and professional life after working "60 hours or more until they got others in and trained." In the small office environment previously experienced as a "mom and pop" kind of business, new faces appeared and "we had to get to know a lot of new people." After coming on board, new staff took "a year to get traction" as they learned MDS organizational history, structure, and management. For those new to disaster relief, their work included rapidly learning about long-term recovery, and how to work bi-nationally with a volunteer base. Numbering nineteen in both Akron and Winnipeg by late 2006, the expanded staff provided a stronger organizational backbone for projects, including "consistency . . . especially for the office work" that had to be done to document expenses, secure supplies, move resources about, and support volunteers. And with people arriving from different backgrounds, they also learned about the diverse Anabaptist constituency.

Anabaptism emphasizes service to one's neighbors. Coupled with increasingly centralized management, concern arose among volunteers, staff, and the Board that staff expansion could potentially undermine the grass roots heritage of MDS. "I was a little afraid of becoming top-heavy." "Prior to Katrina there was a very small staff. Project directors had some freedom to be creative in making decisions." Mindful of its volunteer base, staff consistently viewed their role as supporting the grass roots constituency. They worked to keep the relational core of MDS intact—"Though it is standardized, it is very informal"—and sought ways to play out their roles gently. Staff members generally saw their role in working with the expanded base of long termers as a means to "do some coaching" rather than in directing long-termers in how to do their work, using phrases such as "you might want to think about this" when interacting with volunteers. They walked a careful path between directing long-termers, many of whom were new in a post-Katrina assignment, and understanding that experienced volunteers could get the job done.

Within a short time, the Akron and Winnipeg offices began to function more efficiently within a more specialized division of labor. Looking back, one remarked, "Despite change, we were able to function and get it done. We just kept pushing forward." Despite the significant change — "All those people in one year!"—staff members commented similarly, "But now we are used to it, it's the new normal." Everyone agreed that new hires reinvigorated an already dynamic environment as they "breathed new life into our organization and pushed it forward."

As the Katrina years unfolded, the new normal became familiar. Staff members checked on other's family members who were ill, scheduled joint outings for lunch, and "remembered to check with" the U.S. or Canada offices. One could always find home-baked cookies, whoopie pies, pretzels, or chocolate in Akron or Winnipeg. Staff members celebrated birthdays, weddings, anniversaries, and births of new children and grandchildren both formally and informally. They became a family again.

Ramping Up Resources

A voluntary organization must be accountable to its donors, a concern that permeated the interviews of staff, who were heartened by donor trust. Recognizing their common concern over financial stewardship, one staff member wondered "if it is an Anabaptist thing [to be] always very careful with money and not to be too proud and showy." Letters from donors revealed their appreciation for this core value, as one staff member reported: "I do not get letters that say you are wasteful." Rather, donors write "I give because we know it will be well spent."

As a valued Mennonite trait, thriftiness results in good financial stewardship. Accordingly, staff members take pains to buy something at low cost and "the philosophy is buy what you need, not what you could have." Frugality permeates this grassroots organization, as "get a volunteer to do it instead of paying for it" is commonly heard from staff, board members, and volunteers. Staff also recognize that "our volunteers are incredibly conscientious; they treat it [the donations] as though it is their own money," adding that "many bills were paid personally" by volunteers as well, contributions that do not show up in internal budgets—but are noticed and appreciated by clients and community partners. And, in light of the billions of dollars spent by governments on the Gulf Coast storms, some staff said donors wondered "why we still have money two years later." Staff and volunteers simply explain: "We don't use it on ourselves; we don't go out." Another said, "Even buying paper clips, we tried to use it wisely." MDS offices do not stockpile supplies, "I am aware every penny that I spend on supplies is money lost to a victim. "Forget the new copy machine."

Increasing from three to four sites annually to as many as ten for the Gulf Coast storms meant expanding other resources. In 2005, MDS had a limited number of rolling stock including trucks and trailers. To cover the area that would ultimately include Alabama, Mississippi, Louisiana and Texas, MDS bought new resources starting with pickup trucks and vans. To ready vehicles for project deployment, volunteers swarmed the Akron office in the month following Katrina, prepping vehicles for inspection, applying MDS logos, stocking first aid kits, organizing tools, and driving to the coast. Ultimately, MDS increased its inventory (though donated funds, tools, or vehicles) from about two dozen vehicles to 74 by 2010 along with eighty tool trailers, dump trailers, mobile kitchens, and similar support stock.

Core values of frugality probably lay behind some initial concerns over expenditures. In a context where volunteers prefer to make do, purchases for vehicles were questioned by a few. Still, MDS staff felt they kept such items to a minimum, with five to six vehicles and a similar number of cell phones per project when eight trucks and a twelve passenger van "would be great but it's not necessary." MDS also set boundaries to corral spending, yet have an impact: "We ramped up to a place that was sustainable and used those donations for the next five years to make a long-term difference in those communities." MDS now centralizes the majority of its resources through a new online inventory system which tracks use and location of tools and rolling stock. Office managers record mileage weekly along with emerging problems so that staff can schedule maintenance, move stock to needed areas, and ensure readiness for future sites. Ramping up the resource infrastructure for Katrina resulted in more efficient work at more sites with more volunteers than ever before, resulting in a ready stock of resources deployable to the next disaster.

Caching an inventory of tools and resources became even more essential for supporting volunteers crossing the U.S.-Canadian line. Border officials expressed concern that volunteers were taking jobs away from Americans: "The assumption is that if you are bringing tools you are coming here to work and that requires a work permit." Another concern stems from post September 11th with bringing in potential "weapons of mass construction," especially on commercial airlines. Border security concerns became especially problematic for trades volunteers who needed specific tools for plumbing and electrical work. MDS staff eventually secured FEMA letters of support to be used for border crossing, especially for long-termers, though bringing tools and vehicles remained a barrier. Letters had to be in place three weeks prior to border crossing but still long-termers frequently commented that "border crossing is a pain." Increasing the inventory proved essential given the number of projects and the post-September-11th context.

New Procedures

New staff brought additional expertise and time to do things differently. Given the grassroots base that supported thousands of volunteers, the changes were experienced by everyone, not just the staff. Experienced long-termers in particular saw "a lot of changes over the years in how things have been handled, how [resources] are used at the project. Before Katrina, we didn't provide as much." One staff member summarized what many reported, "There has been a growth of guidance and forms, though we did have paperwork and forms for project sites. This is the computer age now, and we do recordkeeping." New paperwork and computerized forms meant that long-termers had to "know the computer system and how to use it." As one illustration, the staff created an "office manager" set of forms to standardize procedures across the project sites. Long-termers then entered information through networked templates covering vehicles, finances, clients, and volunteers along with fax, letterhead, and signup sheets for devotions and washing dishes. Some long-termers never grew comfortable with the computerized system. To help, staff members added new components to leadership training events. Another strategy allowed staff in Akron to take control of computers on a project site while walking a long termer visually and verbally through the record-keeping procedure. On project sites, those more comfortable with computers would print off emails to help fellow long-term team members.

The new procedures and paperwork, though not always loved by more action-oriented work crews, had become necessary. Staff acknowledged that keeping track of "funding is a huge challenge; it comes from lots of sources." Working with each funder required attention as "each source is very specific on how they will release funds." Some grants required fronting the money and then seeking reimbursement through carefully documented procedures. Clients also needed to document purchases for funders. For example, a faith-based organization serving clients must generate an itemized list of expenses for FEMA or Louisiana's Road Home funds, so "MDS gives detail to the client because the client can be audited" and provides a set of "good documents" to them. Even then, "though they might have had funds, [organizations] did not always release them" as clients and organizations became mired in red tape and bureaucracy. Staff also used various data sources to generate reports for funders and as a base for additional grant applications. One staff member summarized the experience for all: "After Katrina there was a big difference in how we managed information because of the volume that was forced upon us. Reports were needed."

For the staff, careful recordkeeping represented good financial stewardship. They understood well the burden it placed on an already busy long-term crew. And the long-termers met the challenge: "They are donors as well; it is their money they are spending too." Another staff member emphasized that volunteers knew they represented the organization through the new procedures, "They know that how they spend [the donations] reflects on them."

Perhaps an even more significant change occurred with the installation of a 1-800 number for volunteers to contact. Previously, project directors had often recruited their own long-term crews, with office managers handling requests from short-termers. When this role shifted to headquarters, some long-termers felt a loss. For others, the 1-800 number reduced the burden of finding and scheduling work crews. MDS staff also standardized and distributed the majority of volunteer forms and procedures, which further streamlined already well-organized project sites.

The tussle between remaining a grassroots organization and creating procedures managed by staff appeared to work out well. The benefits to staff were significant, as careful recordkeeping makes it possible to more easily move tools, kitchen equipment, computers, or vehicles to new sites and to plan out projects and work team rotations in advance. Reports from projects to headquarters allowed central staff to craft communications with donors on the impact of their contribution. Combining project statistics yielded data useful for grant applications. Centralized databases allow MDS to stay in contact with newly experienced volunteers who might be lured back for more service. The combination of new staff with a more streamlined and efficient management system also resulted in MDS being able to create and institutionalize additional programs for a broader cadre of volunteer labor.

New Programs

Gulf Coast donations and the expanded staff permitted MDS to create new programs that brought in an even wider array of volunteers. New programs often involved non-traditional volunteers across a wider age range. New or invigorated programs included programs for pastors, for older and younger volunteers, and for servants unable to leave their work or home area for the coast. As one example, MDS created a new *Pastors to Projects* program. The purpose is to encourage pastors to experience MDS and then go home and talk about MDS to their congregations. They come "to swing a hammer" in a hands-on way that connects the pastors from Anabaptist theology to the physical practice of serving neighbors.

Like many volunteer organizations, MDS struggles at times with securing volunteers. Consistent with research literature, volunteer rates are highest among younger and older persons. At the suggestion of a volunteer, MDS increased its grassroots base by creating a program for volunteers who drove their recreational vehicles to project sites. The "RV Program" typically matched often-retired volunteers with repair-oriented jobs on a reduced-hour work day. Most RV Programs lasted a few months, though some went to six months. Their work often coincided with winter months, when warmer climates in the south lured volunteers to help. Because of their self-sufficiency, these volunteers did not require much food or supervisory support, thus reducing the burden on a long-term leadership team. They stayed on trailer parks, RV sites, and church parking lots, and were a welcome sight to locals struggling to secure help. From Texas, a partner observed, "The RV group was very special, lots of retired couples." He continued in amazement, "An eighty year old man shoveling rock into a cement mixer. If I did that I'd fall over dead."

Still, MDS realized that "our pool of long-term volunteers is not growing fast enough to meet our needs." As volunteers become older and less able to volunteer, "We lose all that experience and wisdom," a realization that compelled MDS to support programs attracting younger volunteers. MDS reinvigorated its youth summer programs and created an internship program for college students. Doing both types of programs was important as Amish youth leave school by the age of 16. And youth serving along the Gulf Coast impressed locals, as one community partner reported: "The Amish teenagers swarmed the roof and had it done in 24 hours. They worked long hours in 95 degree heat." The partner added that the work ethic of teenagers demonstrated valuable peer behavior for local youth: "We are just trying to keep ours from getting into trouble."

Youth and college programs also generated a means to transmit skills and wisdom from generation to generation. During the summer before Katrina, both Hesston College in Kansas and Canadian Mennonite University in Winnipeg started degree programs in disaster management. Both institutions focused on recovery of socially vulnerable populations, an emphasis unique worldwide in disaster management programs. MDS facilitated program development because "a lot of money was being poured into the emergency response and no one was paying attention to the long-term recovery aspect." A staff member described the heart of the degree programs: "We said that we wanted people who can do the financial books, we want people who can communicate well, people who can communicate in public, people who can articulate our mission and our way of going about our mission, people who can help others to broaden their acceptance of people who are different from themselves, people who know the Anabaptist heritage. Hesston had most of those courses already, so there were not a lot of additions to the list of college courses." MDS supported the disaster programs by providing curriculum development support, program advertising, student scholarships, and internships.

Coupled with courses on MDS culture and experiential components in construction, the programs build strong foundations for both future volunteers and staff. As part of their programs, most students intern on an MDS project site, learning the full range of long-termer roles in office management, construction, cooking, volunteer supervision, and leadership. More than roles and structure, students also learn about the disaster recovery process from the MDS perspective. For many long-termers who mentored interns, that process involved case management with clients. The process ranged from inspirational, "using Bible verses to get the interns started," to the mundane "and then showing them the realities of paperwork and bureaucracy." Finding long-termers to lead youth programs, though, can be hard. Most interviewees agreed that just the right kind of long-termer is needed to guide and mentor youth. Many who did so enjoyed mentoring tremendously: "It may take longer but the effort to work with youth is worth it" citing growth in the student and longevity of the MDS organization as key outcomes. Graduates from Hesston College have gone on to careers in social services and construction or on to additional study. The first Canadian Mennonite University students have just begun to graduate.

Another new initiative, the *Partnership Home Program* (PHP), allows people unable to leave home to serve disaster survivors. The effort starts when local partners in affected areas select a client. MDS then connects the partner and client and family to a distant congregation interested in building a home. Designed as a "one church, one family" relationship, the PHP involves congregations in building house sections in their church parking lots, universities, or warehouses. The PHP means that volunteers—normally distant from the Coast because of work, age, ability, or family obligations or who might not be comfortable in a bunkhouse construction site—can build and walk through the future home of a displaced resident. PHP volunteers can spend an hour or a week on the project and hundreds of people might participate. On one such effort, even volunteers reaching 100 years of age hammered in a few nails. Once completed, the home panels are trucked to Louisiana, Alabama, Mississippi or Texas. When the panels arrive, long-term crews secure permits and oversee on-site construction with short-term crews. Sometimes, local PHP participants deliver and erect the homes themselves, further strengthening the bond they experience with Gulf Coast families. The PHP homes often went up faster than the traditional on-site construction.

WORKING AND SERVING ON THE GULF COAST HURRICANES

As MDS changed internally, staff simultaneously supported a rapidly increasing number of projects. They too found themselves explaining who they were as they worked behind-the-scenes with community partners, selected sites, supported volunteers and served clients.

Who Are the Mennonites?

Similar to long-termers, MDS staff found themselves explaining "who are the Mennonites?" As staff also found, most people simply called them "the Mennonites" as opposed to a formal organizational name. Though brand recognition might be essential for many organizations, it is sufficient for MDS that volunteers live out faith-based beliefs. Proselytizing is not the mission either, as "we are not here to plant churches. The mission is to get people back home," according to a staff member. It took some time for communities new to Mennonites to understand this non-evangelical attitude, yet they came to appreciate such interaction and to embrace the volunteers' faithful witness.

From a staff perspective, the organizational mission explains who Mennonites are. Typically, organizations measure how well they accomplish their mission, which can be calculated by the numbers of repairs/rebuilds, volunteers, project sites and donors. When asked about the mission, all staff can easily state the essential core of the mission: to repair, rebuild, and restore through service in time of disaster. But staff members discern more: "Our work is not just pounding a nail." As one said, "We are serving God and people. We need to remember that or we lose the significance of what MDS does." Consistent with what clients and partners revealed, many staff members commented, "We are not just building houses, we are building relationships." Reconstruction thus serves as the vehicle through which "we develop relationships" and represents "a concrete way of indicating our convictions." As one summarized: "We don't just do a quick cleanup and then get out. Rather, we commit to getting to know the people and finish what we begin."

For staff, the mission centers on "restoring hope, like it says on the MDS shirt, not just rebuilding." Most staff understandably focused on the "restore" part of the mission, understanding that "people can become lost after these disasters." Another explained the MDS mission as pulling "people out of despair to get them going. They are just paralyzed and can hardly make decisions." One agreed, "Our being there for people is vital," adding that volunteers "participate in their joy and sorrow." Client selection criteria lay close under the mission's surface: addressing the unmet needs of "low income, elderly, retired, people that can't afford to come back like single parents" and helping "those with special needs." Everyone agreed, "We assist the vulnerable." Some saw the mission as an issue of justice "for those that don't have a say" and as a way "to get people back home. That is it."

Summarizing the mission, one staff member said "service" and then paused reflectively: "It is not just a job. The value is not in what we are doing, but what God is doing through us." To explain further, some turned to Scripture. Citing *1 Corinthians 10:13*, one staff member saw through the darkness of Katrina, "No temptation has overtaken you except what is common to mankind. And God is faithful; He will not let you be tempted beyond what you can bear. But when you are tempted, He will also provide a way out so that you can endure it." Another noted a scripture from *Colossians 3:17* , "And whatever you do, whether in word or deed, do it all in the name of the Lord Jesus, giving thanks to God the Father through Him." In the aftermath of Katrina, another reflected, "Our mission may not have changed but everything connected to the mission may have: Boards, staff, constituency, our understanding, and our knowledge." MDS grew and adapted, with its Anabaptist core intact, as staff entered to serve.

Making Entry

Staff realized early on that MDS would be working in places where "it was important to enter the community, just to be a presence." They felt "deep emotional and spiritual needs" as homeowners and local partners faced complete community destruction, job losses, and scattered families. A first task involved presenting themselves as "one of many" organizations arriving with promises to help. They realized that building trust was a critical first effort, as local partners and clients had "been ripped off so many times in the past" and "worn down by many organizations and bureaucracies." Staff members expressed concern over disreputable companies and organizations there to make "a quick buck." Entering a community, for MDS, meant understanding the apprehension locals felt juxtaposed against a healthy skepticism of outsiders felt by prospective partners.

Finding local partners in the chaos of Katrina also meant "we had to start from scratch including some case management." For the first time, MDS hired a full time Gulf Coast Coordinator with an extensive background as a project director. Together with other MDS staff, the coordinator and his wife moved along the coast meeting with local recovery committees, explaining MDS, and identifying project areas. In concert with other site investigators, a full slate of projects rolled out by 2006. To help, MDS for the first time used some donated and grant funds to help recovery committees get their work started, then built lasting relationships enduring beyond the five year mark, as reflected in partner and client comments in previous chapters.

Echoing Anabaptist approaches, staff worked from a model centered "in partnership. We learn from our clients and receive more from them. It is from the New Testament in Anabaptism, to be Christ-like." Consistent with the low key entry observed by their community partners, a staff member said, "We are more reserved, the quiet in the land." Another agreed, "Our reflection is more on doing and less on speaking." In a context of failed trust in government, frustration with organizational inertia, and the overwhelming amount of destruction, entering quietly and listening built a strong foundation for partnerships. Doing instead of just speaking as a Louisiana partner commented about their community appreciatively, resulted in "overall, about 22 homes being built."

Keeping promises meant a great deal to partners devastated by disaster, disappointed in government, and leery of outsiders. The relationships staff built along the coast strengthened over time as one community partner noted: "Our dependence on the Mennonites was strong; so much so that the standing joke was that God's area code during Katrina was 717," which dialed into MDS and MCC offices in Akron, Pennsylvania. Though the comment might cause some discomfort among Anabaptists, a client explained that feeling in more straightforward words: "MDS was really there for the people who were devastated and who did not understand the process of getting assistance." A community partner in Mississippi framed it in Anabaptist terms: "They like to be your neighbor."

Selecting Sites

Traditionally, MDS has used paid and volunteer site investigators to determine projects. Katrina was different; MDS relied on experienced investigators along with a new Gulf Coast Coordinator, recommendations from other government and non-government organizations, and "divinely inspired" guidance. In addition, the storms solidified four pillars for site selection: a location for volunteer housing, meaningful work, finances/funding, and volunteers. Several staff members said the same: "These four things determined if a site would work out or not."

Still, an article in the MDS publication *Behind the Hammer* (Grosh 2009) described the process as a "bit messy and unclear." Site selection became more cumbersome than usual as Katrina damage limited entry into the worst-hit areas. Pre-Katrina, typical disasters meant concentrating on a "single town where there was one Mennonite church and one long term recovery committee." For Katrina, hundreds of miles of ravaged coastline, with thousands of people trying to come home again meant that choosing project sites required a massive effort. Even experienced MDS staff and investigators, including veterans of relief work in developing nations, felt shocked by the expanse of destruction they faced: "There was so much need; where do you go?" The first site investigators looked for Mennonites affected by the storm and reconnected them with fellow congregational members, hosted reunion meals, delivered relief supplies, and assisted with cleanup. Ultimately, some of these Mennonite locations hosted MDS volunteers.

As with previous disasters, FEMA VALs facilitated the first post-Katrina meeting of voluntary organizations. Participating organizations gathered two weeks after the event rather than the more typical 2–3 days, an indicator of the time needed to assess recovery sites. After months of such meetings, it became clear that every organization was struggling to find the right sites. Just as the long-termers realized, staff also learned that, "towns didn't really work or function." Using familiar procedures, staff looked to local partners, yet "trying to find the right people to work with was hard. Their homes and lives were destroyed as well." To zero in on their preferred clients and find areas of unmet needs, MDS staff consulted with FEMA, faith-based partners, and community leaders. One such meeting took place in New Orleans in December 2005. Facilitated by a University of New Orleans faculty member, MDS staff and Board members met with neighborhood leaders to discuss local needs.

And, despite the distance between the Gulf Coast, Pennsylvania, and Winnipeg, staff members felt the pain of those affected. When individuals called in to MDS offices, "crying . . . we would try to steer them to the local person." The staff "worked day and night" with telephones glued to their ears, having "never been this busy before." One asked, "How could we begin to address immeasurable needs where there were so many in need?" Another agreed: "There was a massive call for assistance. MDS was only a drop in the bucket." Agonizing decisions had to be made over project sites "since it was clear we could not be everywhere."

To finalize decisions, MDS staff and volunteers continued to meet with and listen to local community leaders, many of whom would eventually lead long-term recovery committees and become steadfast partners. Together, they compared the four pillars to local needs and resources. Not surprisingly, they also relied on feeling led by God "opening the doors to the places where MDS should be." And, "in the end, we trust that God leads us to the right places. We look for places of need."

Supporting Volunteers

For Katrina, MDS needed more long-term volunteers than they had, which was a "big strain in ramping up." New staff provided critical support for leadership training, and helped funnel needed new long-termers into service. Central staff viewed their connections to long-termers as a "relational experience" and put forward efforts to get to know their volunteers and their backgrounds. The original "mom and pop" feeling pre-Katrina segued into a familial environment that also flowed into many long-termer relationships. Staff also understood that couples often served as volunteers and worked to insure that husbands and wives could volunteer together.

Katrina enabled changes in long-term training, which had primarily been for project directors. Office managers, cooks, construction supervisors, and crew leaders now came to leadership training. Annual training was broadened from two events to three per year. Training sessions now included up to fifty new long-termers at sessions held in Pennsylvania, Kansas, and Canada. Training focuses first on the MDS mission and culture. Future long-termers also learn about selecting clients and building and communicating within the leadership team. Communication includes conflict management and trauma counseling. Interestingly, the bulk of training remains on working together as a unit rather than on reconstruction techniques. As a staff member indicated, "It doesn't start with the client, it starts with people that connect to clients."

To find additional long-termers, staff relied on "listening and encouragement." For new project leaders, an experienced mentor may provide guidance both onsite and through phone or email contact. To help the team gel, the staff work at putting together the right people, retaining memories of volunteer preferences, such as cooking skills that will enable success between a head and assistant cook. They also seek a balance of Canadians and Americans for long-term teams. Staff consistently expressed concern with the burden borne by long-termers. "MDS is very intense. It is a camp setting with a lot of people coming and going." As long-termers experienced: "The physical and mental challenge of working constantly round the clock with people will cause burn-out after 2–3 months." After a few months, a new team would have to rotate in.

Transitions, a concern reported by community partners and long-termers, became a worry to staff as well. "Turnover for the project directors is tough," commented a staff member. Transition issues included promises made by prior directors and/or misunderstandings with partners and clients over what work remained to be done. Yet transitions had to happen to avoid burn-out and maintain the cadre of long-termers capable of leading construction projects. Staff tried to ease transitions in part by overlapping project teams, particularly for those new to the position. Yet without clear communication during the transition, they realized "that is where overlapping fails."

Katrina also prompted the MDS Board of Directors to involve staff in debriefing long-term volunteers, a strategy that resulted in making long-termers feel "empowered." The acute fatigue experienced by many long-termers at the end of their volunteer stint could be countered through their debriefing by realizing the extent of their contributions. "It is one reason why Canada supplies so many of the long-term volunteer leaders" staff believed. From recruiting, mentoring, and debriefing long-termers, staff realized "we always worked with seasoned, experienced people" who were "hard workers and dedicated to their tasks." The combination resulted in "many, mostly positive experiences."

A massive influx of over 5,000 short-term volunteers in a year put the staff as well as the long-termers to work. Volunteers arrive with varying skills and as one project director said, "There was always an element of uncertainty each week wondering what skills we will get when the group arrives." Another, though, explained how things worked out: "God always sends the right people for the job at the right time." He added, "and very good crew leaders." A long-term couple agreed: "We put a lot of faith in God because things generally worked out better than our preparation would indicate." Yet another observed, "My philosophy is that God always sends the right volunteers, so don't sweat it."

Another issue staff contended with came from the seasonal nature of constituent volunteerism. Seasonality in MDS is affected by several things. Historically, MDS volunteers have been primarily farmers who must attend to planting and harvesting time in the spring and fall. Amish weddings also occur in November, which reduces availability. Another seasonal factor concerns climate. For the Gulf Coast, projects often shut down in the severe heat and humidity of the summer followed by an increasing hurricane threat in August and September. Such weather could be dangerous to work in, though many sites were open through July. Canadians, especially retirees, preferred volunteering in the winter to enjoy the warmer coastal climate. A staff member observed, "the seasonal ups and downs are a challenge. It is like shutting down a factory for months at a time; it is inefficient."

Staff dedicated themselves to the experience which would provide meaning to volunteers, knowing that: "They pass it on to their congregation. They get it now about why people live where they live, why they stay and they rebuild on the bayou." After volunteering, "That is so important, to bring a new worldview back." The experience of volunteering does indeed "get into your blood" as one staff member explained. When volunteers return for another stint, "they often go back to the same place." Between 2005 and 2010, 36.7 percent of volunteers went once, with another 34.2 percent returning two to three times. A total of 115 individuals (14.9 percent) volunteered four to five times with another 110 (14.2 percent) going more than five times. The volunteers just keep coming back, to serve in the Anabaptist framework generated by MDS over its history and through its staff.

WORKING WITH ANABAPTIST PARTNERS

Among Mennonites, there is an earnest, internal honesty to look critically inward and determine ways to improve, a decidedly Mennonite way to think and behave. Within the body of data collected for this study, clients and communities uniformly praised MDS. Among Mennonite partners, a deeper reflection took place over MDS' actions to the Gulf Coast storms. Views transformed over time from some initial confusion and internal critique of MDS. One initial challenge that MDS faced stemmed from focusing volunteer efforts on their mission of helping those in greatest need. With Mennonite churches and families also devastated by the storms, the organization felt stretched to help fellow Mennonites and also fulfill its mission.

MDS collaborated first with Mennonite Central Committee, an action made more fluid because the new MDS executive director had most recently worked with MCC in delivering material aid. Discovering that Bayou la Batre, Alabama had not yet received outside assistance, the director called on MCC to deliver truckloads of food and blankets; the joint MDS-MCC effort represented the first post-Katrina supplies to arrive in the damaged community. MDS and MCC also sent representatives to the coast to locate splintered congregations, help them to reunite, and host initial congregational gatherings. MDS also "connected us to MEDA (Mennonite Economic Development Association) and other long term development organizations which were very helpful in getting our business people back on their feet again." The role of MDS in Katrina was thus to "create an environment in which a collaborative cross-agency response could happen" among Anabaptists. However, doing so was not without challenges as "policies were not in place to guide decisions."

Although MCC, MDS and other Anabaptist organizations discussed disaster collaboration pre-Katrina, the unprecedented event made it clear they would need to "collaborate closely." MDS took the lead and worked with Mennonite partners to find appropriate roles. To do so, they met frequently, aided by geographic proximity between offices in Akron, Pennsylvania (MCC and MDS) and Winnipeg, Canada (MDS Extension Office and MCC-Canada). "We discussed what resources each could bring to the effort and what such participation would look like." They shared resources including personnel, expertise, material goods, and money. "In the context of this cooperation, the role of MDS would be cleanup and housing needs, MCC would work with the churches, and MEDA would support small business initiatives." They signed a formal agreement, and continued to work on their collaborations: "There was no playbook to guide the organizations working together. Arrangements were made up as we went along."

Anabaptist partners went to the coast together: "The initial joint visit to the disaster area was tremendously helpful in setting the whole tone for the disaster response. . . . We needed someone who could relate to the Asian community, someone who could speak their language, someone who would listen to their stories. MCC experience and assistance was crucial in this area." Indeed, past relationships between "MCC and MDS helped to facilitate communication and opened the door to working together."

Perhaps not surprisingly given an Anabaptist culture where listening to each other matters, communication emerged as an area to work on. One concern came from MDS staff initially not being as prepared to deal with the media as needed. One partner, for example, expressed concern over how to present a consistent message to the public, which "has implications on people recognizing and trusting MDS." A particular area of concern stemmed from misunderstanding over the mission of MDS to help those most in need. Yet Mennonites along the Gulf Coast suffered losses too, and turned to Anabaptist brothers and sisters expecting mutual aid. Crews did provide cleanup, repairs, emotional, and spiritual support. MDS volunteers helped congregations relocate each other and face the damage together as a community. Yet many Mennonites (though not all) also carried insurance, and thus did not meet the typical profile for client assistance. And, in a culture where people gathered to rebuild barns through neighborly and mutual aid, the use of criteria to determine the majority of rebuilding scraped a wound already opened by Katrina. Though the confusion over the MDS mission caused some pain, most coastal Mennonites interviewed for this study said that they had worked through the confusion.

At the five year mark, one Mennonite partner observed what most ultimately concluded: "This was a positive experience. There were problems and tensions in working together but these were not connected to our relationship with MDS. We always maintained a good relationship with MDS. . . . We learned how to become effective partners." Partnerships across Anabaptist organizations also showed common purpose despite diverse theologies and beliefs: "As [Anabaptists] we will be ready and available with volunteers for MDS. We don't agree with everything MDS does, but we will support it."

The experience, over time, seems to have resulted in meaningful outcomes for Anabaptist partners: "MDS taught me the importance of making a personal connection with people." Another Anabaptist partner said, "Had it not been for MDS, our work would have been even more difficulty; they specifically helped us in connecting with people." As MDS began to close down disaster operations along the Gulf, they toured areas with MCC, assessing the possibility of continued Mennonite support for beleaguered communities facing the 2010 Gulf Coast oil spill.

WORKING IN AN ANABAPTIST ORGANIZATION

MDS staff felt a keen awareness of and appreciation that Anabaptist traditions were the driving value within their organizational culture. Indeed, being Anabaptist permeated daily work: financial stewardship, relational contact, building work teams, communication, decision-making, and dedication to the organization's mission. In analyzing answers made to the question, "Did MDS reflect its Anabaptist heritage during the Katrina years?," staff comments fell into two key themes reflective of Anabaptist beliefs: serving neighbors and following Jesus. It is worth noting that all staff members paused, thoughtfully, before responding—the responses were not rehearsed. Staff did not just work for a service organization, they believed deeply in its faith heritage. One said, "There is something about Anabaptism, to go and serve without a big splash, the Anabaptist emphasis to be in service."

The "service" in Mennonite Disaster Service echoes Anabaptist traditions that are exceptionally meaningful to staff. As one explained, "The Anabaptist will always come and help the neighbor in need." Another said, "People helping people is an Anabaptist heritage; that is what we strive to do—since 1950." Doing so follows guidance from Christ to "love your neighbor, give for others." Staff also saw value in faithful service that brings people together across differences: "We may be far away culturally and ethnically but we enter and leave as friends." One staff member explained further: "If you are from someplace like Indiana, you might think of a Cajun in a bayou: is that my neighbor?" Scripture clearly defines the response: "As an Anabaptist, there is no question. That Cajun is your neighbor." Confirming that belief, a staff member said, "Jesus didn't just love the neighbor, He liked them too." Reaching out to others also reflected an embracing sense of connectedness to earlier days when Mennonites experienced persecution-related diaspora. As a staff member said, "We want to create space where community can happen in a healthy way to get people home."

Serving clients with unmet needs by "helping those who fall between the cracks" of available assistance motivates staff. One explained, "I feel a consistency, I believe the MDS leadership was inspired with Anabaptist roots." Service offers a chance to "battle for the Lord against injustice." God, through faithful servants, attends to "His people after the storm, in the sheer silence." As one staff member said, "We wreak havoc on the silence with chain saws and hammers." Staff members supported those who were commanded "to go. God is in His people after the storm." Being Mennonite for many staff means "being a doer of our faith." Faith also means embracing the Anabaptist notion of being the quiet in the land; it does not involve proselytizing. Yet, staff realized that physical presence "often brings out some spiritual awakening in clients because they sense the deep spiritual values that the volunteers bring."

Serving others is also "serving Christ." Doing so represents more than just doing what is commanded, it is a way of life: "Jesus lived so we would behave differently." By volunteering and facilitating service, "we were there, the hands and feet of Jesus." Service also enabled "lay leadership" to emerge, part of the "roots of Anabaptism." Lay leadership, such as serving as a bishop, sharing sacraments, or baptizing adults then "flows to our projects" where lay persons practice leadership.

One staff member saw good in the storm: "Katrina did well for the Anabaptist community—it allowed us to come together." Staff consistently expressed joy in being part of an organization that involved a diverse array of Anabaptists. Though the range from conservative to liberal denominations meant some differences and concerns, "we look past the ways we act out our beliefs and we gather round the larger mission." Consistently, staff expressed a common belief: "What I really appreciate about MDS is that we can attract all kinds of Anabaptists that other organizations cannot." A staff member focused in, "Mennonite Brethren, Amish, Mennonites from Canada—who would never otherwise talk or live together." Involving a diverse set of denominations reflected the essential core of being Anabaptist, a reality from earlier days of refugee efforts: "Yes, we don't want to let anyone go." Staff said that disaster service brought people beyond physical differences such as a head covering or clothing choice. In addition to learning about local cultures on project sites, service also promoted internal growth, "everyone learned that Americans are *a lot like me*—they are not a stereotype—and that all Canadians are not Eskimos." Enabling volunteers to connect through disaster service gave them opportunities "to share our traditions with a wide variety of volunteers."

To summarize, in response to the question of whether MDS reflected its Anabaptist heritage during the Katrina years, one simply said, "Yes, that is who we are." Another concurred: "I can say because of my faith, I am in this group; this is where I am truly faithful with my Anabaptist heritage."

Becoming Servants

MDS allows staff to serve on projects, a normative behavior in a voluntary organization. The executive director told them, "You need that in your gut," meaning the culture of service that permeates MDS from its grass-roots base into the work of the staff. Many staff managed to work on project sites, which meant a great deal to them. Serving also brought project issues into perspective and generated valuable insights such as the importance of acknowledging volunteers more frequently. "No one notices you unless something goes wrong!" Another gained useful insights into other behind-the-scenes work: "Being a cook is sort of a thankless job."

Staff service prompted insights into what brought thousands of others through their office. "Once you have gone out to an MDS site, it gets in your blood." A staff member added, "It's something about being able to help someone, a victim of a disaster, and that you made a difference." Another agreed: "The most important thing may be to lay down your hammer and listen, talk to the homeowner." As one said, "to try to support people and get them back, to provide a listening ear."

"We were very blessed to be able to do that," commented a staff member who realized first-hand what volunteers had written to headquarters. "They [volunteers] always say they were going to bless others but they received so much more." Like other volunteers, staff loved "to hear the stories of the clients, meet the people" which compelled them to return: "Volunteering is like a drug; you have to go back for more!" The volunteer experience inspired their own work: "The most meaningful thing in my position now is getting to go out and meet the clients."

Another agreed: "Getting to know people, seeing lives changed, becoming more deeply connected to people."

Staff also benefited from seeing how "at the end of the work week, volunteers are changed, they are a different person; when they return home, they have a different outlook on life." Again, staff members felt similarly: "It changed my perspective on life and led me to a deeper heart and sense of compassion." Just as their family had passed on a service orientation as part of their faith, some took their children to project sites so that "the kids see us live it out." They socialized their children into volunteerism and returned with families dedicated to explaining local cultures and ways of life criticized by outsiders.

House dedications generated particularly rich, emotional responses. "It was awesome. The family was crying and told us that any time we are in the area not to go to a hotel, to come and stay with them." Another said, "Standing there . . . .you have so many people from the community there, wonderful food and houses being dedicated." In an area like Grand Bayou, being present enabled staff members to experience a community "becoming sustainable and rebuilt." Another described house dedications as "fabulous, very uplifting, and very emotional." One summed it for most, "My volunteering experience with MDS was most meaningful to me. It also helps me see how my work in an office can provide meaning to the mission of MDS." "Yes," said another, "I think this personal understanding of the project site is very helpful" leading staff to work even harder in "sending good, caring people to build houses for those in need."

Meaningful Work

When asked about the "best part" and most successful parts of their work, staff identified several common threads: to work for an organization trusted by donors and volunteers, to be part of a vehicle for Anabaptist service, and ultimately, to serve God through being part of meaningful relationships.

Katrina "opened my eyes to what MDS meant to others," expressed a staff member. They felt confirmation that MDS made a difference for those affected by the storms: "People needed to do something. They could donate money and it would do something." Staff clearly identified helping communities to rebuild, forming relationships with people, and restoring hope as the organization's most successful part of being a vehicle for service: "We built homes, not houses," explained one. To illustrate, the staff member continued, "We put in porches that face each other [so neighbors can visit]. That is building community." Staff also felt the connection experienced by volunteers in places like Grand Bayou and Pass Christian, where MDS was "building houses and community relationships." Especially meaningful, they assisted volunteers going into places forgotten by others: "We went to Cameron Parish; there was no one else there. There was nothing left in Johnson Bayou."

A staff member summed it up for many, "I felt good that I worked for an organization so highly revered in the community." Despite the chaos experienced in the office, "I am blessed to be here," said one. Meeting the challenges of supporting projects from a distance, sometimes when things did not seem like they would come together, confirmed their faith: "It comes together every time and that is very meaningful. There is something, Someone, a master plan." A master plan also meant that volunteers would learn more about God's children, as staff and volunteers both "would 'get it' now about why people live where they live, why they stay, and why they rebuild." Generations came together on projects too: "The older volunteers with the younger; they get to see it and to love it." Creating a vehicle to serve God also brought Anabaptists together: "It is a success when you bring conservatives and non-conservatives together in an environment where it is safe for us all to be on one project with one goal." New programs created by new staff also meant that people could serve from afar, such as the "Partnership Home Program that was done because of Katrina." Overall, staff said that success could best be measured over "the work God enabled us to do" by using them to create opportunities for volunteers to "minister in the lives of people, not the number of houses." Different from a formal organization characterized by hierarchical structure and impersonal relationships, a staff member said, "I never want us to be a corporation, rather to be facilitators." Despite staff growth and centralization of procedures, one said that headquarters "is just a place that houses people to help you get your project started."

Staff felt warmed by seeing the "commitment level of the way everyone worked together in that first year" after Katrina. Recognizing this, one staff member remarked five years after the storm, "I think our greatest success is that we have not pulled out of the area. We are still there, still working and rebuilding." They knew that MDS represented a meaningful vehicle for service and "we were swarmed with volunteers who wanted to help." Despite the newness of many staff, the Katrina years led one to comment, "This is a really, really nice place to work. At all levels, we believe in what we do." Beyond MDS, staff commented frequently as this one did, "Anywhere I go in the Gulf states I find people I know, people who accept me as a good friend. This is the real intention of MDS, to be a good neighbor." One linked MDS service to how earlier generations helped "the Russian Mennonites who had experienced loss, tragedy, famine, hunger." Stories ingrained in them by parents and grandparents taught them "to be compassionate, obedient, and grateful" to refugees and those affected by war, disaster, and displacement. "My dad told me about driving a group of Amish to the Palm Sunday tornadoes in 1965" said one. Above all, staff saw MDS as "an avenue to be the hands and feet of Jesus," building on a tradition generated through faith and family.

NOTES

1. The MDS main office moved into new quarters in Lititz, Pennsylvania; see chapter 8.

2. History of MDS Region V and MCC Separation. Provided by the MDS Binational Extension Office. No date.

3. Binational Extension Office in Canada from 2001 to 2006—a History. Provided by the MDS Binational Extension Office. No date.

4. MCC News Service. February 6, 1970. "President Nixon Praises Mennonites." News Release, MCC, Pennsylvania.

5. U.S. Department of Housing and Urban Development. July 26, 1970. "Mennonite Group Honored by HUD for Public Service." News Release, HUD, Washington D.C.

EIGHT

Building a Therapeutic Community

Bear ye one another's burdens, and in so doing, fulfill the law of Christ.
—Galatians 6:2

INTRODUCTION

Religion supports the broader society through multiple functions. In disasters, faith provides answers and a source of strength (Durkheim 1912). For disaster response and recovery organizations, religion helps to recruit volunteers, provides them with a meaningful framework in which to serve, and offers resources to do so (Nelson and Dynes 1971). Many organizations organize and send resources and volunteers into disaster zones. Lutherans, for example, provide chaplain services along with their volunteers. Baptists send large trailers to feed thousands of people daily. Seventh-Day Adventists manage large warehouses of donations for short and long-term recovery purposes. Muslims transport materials across long distances to those in need. Jews rebuild the churches of other denominations. Buddhists organize relief distribution. Methodists help with case management and Catholics fund dozens of local projects in any given event. Faith matters in a post-disaster context and not only for providing comfort to the bereaved. As any long-term recovery committee knows, you cannot bring people back home or heal their hurt without an organized effort that includes the faith-based community.

Reconstruction allows people to return home, but significant intangible benefits accrue as well. As one MDS volunteer said in the early 1950s: "Often the work we do doesn't give the biggest lift. A man sitting in the midst of the ruins of his earthly possessions often doesn't have the courage to begin over, nor even to salvage what is left. To have men pitch in and help him and show him that there are people who care about his welfare usually brings a mental change that is worth more than the little bit of physical assistance."[1] Disaster researchers have named such a phenomenon the "therapeutic community" (Barton 1970, see also Fritz 1996 and Gurney 1977). To date, studies that document and analyze the therapeutic community do so in an immediate post-disaster response period (e.g., see Lowe and Fothergill 2003; Michel 2007). This study demonstrates the longitudinal development of a therapeutic community and the mechanisms that made it possible.

THE THERAPEUTIC COMMUNITY

Most disasters generate altruistic behavior, which is demonstrated when volunteers arrive to help (Dynes 1994). Events like hurricanes can actually pull communities together as they move to shelter those displaced, form recovery committees, and rebuild neighborhoods. Such a connection may be short-lived though, as blaming may erupt over broken levees, perceived government failures to address unmet needs, or when local leaders grow exhausted from nonstop efforts to help their neighbors. Known as the "corrosive community," such an environment fractures post-disaster harmony, sending a community into turmoil and making recovery even harder (Barton 1969; Erikson 1994; Peek 2011). The immediate post-Katrina period witnessed both, with blaming erupting around socially vulnerable populations and the associated loss of life.

Alternatively, the appearance of a "therapeutic" or "altruistic" community can promote more positive effects (Erikson 1994; Quarantelli and Dynes 1976; Barton 1970; Fritz 1961; Gurney 1977). Several conditions seem to promote the development of a therapeutic community. First, people must learn about an event, which they do through both informal and formal communications. Second, people who want to help gain "sympathetic identification" with victims, a feeling that grows when helpers sense a moral obligation (called a "normative mechanism") to respond. The random, sudden shock of a disaster also generates concern for those who were harmed; the perception that such impacts were not the fault of the victim increases a desire to help. Third, ideologies and values compel people to converge altruistically in a "snowball effect" (Barton 1969). Faith serves as an important part of such ideologies and values, a resource that produces "cultural capital" fueling volunteer commitment (Wilson and Musick 1997). Beyond these key conditions, human actions trigger the development of a therapeutic community. Key to these is the act of sympathetic listening, an active rather than a passive act that connects survivors and their stories to those who arrive to help.

Hearing the Call

The media, which covered Katrina, Rita, and Ike extensively, disseminated information spawning the convergence of volunteer efforts across hundreds of civic, community, and faith-based organizations. The size of the event can increase media coverage, further disseminating concerns about those harmed. This was certainly true with the Gulf Coast storms, which generated a record turnout especially among volunteers in faith-based disaster organizations. In disasters, people response to media calls out of a sense of obligation for the broader community and to right what has gone so wrong (Michel 2007; Lowe and Fothergill 2003).

Beyond the media, faith-based organizations facilitate communications among like-minded people and provide value-driven ideologies that spur people to act. For example, churches responding to Katrina in the Baton Rouge, Louisiana area indicated that, for them: "helping those in distress was not a choice but a duty and a call" (Cain and Barthelemy 2008, p. 39). Media campaigns that occur within the context of a faith tradition link deeply embedded belief systems to normative behaviors such as organizing mission teams, calling one's friends to form a long-term recovery crew, or institutionalizing service within a college curriculum. Such communications in faith-based settings occur in the context of a socially integrated network which spurs volunteerism (Michel 2007). MDS, through its internal communications (e-mail distribution lists, web site, newsletters, direct invitations) and formal structure (regions, units, congregations) further distributed information about the event and related needs to its constituents.

Disaster-focused FBOs thus offer a critically important framework in which to motivate and structure service through deeply held, time-worn religious belief systems. Structurally, FBOs provide institutionalized and often specific roles that people fill as long-term and short-term volunteers, Board members and staff. For MDS, behavioral expectations have become uniform within those roles, and are handed down through critical agents of socialization: church, family, and peers. Training further instills normative behaviors, as does the mentoring that takes place on construction sites from project directors, construction supervisors, crew leaders, office managers, and cooks. To form long-term crews, many MDSers called on people they knew from previous disasters, regenerating the social capital they knew to be effective. With a consistent organizational structure and well-established base of cultural capital, the potential therapeutic community and its healing effects can be significant.

Sympathetic Identification

Therapeutic communities are believed to "compensate for the sorrow and stress under which many members are living with an unexpected abundance of personal warmth and direct help" (Barton 1969, p. 207). Sympathetic identification drives those who extend such compassion. Volunteers' willingness to do so stems from their own primary groups, like families and church groups, where they learned to care for each other. One's culture and history also plays a role in generating sympathetic identification. Anabaptists, for example, share a long legacy of caring for others harmed by political repression and social injustice. Sympathetic identification also forms out of feeling connected to people who are perceived as "neighbors." For Mennonites, who view strangers in need as "neighbors," reaching out fits consistently within a theological framework. A third sympathetic tie forms when volunteers see victims as being like themselves: farmers, for example—or, in the case of the coast— shrimpers and fishers.

It is clear that MDS arose out an Anabaptist core that compelled founders and those who followed to create an effective organization, whether for refugee work, social justice efforts, or disaster relief and recovery. Such a faith-based structure arose not just from theological principles but from shared history and tradition. That Mennonites would understand the diaspora generated by the Gulf Coast storms and the pain that coastal residents experienced fits within their collective memory. Such forced dislocation has permeated much of Mennonite history. Just as Acadians fled Canada to the Louisiana "Cajun" coast (Brasseaux 1992), Mennonites experienced traumatic displacement as well. Diasporic similarities tie back to Mennonites leaving Germany and Russia to eke out new livelihoods under harsh conditions in Peru and in the unfamiliar lands of North America. That they reach out to others so affected resonates from memories of Dirk Willem turning back on the ice to saving refugees fleeing modern war and from the brink of starvation to rescuing those harmed by natural disasters, socioeconomic injustice, or government inadequacies. Anabaptist history and theology forms a solid foundation for sympathetic identification.

Sympathetic Listening

Personal contact enables volunteers to find even more commonalities with those they serve (Barton 1969). Indeed, studies reveal that: "Mere talk can be a constructive and therapeutic activity. Talking helps to ventilate anxiety. There is a cathartic potential in the expression of memories. What people need, then, is a listener, someone to talk to" (Reed 1977). As survivors tell their story, and volunteers listen, they build intense connections. It is this connective relationship that produces a basis for healing and in this study, served as the normative mechanism to produce a therapeutic community.

What do people need to talk about? Common needs include listening to expressions of grief over lost possessions and pets, fear of storms, worry over the future, concern about loved ones, stress over economic livelihoods and a survival guilt (Chinnici 1985). Unfortunately, those affected by disasters often stop sharing their stories after a few weeks when they are just beginning to process their emotions around loss (Pennebaker 1997; Reed 1977). Such self-censorship internalizes the trauma (Mitchell et al. 2004). To feel better and move forward after crisis, we need to tell others about our experiences and they need to listen. Personal needs to self-disclose may vary with the magnitude of the event, the scope of the destruction, and the amount of exposure we experience (Norris et al. 2002a and b). The worst disasters, particularly those that disrupt our social networks, seem to cause the most damage. In an event like Katrina, where people lost their neighbors, faith community, co-workers and broader community ties, trauma can cause debilitating immobility. While a minority may experience the worst of psychological trauma, many may experience varying levels of stress that make even the easiest of chores (like picking out a paint color for a new house) feel overwhelming. People needed sympathetic listening to take place beyond the period of self-censorship and throughout the lingering years of recovery.

How have disaster volunteers provided sympathetic listening? After the 1995 Great Hanshin-Awaji earthquake in Kobe, Japan, faculty from a nursing college reached out to elderly residents displaced from their homes. Most had moved out of shelters two to six months after the event. Hoping to prevent "kodokushi" or death alone, the volunteers visited the elderly and just listened. Such visits reduced over-use of alcohol as well as associated chronic diseases and stress-related illnesses (Kaho and Ikeda 2009). In the 1970s, Chaplains associated with Appalachian Regional Hospital responded to a disaster through providing ecumenical counseling and long-term pastoral care (Jordan 1976). Their efforts ranged from home visits to office counseling and listening to feelings and grief associated with the loss of community. Over time, their work transitioned into advocacy and identifying unmet needs. As one author observed: "One needs to listen with an even greater intensity than in the average pastoral care situation" including sensitivity to local cultural contexts (Jordan 1976, p. 170).

One particular form of listening may involve an act of faith. Clergy surveyed after a storm in South Carolina reported that they used prayer and Scripture to ask God for protection, to reduce losses, to persevere, and to have faith in God's plan (Mitchell 2003). Prayer, and other rituals associated with faith traditions, has been found to help people psychologically (Smith et al. 2000; Koenig 2006; DeSilva 2006). One pastor who offered disaster spiritual care after a Kentucky tornado concurred after he held funeral services for the house and dedicated temporary or new homes, finding that such events "might offer the person some sense of stability in the face of up-rootedness" (Reed 1977, 101). In Moore, Oklahoma after the May 2013 tornadoes, the community held a memorial service for pets. Conversely, house dedications to start a new life serve the same function and ease transitions. Symbolically, they also move the volunteer organization along to the next client albeit with lingering effects.

MDS accomplished sympathetic listening effectively. All along the coast after the 2005 and 2008 storms, clients made similar statements: "We really needed a friend to talk to." In Alabama, a client thanked the volunteers "for everything they did, but most of all just for being here with me. Knowing that someone cares is so helpful." A family in Texas described the connection they experienced with volunteers: "When I had a bad day, it was like they felt it." A woman in Mississippi represented the feelings for many: "They responded to our agony and hurt and what went on with Katrina." The non-judgmental approach mattered to her as well: "Lord, I had no idea these kind of people was in this world. They didn't look down on you, they made you think you was somebody. I couldn't stop singing their praises." For clients and communities, sympathetic listening was not just an act, it was a central element of a consistently presented way of life.

Cultural Capital

What generates the ability to sympathetically listen, to even consider heeding the call to volunteer? Scholars have consistently found that religion influences volunteer turnout, giving "people a broader rationale for service that goes beyond meeting their own instrumental and emotional needs of the moment" (Becker and Dhingra 2001, p. 332). Religious networks, found through regular worship attendance and social networks, produce social capital (Wilson and Musick 1997). Particularly important is intergenerational transmission of normative behaviors, in essence, the passing on of cultural traditions from parent to child (Park and Smith 2001). Such intergenerational connections can be found in MDS, organized in 1950, and institutionalized as yet another extension of a theologically based service orientation.

Throughout the research for this volume, clients, community leaders, and various officials consistently remarked on the theological foundation of MDS. Similar to other FBOs, MDS volunteers have felt called by faith to serve as the "hands and feet of Jesus." In a frequently used lesson from Matthew 25: 35–40, a scriptural mandate emerges:

> [35] For I was hungry and you gave me something to eat, I was thirsty and you gave me something to drink, I was a stranger and you invited me in, [36] I needed clothes and you clothed me, I was sick and you looked after me, I was in prison and you came to visit me. [37] "Then the righteous will answer him, 'Lord, when did we see you hungry and feed you, or thirsty and give you something to drink? [38] When did we see you a stranger and invite you in, or needing clothes and clothe you?

[39] When did we see you sick or in prison and go to visit you?' [40] "The King will reply, 'Truly I tell you, whatever you did for one of the least of these brothers and sisters of mine, you did for me.'[2]

Faith-based partners confirmed this MDS connection to Matthew 25. For one Texan: "The Gospel and ancient prophets said that God was on the side of the marginalized. Jesus says to help them. There are ways, various philosophies of how to help people, like government or through church. MDS doesn't get hung up on a philosophy, they just do it." From Louisiana, a faith-based partner concurred: "MDS was a tremendous beacon of hope to poor people in trouble. Their service in following Jesus in a practical manner was most impressive and a great example to me." And a Mississippi partner confirmed, "MDS helped a lot of people and did very good work. We were very thankful to see they really cared for the people who were in need of help. We much appreciated that their work was done in the name of Jesus. We are extremely thankful for what MDS has done. MDS was/is an answer to prayer, a gift from God."

Community partners, faith-based organizations and Mennonite partners confirmed client observations that the volunteers acted faithfully. A community partner in Mississippi said, "A good portion of our congregation was unaware of Anabaptism. The work of MDS was inspiring and made people more aware of Anabaptist theology and practice." The clearest demonstration of Anabaptist heritage came through servant action: "MDS is clearly driven by the idea of serving—it is part of their faith," said a resident in New Orleans. Another partner described the effort it took to rebuild in Plaquemines Parish: "What they did in Grand Bayou: the dedication, the gifts, the whole process is important. It does say ministry." Another partner from Cameron Parish observed: "They are committed to the Lord. Their purpose is to help people in need, it is their calling. They ask nothing; they just show up." Faith in action came through to recipients all along the coast: "Christianity is more than believing, it is more than talk, and what MDS does as action is far beyond what most organizations do. They have a commitment to God and a belief that wants them to assist when people are in need. They helped every way they could and they are coming back again this fall. They were good representatives of their faith."

Mennonite partners confirmed the MDS' role "as a ministry of the church" and "the face of the Mennonite church in the disaster area." One Mennonite organizational partner focused squarely on the Anabaptist value of MDS: "What was important was being in the mind of a servant." Mennonite and non-Mennonite partners made connections to a key piece of Anabaptist heritage: "Many of the churches requested input from Mennonites on peace theology." More than one partner also linked MDS volunteerism to scriptural mandate: "being the hands and feet of Jesus. In this way [volunteering], MDS teaches Anabaptist thinking by example."

A faith-based partner from Plaquemines Parish, where thousands lost their homes to a 30 foot storm surge, urged MDS to continue its witness through service. Quoting 1 Corinthians 15:58, the partner shared: "Therefore, my dear brothers, stand firm. Let nothing move you. Always give yourselves fully to the work of the Lord, because you know that your labor in the Lord is not in vain."

People on the coast learned about a faith tradition new to them and overcame their own stereotypes. One client who had heard of the practice of separatism among Anabaptists realized: "I always thought they wasn't nice. They stayed to their world and didn't want to be in ours. I was wrong. You have to lose everything to know."

Clients observed a consistent behavioral response mandated by Anabaptist theology: "They talked to my family Christian-like. There is Godliness inside of them. . . . They are truly God's people." A male client provided further context to the power of their witness saying, "I have never met a group of people like that. I have visited several churches around here [since the house was finished] but none like them. I am still looking." A Texas family confirmed: "They take time to travel, they don't know where they are going. There's so much God in them. I think of Psalm 23 'my cup runneth over' and theirs does to other people. The other verse is 'let your light so shine.'" A Louisiana couple observed: "There was no doubt the Spirit was in them, we were all agreed we could feel it in them. They came to help. You can't help but love them. You don't worry, it is going to be all right." A family member who agreed leaned forward, emphasizing: "Those Mennonites have a big torch."

Clients came away "impressed with their unspoken religion which came from the heart." One client felt compelled to: "tell all my friends at church about Mennonites and even phone up people that I know to tell them about the work of Mennonites." The demonstration of faith through action came through clearly: "Lots of people talk religion, these people do religion." Another client quoted from 1 Corinthians 24: "'I come not with enticing words but a demonstration.'"

Clients expressed complete astonishment that people would come from so far away to help a complete stranger. In one way or another, nearly all clients said the same thing: "There is no greater love than to have someone lay down their life for you. What better example of Jesus?" The arrival of faithful volunteers on the coast transformed tragedy and exploitation to learning: "how nice people can be." A woman in Louisiana summarized the effects: "The sweetness and kindness really helps you sleep through the night." A self-described loner who overcame deep personal depression after his encounter with MDS volunteers said: "They restored my faith in humanity."

Wilson and Musick (1997, p. 699) accurately predicted that religiosity "prepares people for participation in volunteer work." Religious values that compel service to others, and religious structures that provide for organized volunteerism, produce invaluable sources of cultural capital necessary to heal stricken communities.

PRACTICAL INSIGHTS FOR DISASTER VOLUNTEER ORGANIZATIONS

Disaster researchers conclude most scholarly works by examining findings vis-à-vis extant literature and by identifying practical applications. For this volume, an appropriate question to ask is whether any disaster or volunteer organization can foster a therapeutic community? The approach of MDS to disaster recovery suggests several practical insights.

First, what local leaders seem to appreciate the most is the way in which MDS made entry to their community. Starting with the question "What would be helpful to you?" MDS placed ownership of the recovery process into the hands of the local community. MDS then went on to explain who they were and what they could do, embarking on a course of mutual discernment with the local community regarding their long-term commitment. In a context of near-total devastation, an entry effort that began and continued in a low-key manner relieved local leaders. Exhausted by individual and collective losses, locals needed external organizations to arrive self-contained and to not impose further on already-beleaguered communities.

A second key best practice stems from a philosophical stance of going on the journey together with locals. As long-term recovery committees (LTRCs) and officials work out how they will organize rebuilding efforts, external organizations must remain mindful that such an effort will proceed in fits and starts. While most spontaneous volunteers arrive in the first few weeks after a disaster, experienced organizations walk with local leaders down a slowly unfolding road to recovery. Because most locals lack experience with disaster recovery, offering gentle suggestions on what worked in other locations allows LTRCs to assess how well the approach fits in their community. Slow and steady approaches benefit locals as ultimately such efforts empower people who know their community best to establish a viable process.

Third, disaster recovery volunteer organizations need to be at the LTRC table. MDS, with its long-term volunteer structure and strong ties back to headquarters, allows for such a presence. Over time, that steadfast presence builds a more effective working relationship. To further that connection, answering phone and email inquiries and being willing to adhere to local practices matters. MDS enjoys a strong reputation in producing quality home construction in part because of their organizational willingness to adhere to post-disaster building practices. They also put in extra efforts to build it right. Providing construction oversight thus helps to insure that things are done well, including willingness to re-do something that is less than desirable. Beyond construction, participating in the LTRCs integrates an external organization into the case management process. Locals shoulder responsibility for finding and recommending clients, which MDS could accept or reject based on the client's fit with the MDS mission.

Fourth, external organizations need to be willing to listen—actively and sympathetically—to the clients with whom they interact. MDS volunteers practice such listening, and value the stories that local people shared with them. Listening promotes a therapeutic response within those harmed by disasters and lessens the burden with which they may struggle. As more than one long-term volunteer said, sometimes you need to lay down the hammer and just listen. Local leaders and officials require the same act of listening, as many on the coast not only worked to rebuild neighbors' homes but their own as well. Local leaders also struggle through a multi-year process, as watching the slow return of homes, livelihoods, and environmental familiarity can take a toll. Too often, locals did not see their neighbors return home from the widespread diaspora. Both leaders and clients need sympathetic listening.

Fifth, taking the time to understand local cultures and ways of life is deeply appreciated by locals. Not questioning why someone would want to return home to a place that has been devastated makes a difference to people who miss their neighbors, their familiar voices and accents, and economic livelihoods. People on the coast felt that Mennonites took the time to learn about their way of life and built meaningful, lasting relationships as a consequence. Outsiders who express interest in local ways to earn a living and eagerly take opportunities to learn firsthand were greatly appreciated. Not everyone is invited to gumbo.

Sixth, finding informal ways for locals and outsiders to interact helps to build enduring ties. People felt comfortable at the MDS camp. Going to camp served as a way for clients to pay back an external organization by telling their story to volunteers. But those informal visits resulted in even more. Visiting camp helped to foster a trusted relationship. Clients even left their children at the camp to play, comfortable in the thought that a safe place existed after the violence of the storms, the distance of government bureaucracy, and the unscrupulousness of contractors. On project sites, intangible ties developed between volunteers and clients from pulling debris out of the muck of the bayou to singing hymns of celebration at house dedications. Key practices that mattered to clients included praying with and for them, and sharing meals. For local leaders, it meant a great deal that an external organization bought local and attended local worship services.

Seventh, it matters to involve clients in picking out their own colors, countertops, and cabinetry. Being empowered to do so, even when they first expressed reluctance, brought the first real happiness that many had experienced for years. Clients began to own the process of reconstruction by becoming involved in decision-making. They found not only joy at the prospect of going home, but in having control over their lives after years in temporary housing and at the mercy of a bureaucratized relief process. Choosing and deciding enables problem-solving and helps people to move forward out of disaster-generated inertia.

Eighth, a signature characteristic of MDS is the organizational culture that promotes deep internal reflection. Although local leaders and clients interviewed for this volume clearly said "tell them not to change a thing," MDS constantly looks internally for things that need change. Tinkerers at heart, MDS embodied an ability to engage in thoughtful self-examination at all levels and to face bravely critiques to build the organization better. Doing so resulted in a painful realization about five years after Katrina that they would need to reduce their numbers of paid post-Katrina staff. Doing so represented good financial stewardship although painful both organizationally and personally as members of the family moved on. Through a dedicated internal reflection, MDS also renewed its mission to the broadly based and historic grass roots constituency.

Ninth, disaster-prone communities would be well-advised to turn to religions to recruit volunteers. Higher levels of volunteerism are generated by the faithful. Stronger and integrated social networks exist within religious communities. Resources to fund volunteer efforts can be tapped from the same place. Disaster-specific FBOs provide working social structures to organize work teams. Not only labor can be found within the faith-based sector, but historic, cultural and theological foundations that motivate volunteer turnout. Consistent behavioral response tied to those foundations can produce therapeutic effects.

Finally, volunteer, civic, community and faith-based organizations that want to help in disasters need to coordinate within the long-term recovery partnerships. Showing up may demonstrate caring, but such spontaneity often wanes as media coverage disappears. Volunteers who want to help need to coordinate within experienced disaster organizations. Such organizations need to find ways to stay in place for the long-haul. Traumatic responses, which can be effectively addressed by the therapeutic community, may not appear for six to twelve months or even longer. Most volunteers have disappeared by then. Long-term recovery requires long-term commitment.

LINGERING EFFECTS OF A THERAPEUTIC COMMUNITY

A Texas client offered: "The only bad thing I can say is they left. I wish they would have stayed longer." As tears welled up, he said quietly to tell the volunteers: "Keep doing it the same." Some found ways to keep their volunteers close by. One Louisianan asked volunteers to sign their names onto garden beds, adding "Some of the names are wearing off. I would like them to come back and sign their names again." In describing "their" volunteers, clients' faces would light up as they described how volunteers made return visits, called on the phone, wrote or e-mailed. A Louisiana man said: "I still keep in touch with everybody. I send them Christmas cards every year." To prove his point, he pulled out a sheet of paper with the names and addresses of his volunteers, as did one client after another across the coast. Holidays contact emerged as the time when clients usually heard from their volunteers. One New Orleans client said he "gets lots of Christmas cards" and, without prompting, immediately named off at least ten volunteers.

Clients formed especially close ties with the long-term volunteers. One said that her project director "called me just the other day to see how I was doing. A very special friend!" Another woman in Louisiana continually referred to her project director as "my angel" who continued checking on her, despite the passage of several years. International borders and long-distance calls did not deter contact, either. A Texas couple said that regardless of the project director being from Manitoba and the volunteers from the east coast, they remained in touch "almost weekly and definitely monthly." A New Orleans client said she had exchanged photos with one volunteer who "still calls me up."

Clients especially loved return visits from their volunteers, saying: "Our door is always open!" said people in Alabama, Mississippi, Louisiana and Texas. And the client open-door policy worked, especially for repeat volunteers: "Some of the volunteers stop by and visit when they come to work on another house. One time a group of eight showed up!" A Texas family told with delight, "A whole bus load came by a month ago just to say hi!" Another expressed surprise when one of the volunteers showed up unexpectedly: "I just came by to see how you are and if you needed anything." One resident in Louisiana said his volunteers, "came to visit me just last month and stayed for five hours." With eyes still expressing wonderment, he emphasized, the volunteers "came from Kansas just to visit *me*." A couple in Louisiana recovering from Rita had the same experience: "Every winter we get visits from people who had worked on the house but had not seen it when it was finished. They are very welcome."

Some clients even visited their volunteers. One family traveled to the church that had provided funds for rebuilding saying, "It was a grand welcome." Another couple told about neighbors who traveled to Pennsylvania, learning about "their way of life up there and really enjoyed it." MDS invited several clients to visit Mennonite churches and tell their story, a trip the clients greatly enjoyed. Some clients from Mississippi visited the Illinois Rotary that paid for materials MDS used to build homes in Pass Christian. A few clients spoke at Mennonite colleges and conferences about their way of life on the coast.

Perhaps not surprisingly, some clients reported that the interaction had tapered off: "I wish I could see every one of them again. Now and then they write," said a Louisiana woman. In Mississippi, an older woman said that her volunteers "sent cards and presents at Christmas though I don't hear from them anymore." Some experienced difficulties staying in touch due to life circumstances or as the years passed. A Louisiana woman tried to maintain contact but discovered that her writing had failed with age. Many of the elderly clients did not use e-mail though some found the Internet a way to remain in touch with volunteers. In other circumstances, phone numbers had changed or some clients had moved into assisted living. It just became harder to stay in touch.

Clients did not see the relationship as just surrounding the reconstruction. As a Texas client said: "I want to see them again." A woman in Louisiana said to tell the disaster volunteers: "This house is always open for you to come back, anytime." Yes, said someone from Grand Bayou: "I love them coming back."

NOTES

1. No author. Note in folder, filed in 1954. *Report of the Activities of the Mennonite Service Organizations Kansas Area*. Mennonite Library and Archives, Newton, Kansas.

2. New International Version, 2010.

Appendix A: Methodology

RESEARCH DESIGN

This study relied upon a mixed-methods approach that incorporated traditional disaster qualitative and quantitative methods (Phillips 2013; Phillips 1997; Quarantelli 2002; Stallings 2002). Qualitative methods included data generated from in-depth interviews (n = 162), focus groups (n = 59), archival documents, and participant observation. Quantitative methods generated survey data yielding 852 total respondents. The timeline for the data collection occurred from May of 2010 through May of 2011, designed to cover the fifth-year anniversaries of hurricanes Katrina and Rita and the three-year anniversary of Ike. Typically, anniversaries evoke memories useful to researchers as people reflect on the meaning of the event in their lives (Eyre 2006). Anniversaries also prompt recall and often enable people to place the past in perspective and to allow them to see progress or the lack thereof.

At the invitation of Mennonite Disaster Service (MDS), this study evaluated if MDS accomplished their mission to repair, rebuild and restore after disaster. Their concern emanated from having more donations, projects, volunteers, and new staff generated by hurricanes Katrina and Rita. MDS wanted to know: did the quantity of resources they received affect the quality of services they delivered? To research this question, a small team of researchers interviewed MDS clients, as well as community-based, faith-based, and Anabaptist partners who worked with MDS and MDS staff and board members. An MDS staff member coordinated logistics while the author led efforts to construct data-gathering instruments, train, and supervise the field team. Members of the research team included Ron Dueck, a skilled educator and former Director of the Board for Mennonite Central Committee, along with students from Hesston College in Kansas and Canadian Mennonite University in Winnipeg. The evaluation team coordinated with the MDS Board to deploy a survey. In addition, the author collected and analyzed internal organizational documents, archival records, publications and other relevant materials to understand the organization and its efforts. Finally, the author participated in MDS volunteer work at several project sites and spent extensive time at MDS headquarters in Pennsylvania.

In order to enhance usefulness of an evaluation project for academic research, I used a naturalistic paradigm (Erlandson et al. 1992; Lincoln and Guba 1985). Naturalistic inquiry directs the researchers to plan for data collection and analysis while allowing for flexibility in the research design. Being open enables the researcher to adapt the data collection process as needed by adding or subtracting questions to interviews and focusing in to think and perceive in new ways. After pilot testing the instrument and fine-tuning the questions, we retained a primary set of questions throughout the study. However, we remained open to additional information that respondents volunteered. Doing so revealed a therapeutic community.

Qualitative approaches that use naturalism direct the researcher to gather data so that they can construct reality in ways that emanate realistically from actors embedded in settings and contexts. We experience their world by capturing their perspectives and verifying our perceptions of their thoughts through several techniques. Substantial depth and richness developed. For example, in asking respondents to "tell us about your house," clients and partners talked about the *people* who worked on their home and the meaningful *relationships* they experienced.

Recording data (people's responses) is vitally important. To do so, researchers need to capture 'native language'—the words of the people and the context that gives it meaning (Spradley 1980). This requires understanding local meaning—such as "everyone is invited to come, but few are invited to gumbo." Researchers must record words, phrases and their meaning as well as non-verbal content that infuses the verbal messages being delivered. To illustrate, one respondent leaned forward making intentional eye-contact as he described the way in which volunteers worked *with* him rather than *for* him. His eyes filled with tears and he punctuated certain words with nods. His meaning grew clear through both verbal and non-verbal behaviors: building the house meant security for his family and peace of mind as he battled a pernicious disease. Nearly every client we interviewed shed tears, demonstrating how volunteer efforts moved them emotionally. Given that the researchers were complete strangers to the respondent(s) just minutes prior to the tears, recording this non-verbal behavior seemed not only relevant but also suggested a sincere presentation of their beliefs. The emotional context promotes a high degree of confidence that participants shared a deeply held sentiment far beyond a hospitable or polite response to the evaluation. In 30 years of disaster research, this emerged as the most powerful and emotionally sincere research experience I have ever encountered.

Recording data requires the researcher reflect on "criticality" within the respondent's context. To enhance success, I appreciate and acknowledge the influence of local researchers Pam Jenkins, Shirley Laska, Joselin Landry, Patricia Stukes, and Kristina Peterson—all of whom helped me to understand context well before Katrina and continued to serve as helpful interpreters and debriefers throughout the project. I am particularly indebted to Dr. Jenkins, a gifted qualitative researcher and stalwart Katri-

na survivor, who saw value in the project from inception to completion—
and pushed me diligently to record, reflect, and analyze data with rigor.

Another dimension required to record data is to listen to what people
say with theoretical sensitivity, which stems from several bases. The first
base comes from research literature that supports, refutes, or transforms
scientific knowledge. When we document such insights, we move forward what we know about a given topic, like volunteerism. Second,
knowing how the disaster recovery process is designed to function as
well as how faith-based organizations operate in disasters helps. To illustrate, there are multiple common organizational forms that emerge after a
disaster, such as a long-term recovery committee or an interfaith. By
listening to community partners describe their organizations and process,
it is possible to ascertain not only their organizational interactions with
MDS but the meaning of the relationships that emerged. When one of
them says "[this MDS person] is an honorary Cajun" they are saying that
this person fit in well, understood local need, appreciated their culture,
and can "come back anytime and stay." A third basis is simply research
experience. After thirty years in the field, it is far easier to "hear" something that is relevant than it is just starting out as a novice investigator.
For students reading this, know that the third base for developing theoretical sensitivity will come.

QUALITATIVE DATA COLLECTION

Interviews and Focus Groups

Focus groups were used to gather information from long-term volunteers, including cooks, office managers, and project directors. Focus
groups took place during a Project Director's Forum that allowed for
written and verbal content to be provided on various topics. A total of 59
individuals participated in these focus groups with the largest such
group being project directors. Smaller groups of office managers and
cooks also contributed. Analysis involved capturing the comments of
participants and then writing up their thoughts. Interviews captured perceptions and experiences in depth from clients, community partners,
long-term volunteers, MDS staff, and MDS Board members. Interviews
followed general semi-structured, open-ended schedules designed as
"guided conversations" to put participants at ease, solicit richer data and
enable both qualitative and quantitative coding (Weiss 1994; Gorden
1992). We had very little difficulty gaining access to most of the interviewees with some exceptions noted below in the section on sampling.
Only one person declined an interview, presumably because they were
displeased with their repair though that could not be confirmed. Over

and over, people opened their doors to the research team. We were even served gumbo on several occasions.

Participant Observation

Although the research design initially centered on interviews, it became clear that time spent conducting observations would generate beneficial insights for the book. Accordingly, I observed on project sites in Mississippi and Louisiana while taking care to not record personal comments or experiences of the volunteers. Rather, I wrote up nightly notes on the lived experience of volunteer life on a project site. To capture my experiences systematically, I relied on a matrix created originally by Spradley (1980) which focuses attention on places, acts, actions and interactions. Spradley tells us to create "mini-tours" within the places we observe, such as the arrangement of a kitchen, and a grand tour like the layout of the camp. Comparing such tours enabled me to discern the various ways in which MDS established camps and their phenomenal ability to transform nearly destroyed facilities into functional volunteer housing.

While on project sites (whether passing through as an evaluator or there as a volunteer), I lived, ate, and shared chores with MDS volunteers. I also spent a week volunteering in Plaquemines Parish where I rotated through the jobs of office manager, assistant cook, and crew member. Being on site enabled me to see clearly that the organizational structure of MDS varied little across project sites which surely laid a foundation for organizational success and consistently positive volunteer experiences. Participant observation data were analyzed using the Developmental Research Sequence that results in increasingly nuanced domain, taxonomic and componential analyses as described above in the observation section (Spradley 1980).

Visual Documentation

Another way to capture data is through visual documentation including photography or videography (David 2010; Banks 2007; Blinn 1987; Collier and Collier 1986). I photographed the interiors and exteriors of MDS volunteer sites. Examples included dining rooms (with tabasco bottles on all project sites), housing (including handmade bunk beds), and work spaces. In each location, I photographed the daily job board which revealed a consistency in how MDS organized work crews and tasks. Additional photography produced insight into the careful way that tools are organized and maintained, efforts to recycle, and the weekly routine that evolved over time—and varied little from site to site.

Archival Research

A final data source, archival records, served to complete the data collection process. I have spent years (including time prior to the onset of the formal evaluation) studying internal records at MDS headquarters. Those records shed light into the historical character and consistency of MDS in establishing project sites. Historic materials also made it possible to understand that MDS had been present in some of the sites prior to the Gulf Coast storms, including for hurricane Camille in 1969 and hurricane Audrey in 1957.

Historic materials are subject to several kinds of issues, particularly selective deposit (Webb et al. 2000). This is particularly true in more official archives. Those who send materials to archives may not send everything or documents may simply have been lost over time. Archives may also have partial records, requiring the researcher to go to many places. Such travel occurred with this research and I found it necessary to visit the Mennonite Library and Archive in Newton, Kansas; the Mennonite Central Committee Library and Archive in Akron, Pennsylvania; and the Mennonite Church USA Archive in Goshen, Indiana. I found useful documents at each location and the journey was made particularly worthwhile by dedicated librarians and archivists who diligently searched their files for treasures. Analyzing documents required effort to compare and contrast what archives had available in order to discern themes pertinent to the history, culture, and theology of MDS.

Sampling

Researchers must make selections over who to talk to and where to observe, a process called sampling. Our evaluation team went to all sites where MDS established projects for Katrina, Rita, and Ike. MDS also provided a list of clients, community partners, and faith-based partners. We attempted to contact all clients on the lists though some remained unavailable because phone numbers had changed or because clients had moved (often to nursing homes). In a few cases, we learned that some clients had died. We contacted all community partners on the list provided, typically 3–10 such contacts per community and identified additional interviewees not on the list of recommendations. For those not on the list, they had to be familiar with MDS such as elected and appointed officials and members of the faith community. No one was excluded from selection in sampling unless they were simply unavailable. However, members of a Vietnamese-American community (fearful of the human subjects form) declined to participate. No one in the community or faith-based partners declined an interview request. A total of 162 interviews were conducted, written up as summaries, and then assessed using NVivo qualitative software.

DATA ANALYSIS

Qualitative Analysis

A grounded theory approach was used to analyze qualitative data where the researcher identifies and codes bits of data, compares them to each other systematically, and then builds an explanation (Glaser and Strauss 1967; Lincoln and Guba 1985). Called the "constant comparative process," the process provides a higher degree of confidence that the data are coded correctly. The process results in an inductively generated explanation of what happened—in this case, the emergence of a therapeutic community. Data analysis began with "open coding" as suggested by Glaser and Strauss (1967) to reveal what is meaningful to those interviewed. Selective coding then follows on an identified code. For example, open coding revealed the category of "building relationships" which was then selectively coded for the stages and means through which clients and volunteers constructed relationships.

Quantitative Analysis

The project also relied on data captured in a survey which was offered to MDS volunteers via online and paper forms. A total of 852 surveys were captured representing over a dozen Anabaptist denominations. Those data were prepared for use by importing them into SPSS, a software package that expedites analysis. Open-ended questions were also coded to reveal themes across the hundreds of volunteers who responded.

CREDIBILITY AND TRUSTWORTHINESS OF THE DATA

Qualitative researchers use several methods to assess the credibility and trustworthiness of the data and the analysis. In the present study, techniques used included triangulation, negative case analysis, referential adequacy, peer debriefing, member checks, and an audit trail (Lincoln and Guba 1985; Erlandson et al. 1992). Triangulation refers to the use of multiple data sources focused on the research question. To illustrate, the combination of qualitative and quantitative data allow the researcher to study a question statistically and in-depth. Statistics offer the potential to use pre-determined statistical tests with firm decision points regarding the power of the finding and the possibility that it occurred due to chance. Qualitative methods produce thick, rich description that can be coded systematically to identify themes and produce theoretical insights. For example, one can ask someone about the meaning of Anabaptism to volunteers using both a survey and an in-depth interview. The survey tells you the number of people in agreement and the intensity of their concurrence. The interview sheds light on the personal significance and meaning of the theology. To strengthen confidence in the findings, multiple methods were used within the qualitative research design. As one example, a respondent might say "it's in our DNA" to express the meaning of service in their lives and a researcher can contrast that with archival records, participant observation, and organizational records. If the multiple methods lead the researcher analytically to similar results from varying angles, the triangulation supports the findings. In this case, remarkable consistency resulted from a mixed methods approach that triangulated the research findings.

Another technique, called negative case analysis, engages the analyst in searching for cases and findings contrary to what has been found. The positive depiction of volunteers in this volume serves as an example. Could one organization produce such remarkably consistent images of volunteers? By using Nvivo, it is possible to examine that question across various factors. I did so by looking at possible differences across states, size of communities (urban, small town, rural), racial and ethnic groups, and by contrasting sampling groups such as clients versus community partners. The findings remained consistently positive. In a few cases where negative comments occurred, it was actually hard to determine if the problem stemmed from MDS volunteers or from a situation where multiple organizations (i.e., another organization was the problem) worked on a site. Nearly all clients who told of a problem with their home said that a project director stopped by to fix it or the problem occurred due to another storm (such as Ike pushing moisture under some floors) or from normal household repairs (an air conditioner breaking down). The negative case analysis also revealed that as the interviews moved from outside the organization (clients, community partners) to inside (Mennonite partners), critique of MDS became a little more common. However, at the five year mark most Mennonite partners also indicated that problems and concerns had, for the most part, been successfully addressed or were chalked up to the significant impact that Katrina brought on all response and recovery organizations.

Referential adequacy is another technique whereby the researcher sets aside some of the data (such as 10 interviews out of 100) and then analyzes them separately to see if the same results or themes are present. Referential adequacy produced exactly that: consistency of findings. Researchers conducting qualitative studies also work toward "saturation" when it is possible to predict what the next respondent will say. Saturation occurred fairly quickly. The instance of respondents referring to volunteers as "like family" serves as one example as it became quickly possible to anticipate respondents would use the phrase.

Peer debriefing, another technique, took place in multiple ways. First, the research team met nearly every night while in the field to discuss findings and see what they were discovering, to identify anomalies, and to see if the instrument needed to be adapted. Second, the research team met at the end of a field trip to identify themes and generate field trip reports to summarize impressions (Quarantelli, no date). Third, an MDS staff member debriefed the research team separately and together on multiple occasions. Finally, a most useful form of peer debriefing came from speaking with fellow researchers about the methodology and techniques. For that, I particularly thank Dr. Pam Jenkins of the University of New Orleans, Dr. Walt Peacock of Texas A&M University, and Dr. David Neal of Oklahoma State University. Their good sensibility of methodology coupled with Dr. Jenkins' thorough knowledge of the storms, Louisiana culture, populations, and social systems served to focus inquiry in productive directions. Furthermore, they kept the research team honest about their findings by asking for anomalies and contrasting initial analyses with existing studies. As a final check, I sent interview summaries to key respondents for their review and invited review of written chapters by MDS staff, long term volunteers, and fellow researchers for their scrutiny. Involving respondents in review of content is called a member check and serves as yet another means to confirm trustworthiness and credibility of the analysis.

Finally, I created an audit trail. The purpose of the audit trail is to create a set of files that an outside reviewer can look through and determine if methodological rigor represented the research efforts. The audit trail includes interview summaries, Nvivo coded reports, documents, memoes (Lofland et al. 2006), photographs and analyses.

References and Recommended Readings

Airriess, Christopher, et al. 2007. "Church-based Social Capital, and Geographical Scale: Katrina evacuation, relocation and recovery in a New Orleans Vietnamese American community." *Geoforum* 39: 1333–1346.

Ahler, James G. and Joseph B. Tamney. 1964. "Some Functions of Religious Ritual in a Catastrophe." *Sociological Analysis* 25: 212–230.

Amato, P., R. Ho and S. Partridge. 1984. "Responsibility Attribution and Helping Behaviour in the Ash Wednesday Bushfires." *Australian Journal of Psychology* 36/2: 191–203.

Banks, Marcus. 2007. *Using Visual Data in Qualitative Research*. Thousand Oaks, CA: Sage.

Barton, Alan. 1970. *Communities in Disaster: A Sociological Analysis of Collective Stress Situations*. NY: Doubleday.

Bayou la Batre Chamber of Commerce. 2010. "Welcome to the Bayou." Bayou La Batre, AL. Bayou la Batre Chamber of Commerce.

Becker, Penny E.. 1999. *Congregations in Conflict: Cultural Models of Religious Life*. NY: Cambridge University Press.

Becker, Penny Edgell and Pawan H. Dhingra. 2001. "Religious Involvement and Volunteering: Implications for Civil Society." *Sociology of Religion* 62(3): 315–335.

Blinn, Lynn. 1987. "Phototherapeutic Intervention to Improve Self-concept and Prevent Repeat Pregnancies among Adolescents." *Family Relations* 36: 252–257.

Bolin, Robert C. 1994. *Household and Community Recovery after Disaster*. Boulder, CO: Natural Hazards Center Monograph 56.

Bolin, Robert C. 2006. "Race, Class, Ethnicity, and Disaster Vulnerability." In *Handbook of Disaster Research*, edited by Havidán Rodriguez, Enrico L. Quarantelli, and Russell R., 113–129. NY: Springer.

Bolin, R. C. and L. Stanford. 1998. "The Northridge Earthquake: community-based approaches to unmet recovery needs." *Disasters* 22/1: 21–38.

Bowditch, James L., Anthony F. Buono, and Marcus M. Stewart. 2008. *A Primer on Organizational Behavior, 7th edition*. Hoboken, NJ: Wiley.

Britton, Neil. 1991. "Permanent Disaster Volunteers." *Nonprofit and voluntary sector quarterly* 20/4: 395–415.

Cain, Daphne S. and Juan Barthelemy. 2008. "Tangible and Spiritual Relief after the Storm: The religious community responds to Katrina." *Journal of Social Service Research* 34(3): 29–42.

Callaway, Cassie and Moore, Ariana. 2006. "Serious Oversight: Bayou La Batre." *Baykeeper Magazine*, Spring 2006.

Childers, Cheryl. 2008. "Elderly Female-Headed Households in the Disaster Loan Process." Pp. 182–193 in *Women and Disasters: from Theory to Practice*, edited by Brenda Phillips and Betty Morrow. Philadelphia, PA: Xlibris/International Research Committee on Disaster.

Chinnici, Rosemary. 1985. "Pastoral Care Following a Natural Disaster." *Pastoral Psychology* 33/4: 245–254.

Clive, Alan, Elizabeth Davis, Rebecca Hansen and Jennifer Mincin. 2010. "Disability." Pp. 187–216 in *Social Vulnerability to Disasters*, edited by Brenda Phillips, Deborah S. K. Thomas, Alice Fothergill and Lynn Blinn-Pike. Boca Raton, FL: CRC Press.

189

Clizbe, John. 2004. "Challenges in Managing Volunteers During Bioterrorism Response." *Biosecurity and Bioterrorism: Biodefense Strategy, Practice, and Science* 2/4: 294–300.

Collier, John and Malcolm Collier. 1986. *Visual Anthropology*. Albuquerque: University of New Mexico Press.

Comerio, Mary. 1997. "Housing Issues after Disasters." *Journal of Contingencies and Crisis Management* 5: 166–178.

Comerio, Mary. 1998. *Disaster Hits Home: New Policy for Urban Housing Recovery*. Berkeley: University of California Press.

Cutter, Susan L. 1996. "Vulnerability to Environmental Hazards." *Progress in Human Geography* 20/4: 529–539.

Cutter, Susan. 2006. "The Geography of Social Vulnerability: Race, Class and Catastrophe." Available at http://understandingkatrina.ssrc.org/Cutter/, last accessed January 12, 2011.

De Silva, Padmal. 2006. "The Tsunami and its Aftermath in Sri Lanka: explorations of a Buddhist perspective." *International Review of Psychiatry* 18/3: 281–297.

Dash, Nicole. 2010. "Race and Ethnicity." Pp. 101–122 in *Social Vulnerability to Disasters*, edited by Brenda Phillips, Deborah S. K. Thomas, Alice Fothergill and Lynn Blinn-Pike. Boca Raton, FL: CRC Press.

Dash, Nicole, Betty Morrow and Juanita Mainster. 2007. "Lasting Effects of Hurricane Andrew on a Working-Class Community." *Natural Hazards Review* 8(13): 13–21.

David, Gaby. 2010. "Camera Phone Images, Videos and Live Streaming." *Visual Studies* 25/1: 89–98.

Detweiler, Lowell. 2000. *The Hammer Rings Hope*. Scottdale, PA: Herald Press.

Dreier, Peter. 2005. "Katrina in Perspective: the Disaster Raises Key Questions About the Role of Government in American Society." *Dissent Magazine*, available at http://www.commondreams.org/views05/0915-27.htm, last accessed March 9, 2011.

Durkheim, Emile. 1912. *The Elementary Forms of Religious Life*. New York: Oxford University Press.

Dyck, Cornelius J. 1993. *An Introduction to Mennonite History*, third edition. Scottdale, PA: Herald Press.

Dyck, Peter J. and Elfrieda Dyck. 1991. *Up From the Rubble*. Scottdale, PA: Herald Press.

Dynes, Russell R. 1994. "Situational Altruism: toward an explanation of pathologies in disaster assistance." Preliminary paper #201 of the University of Delaware, Disaster Research Center, Newark, Delaware.

Dynes, Russell R. 1970. *Organized Behavior in Disaster*. Lexington, MA: Health Lexington Books.

Dyregrov, Atle, Jakob Kristoffersen, and Rolf Gjestad. 1996. "Voluntary and Professional Disaster Workers: Similarities and Differences in Reactions." *Journal of Traumatic Stress* 9/3: 541–555.

Eden Mennonite Church Historical Committee. 2010. "Historical Committee - Church History." Available at http://edenmennonite.org/Historical_Committee, last accessed December 3, 2010.

Elliot, Debbie. 2006. "Can Bayou la Batre Bounce Back?" *NPR*, 28 May 2006.

Ellis, Dan. 2001. "First People of the Pass: Black heritage, free persons of color." Available at http://pc.danellis.net/index.htm, last accessed July 1, 2010.

Ellis, Dan. 2001a. "First People of the Pass Black Heritage: free persons of color." Available at http://history.passchristian.net/pass_time_line.htm, last accessed July 1, 2010.

Ellis, Dan. 2001b. *Images of America: Pass Christian*. Charleston, SC: Arcadia Publishing.

Ellis, Dan. 2005. "Historical Pass Christian, Mississippi: History 101—-a Glimpse of Pass Christian." Available at http://pc.danellis.net/index.htm, last accessed July 1, 2010.

Ellis, Dan. 2005. "Pass Christian—Significant Dates." Available at http://history.passchristian.net/pass_time_line.htm, last accessed July 1, 2010.

Enarson, Elaine. 2010. "Gender." Pp. 123–154 in *Social Vulnerability to Disasters*, edited by Brenda Phillips, Deborah S. K. Thomas, Alice Fothergill and Lynn Blinn-Pike. Boca Raton, FL: CRC Press.

Enarson, Elaine. 2008. "Women and Housing Issues in Two U.S. Disasters: Case Studies from Hurricane Andrew and the Red River Valley Flood." Pp. 155–181 in *Women and Disasters: from Theory to Practice*, edited by Brenda Phillips and Betty Morrow. Philadelphia, PA: Xlibris/International Research Committee on Disaster.

Enarson, Elaine. 2001. "What Women Do: Gendered Labor in the Red River Valley Flood." *Environmental Hazards* 3:1–18.

Enarson, Elaine, Alice Fothergill and Lori Peek. 2006. "Gender and Disaster: foundation and directions." Pp. 130–146 in *Handbook of Disaster Research*, edited by Havidán Rodríguez, Enrico L. Quarantelli, and Russell R. Dynes. NY: Springer.

Enarson, Elaine and Betty Morrow. 1997. "A Gendered Perspective: The Voices of Women." Pp. 116–140 in *Hurricane Andrew: Ethnicity, Gender and the Sociology of Disasters*, edited by Walter. G. Peacock, Betty. H. Morrow and Hugh. Gladwin. London: Routledge.

Environmental Sciences Service Administration Weather Bureau (ESSA). 1969. *Hurricane Camille Preliminary Report*. Washington D.C.: U.S. Department of Commerce.

Erikson, Kai. 1994. *A New Species of Trouble*. NY: Norton.

Erlandson, David, et al. 1993. *Doing Naturalistic Inquiry*. Thousand Oaks, CA: Sage.

Evans-Cowley, Jennifer S. and Meghan Zimmerman Gough. 2010. "Evaluating New Urbanist Plans in Post-Katrina Mississippi." *Journal of Urban Design* 14/4: 439–461.

Eyre, Anne. 2006. "Remembering: community commemoration after disaster." Pp. 441–455 in in *Handbook of Disaster Research*, edited by Havidán Rodríguez, Enrico L. Quarantelli, and Russell R. Dynes. NY: Springer.

Farris, Anne. 2006. *Katrina Anniversary finds Faith-based Groups Still on the Front Lines, Resilient but Fatigued*. http://www.religionandsocialpolicy.org. Accessed January 15, 2008.

Federal Emergency Management Agency. 1999. *The Role of Voluntary Agencies in Emergency Management*. Independent Study 288. http://www.fema.gov.

Federal Coordinator for Gulf Coast Rebuilding. 2006. *Current Housing Units Damage Estimates Hurricanes Katrina, Rita and Wilma*. Washington, D.C.: Department of Homeland Security.

Federal Emergency Management Agency (FEMA). No date, a. "National Response Framework" Resource Center. Available at http://www.fema.gov/emergency/nrf/aboutNRF.htm, last accessed March 14, 2011.

Federal Emergency Management Agency (FEMA). No date, b. "FEMA Voluntary Agency Liaison." Washington D.C.: FEMA Handout.

Federal Emergency Management Agency. 2010. *Hurricane Ike in Texas and Louisiana: Mitigation Assessment Team Report, Building Performance Observations, Recommendations, and Technical Guidance*. Washington D.C.: FEMA.

Federal Emergency Management Agency (FEMA). 2002. "Testimony of Federal Emergency Management Agency Director Joe M. Allbaugh." Available at http://www.fema.gov/about/director/allbaugh/testimony/051601.shtm, last accessed March 9, 2011.

Fernandez, Lauren. et al. 2000. "Frail Elderly as Disaster Victims: Emergency Management Strategies." *Prehospital and Disaster Management* 17/2: 67–74.

Fothergill, Alice. 2008. "Domestic Violence after Disasters." Pp. 131–5154 in *Women and Disasters: from Theory to Practice*, edited by Brenda Phillips and Betty Morrow. Philadelphia, PA: Xlibris/International Research Committee on Disaster.

Fritz, Charles E. 1961. "Disaster." *Contemporary Social Problems*: 651–694.

Fritz, Charles E. and J. H. Mathewson. 1956. *Convergence Behavior: a Disaster Control Problem*. Special Report prepared for the Committee on Disaster Studies, National Academy of Sciences, National Research Council.

Fritz, Herman M., Chris Blount, Robert Sokoloski, Justin Singleton, Andrew Fuggle, Brian G. McAdoo, Andrew Moore, Chad Grass, and Banks Tate. 2007. "Hurricane

Katrina Storm Surge Distribution and Field Observations on the Mississippi Barrier Islands." *Estuarine Coastal and Shelf Science* 24: 12–20.

GAMEO. No date. "Civilian Public Service." Available at http://www.gameo.org/encyclopedia/contents/C52.html, last accessed December 3, 2010.

Garrison, Jean L. 1985. "Mental Health Implications of Disaster Relocation in the United States: A Review of the Literature." *International Journal of Mass Emergencies and Disasters* 3/2: 49–65.

Gingerich, Melvin. 1949. *Service for Peace: A history of Mennonite Civilian Public Service*. Akron, Pa.: Mennonite Central Committee.

Glaser, Barney and Anselm Strauss. 1967. *The Discovery of Grounded Theory*. NY: Aldine.

Gorden, Raymond L. 1992. *Basic Interviewing Skills*. Itasca: Peacock.

Graber, Chris. 1970. *Camille Disaster Summary*. From the MDS Archive files on Hurricane Camille.

Gaillard, Frye. 2007. "After the Storms: Tradition and Change in Bayou La Batre." *The Journal of American History* 94(3): 856–862.

Graumann, Alex, Tamara Houston, Jay Lawrimore, David Levinson, Neal Lott, Sam McCown, Scott Stephens, and David Wuertz. 2005 (Updated 2006). *Hurricane Katrina: A Climatological Perspective*. Washington, D.C.: U.S. Department of Commerce/ NOAA.

Greater New Orleans Community Data Center. 2010. *Active Zip Codes, November 2010* Available at http://www.gnocdc.org/ZipcodeRepopulation/index.html, last accessed January 11, 2011.

Greater New Orleans Community Data Center. 2002. *Lower Ninth Ward Neighborhood Snapshot*. Available at http://www.gnocdc.org/orleans/8/22/snapshot.html, last accessed January 11, 2011.

Grosh, Jerry. 2009. "How Does MDS Decide Where to Work?" *Behind the Hammer* (March): 4–5.

Gurney, Patrick. 1977. "The Therapeutic Community Revisited." Preliminary Paper #39. Newark, DE: Disaster Research Center, University of Delaware.

Handmer, John. 1985. *Local Reaction to Acquisition: An Australian Study*. Working Paper #53, Centre for Resource and Environmental Studies, Australian National University.

Haines, Aubrey, B. No date (August 22, possibly 1970). "They help disaster areas but they do more than help remove debris." From the MDS Archive files on Hurricane Camille.

Haury, David A. 1979. *The Quiet Demonstration: The Mennonite Mission in Gulfport, Mississippi*. Newton, Kansas: Faith and Life Press.

Hearn, Philip D. 2004. *Hurricane Camille*. Jackson, MS: University Press of Mississippi.

Heinz Center. 2002. *Human Links to Coastal Disasters*. Washington D.C.: The Heinz Center Foundation.

Hummon, David. M. 1986. "Place Identities: Localities of the Self." Pp. 34–37 in *Purposes in Built Form and Culture Research,* edited by J. William Carswell and David Saile. Proceedings of the 1986 International Conference on Built Form and Culture Research, University of Kansas Press.

Hummon, David. M. 1990. *Commonplaces: Community Ideology and Identity in American Culture*. Albany, NY: SUNY Press.

Jenkins, Pam. 2012. "After the Flood: faith in the diaspora." Pp. 218–230 in *Displaced,* edited by Lynn Weber and Lori Peek. Austin: University of Texas Press.

Jenkins, Pam and Brenda Phillips. 2008. "Domestic Violence and Disaster." Pp. 65–69 in *Katrina and the Women of New Orleans,* edited by Beth Willinger. New Orleans: Tulane University, Newcomb College Center for Research on Women.

Jordan, Craig. 1976. "Pastoral Care and Chronic Disaster Victims: The Buffalo Creek Experience." *The Journal of Pastoral Care* 30/3: 159–170.

Kako, Mayumi and Sugako Ikeda. 2009. "Volunteer Experiences in Community Housing During the Great Hanshin-Awaji Earthquake, Japan." *Nursing and Health Sciences* 11: 357–359.

Keim, Barry D. and Robert A. Muller. 2009. *Hurricanes of the Gulf of Mexico.* Baton Rouge: Louisiana State University Press.

Koenig, Harold. 2006. *In the Wake of Disaster: religious responses to terrorism and catastrophe.* Philadelphia: Templeton Foundation Press.

Knabb, Richard B., Jamie R. Rhome, and Daniel P. Brown. 2005 (Updated 2006). *Tropical Cyclone Report Hurricane Katrina 23–30 August 2005.* Miami, FL: National Hurricane Center.

Kraus, Nicholas C. and Lihwa Lin. 2009. "Hurricane Ike along the Upper Texas Coast: An Introduction." *Shore and Beach* 77/2: 3–8.

Kraybill, Donald. B. 2010. *Concise Encyclopedia of Amish, Brethren, Hutterites, and Mennonites.* Baltimore, MD: Johns Hopkins University Press.

Lam, Pui-Yan. 2002. "As the Flocks Gather: how religion affects voluntary association participation." *Journal for the Scientific Study of Religion* 41/3: 405–422.

Lincoln, Yvonne and Egon Guba. 1985. *Naturalistic Inquiry.* Newbury Park, CA: Sage.

Lofland, John, David Snow, Leon Anderson, and Lyn H. Lofland. 2006. *Analyzing Social Settings: a guide to qualitative observation and analysis.* Belmont, CA: Thomson.

Lowe, Setha and Alice Fothergill. 2003. "A Need to Help: Emergent Volunteer Behavior after September 11th." Pp. 293–314 in *Beyond September 11th: an Account of Postdisaster Research,* edited by Jacque Monday. Boulder, CO: Natural Hazards Research and Applications Information Center.

Louisiana Speaks. No date. "Cameron Parish—damage impact and needs assessment." Available at http://www.louisianaspeaks-parishplans.org/IndParishHomepage_BaselineNeedsAssessment.cfm?EntID=5, last accessed August 2, 2011.

Liu, Amy and Allison Plyer. 2010. "An Overview of Greater New Orleans: from recovery to transformation." Washington: Brookings Institution and Greater New Orleans Community Data Center (*The New Orleans Index at Five*).

Lu, Jing-Chien, Walter Gillis Peacock, Yang Zhang, and Nichole Dash. 2007. "Long-Term Housing Recovery: Does Type Really Make a Difference?" pp. 1–8 in *Proceedings of 2nd International Conference on Urban Disaster Reduction, Tiape, Taiwan , November 27–29, 2007.* Available at http://ncdr.nat.gov.tw/2icudr/2icudr_cd/2007BOOK.html.

Marus, Robert. 2005. "In Bayou la Batre, Hit by Katrina, Movie Drama Becomes All too Real." *Associated Baptist Press,* 6 September 2005.

McAdam, Doug. 1988. *Freedom Summer.* NY: Oxford University Press.

McIntosh, Barbara R. and Nicholas L. Danigelis. 1995. "Race, Gender and the Relevance of Productive Activity for Elders' Affect." *Journal of Gerontology* 50B/4: S229–S239.

McCullough, David. 1987. *The Johnstown Flood.* NY: Simon and Schuster, Inc.

Michel, Lacie M., et al. 2007. "Personal Responsibility and Volunteering after a Natural Disaster." *Sociological Spectrum* 27/6: 633–652.

Mitchell, Jerry T. 2003. "Prayer in Disaster: Case Study of Christian Clergy." *Natural Hazards Review* 4/1: 20–26.

Murray, Stuart. 2010. *The Naked Anabaptist: the Bare Essentials of a Radical Faith.* Scottdale, PA: Herald Press.

Musick, Marc, John Wilson, and William B. Bynum, Jr. 2000. "Race and Formal Volunteering: The Differential Effects of Class and Religion." *Social Forces* 78/4: 1539–1571.

National Council on Disability. 2009. *Effective Emergency Management: Making Improvements for Communities and People with Disabilities.* Washington D.C.: National Council on Disability.

National Council on Disability. 2010. "Lessons Learned from National Emergencies Regarding the Provision of Accessible and Affordable Housing." Pp. 123–140 in *The State of Housing in America in the 21st Century: A Disability Perspective.* Washington D.C.: National Council on Disability.

National Oceanic and Atmospheric Agency. 2005. "Hurricane Rita." Retrieved from http://www.ncdc.noaa.gov/special-reports/rita.html, August 1, 2010.

National Oceanic and Atmospheric Agency. 2009. "Meteorological Comparison of Hurricanes Audrey and Rita." Available at http://www.srh.noaa.gov/lch/?n=rita_audrey, last accessed August 2, 2011.

National Oceanic and Atmospheric Agency. 2010a. "Udall, Kansas." Available at http://www.crh.noaa.gov/ict/udall/stormreport2.php, last accessed December 1, 2010.

National Oceanic and Atmospheric Agency. 2010b. "Top Ten Weather Events of the Twentieth Century." Available at http://www.crh.noaa.gov/ict/climate/topten.php, last accessed December 2, 2010.

National Organization on Disability. 2002. "Special Needs Assessment of Katrina Evacuees." Washington D.C.: National Organization on Disability.

National Voluntary Organizations Active in Disaster. No date. *Managing Spontaneous Volunteers in Times of Disaster.* http://PointsofLight.org/Disaster. Accessed January 15, 2008.

Neal, David M. 1993. "Flooded with Relief: Issues of Effective Donations Distribution." In *Crosstraining: Light the Torch*, proceedings of the 17th Annual Conference of Floodplain Managers.

Neal, David M. 1994. "The Consequences of Excessive Unrequested Donations: The Case of Hurricane Andrew. *Disaster Management* 66/1: 23–28.

Nelson, L.D. & Dynes, Russell. 1976. "The Impact of Devotionalism and Attendance on Ordinary and Emergency Helping Behavior." *Journal for the Scientific Study of Religion* 15: 47–59.

Newton County Historical Commission. No date. "Newton's Historic Walking Tour." Pamphlet, Newton, Texas.

Newton County Historical Commission. 1986. *Newton County Nuggets.* Austin, TX: Eakin Publications.

Newton County Historical Commission. 1996. "Sketches of Newton County History." Newton, TX: Newton County Historical Commission.

Neufeld, Thomas R. Yoder. 2007. "From 'die Stillen im Lande' to 'Getting in the Way': A Theology for Conscientious Objection and Engagement." *Journal of Mennonite Studies* 25: 171–181.

Norris, Fran. H., Matthew. J. Friedman, and Patricia. J. Watson. 2002a. "60,000 Disaster Victims Speak: Part II." *Psychiatry* 65/3:240–260.

Norris, Fran. H., Matthew. J. Friedman, Patricia. J. Watson, Christopher. M. Byrne, Eolia. Diaz, and Kryszytov Kaniasty. 2002b. "60,000 Disaster Victims Speak: Part I." *Psychiatry* 65/3:207–239.

Park, Jerry Z. and Christian Smith. 2000. "To Whom Much Has Been Given: Religious Capital and Community Voluntarism Among Churchgoing Protestants." *Journal for the Scientific Study of Religion* 39/3: 272–286.

Paris, Barry. No Date. "Mennonites Tell of Tragedies in Camille's Wake." The *Wichita Eagle*, page 61. From the MDS Archive files on Hurricane Camille.

Paton, Douglas. 1996. "Training Disaster Workers: Promoting Wellbeing and Operational Effectiveness." *Disaster Prevention and Management* 5/5: 11–18.

Paton, Douglas. 1994. "Disaster Relief Work: an Example of Training Effectiveness." *Journal of Traumatic Stress* 7/2: 275–288.

Peacock, Walter, Nicole Dash, and Yang Zhang. 2006. "Sheltering and Housing Recovery Following Disaster." Pp. 258–274 in *Handbook of Disaster Research*, edited by Havidán Rodríguez, Enrico L. Quarantelli, and Russell R. Dynes. NY: Springer.

Peacock, Walter and Kathleen Ragsdale. 1997. "Social systems, Ecological Networks, and Disasters: Toward a Socio-political Ecology of Disasters." Pp. 29–35 in *Hurricane Andrew: Ethnicity, Gender and the Sociology of Disasters*, edited by W. G. Peacock, B. H. Morrow and H. Gladwin. London: Routledge.

Peacock, Walter and Chris Girard. 1996. "Ethnic and Racial Inequalities in Hurricane Damage and Insurance Settlements." Pp. 171–190 in *Hurricane Andrew: Ethnicity,*

Gender and the Sociology of Disasters, edited by W. G. Peacock, B. H. Morrow and H. Gladwin. London: Routledge.

Peek, Lori. 2010. "Age." Pp. 155–180 in *Social Vulnerability to Disaster*, ed. Brenda Phillips, Deborah S. K. Thomas, Alice Fothergill and Lynn Pike. Boca Raton, FL: CRC Press.

Peek, Lori. 2010. *Behind the Backlash: Muslims after September 11th*. Philadelphia: Temple University Press.

Peek, Lori, Jeannette Sutton, and Judy Gump. 2008. "Caring for Children in the Aftermath of Disaster: The Church of the Brethren Children's Disaster Services Program." *Children, Youth and Environments* 18/1: 408–421.

Pennebaker, James. 1997. *Opening Up*. NY: Guildford Press.

Phillips, Brenda D. 1997. "Qualitative Disaster Research," *International Journal of Mass Emergencies and Disasters* 15/1: 179–195.

Phillips, B. and P. Jenkins. 2009. Pp. 215–238 in "The roles of faith-based organizations after Hurricane Katrina." In *Meeting the Needs of Children, Families, and Communities Post-disaster: Lessons learned from Hurricane Katrina and its Aftermath*, edited by Ryan Kilmer, Virginia. Gil-Rivas, Richard Tedeschi, & Lawrence Calhoun. Washington, D.C.: American Psychological Association.

Phillips, Brenda D. 1996. "Homelessness and the Social Construction of Places: the Loma Prieta earthquake." *Humanity and Society* 19/4: 94–101.

Phillips, Brenda D. 2009. *Disaster Recovery*. Boca Raton, FL: CRC Press.

Phillips, Brenda and Maureen Fordham. 2010. "Introduction." Pp. 1–16 in *Social Vulnerability to Disasters*, ed. Brenda Phillips, Deborah S. K. Thomas, Alice Fothergill and Lynn Blinn-Pike. Boca Raton, FL: CRC Press.

Phillips, Brenda, Pamela Jenkins, and Elaine Enarson. 2010. "Violence and Disaster Vulnerability." Pp. 279–306 in *Social Vulnerability to Disasters*, edited by Brenda Phillips, Deborah S. K. Thomas, Alice Fothergill and Lynn Blinn-Pike. Boca Raton, FL: CRC Press.

Phillips, Brenda D. 2013/Forthcoming. *Qualitative Disaster Research*. NY: Oxford University Press.

Pike, Lynn. 2010. "Households and Families." Pp. 257–278 in *Social Vulnerability to Disasters*, edited by Brenda Phillips, Deborah S. K. Thomas, Alice Fothergill and Lynn Blinn-Pike. Boca Raton, FL: CRC Press.

Piliavin, Jane Allyn and Hong-Wen Charng. 1990. "Altruism: A Review of Recent Theory and Research." *Annual Review of Sociology* 16: 27–65.

Plyer, Allison. 2010. Hurricane Katrina Recovery. Available at http://www.gnocdc.org/Factsforfeatures/HurricaneKatrinaRecovery/HurricaneKatrinaRecovery.pdf, last accessed January 11, 2011.

Post, Cathy C. 2007. *Hurricane Audrey*. Gretna, LA: Pelican Publishing Company.

Preservation Resource Center of New Orleans. No date. "Living with History in New Orleans Neighborhoods: Holy Cross." Brochure, available at http://understandingkatrina.ssrc.org/Cutter/, last accessed January 12, 2011.

Quarantelli, E. L. No date. "The Early History of the Disaster Research Center." Available at http://www.udel.edu/DRC/aboutus/Early%20History%20of%20DRC%20%282%29.pdf, last accessed 12 June 2013.

Quarantelli, E. L. and Russell R. Dynes. 1976. "Community Conflict: its presence and absence in natural disasters." *Mass Emergencies* 1: 139–152.

Quarantelli, E. L. 1998. "The Disaster Recovery Process: What We Do and Do Not Know from Research." Available at http://dspace.udel.edu:8080/dspace/handle/19716/309?mode=simple. Accessed March 14, 2011.

Quarantelli, E. L. 2002. "The Disaster Research Center (DRC) Field Studies of Organized Behavior in the Crisis Time Period of Disasters." Pp. 94–126 in Stallings, Robert, editor, *Methods of Disaster Research*. Philadelphia: Xlibris.

Quarantelli, E. L. 2006. "Catastrophes are Different from Disasters: Some Implications for Crisis Planning and Management Drawn from Katrina." Available at http://understandingkatrina.ssrc.org/Quarantelli/, last accessed March 30, 2011.

Rappaport, Ed. 2005. "Addendum, Hurricane Andrew August 16–28, 1992." Available at http://www.nhc.noaa.gov/1992andrew_add.html, last accessed December 3, 2010.

Reed, John O. 1977. "The Pastoral Care of Victims of Major Disaster." *The Journal of Pastoral Care* 31/2: 97–108.

Roberts, Stephen and Willard Ashley. 2008. *Disaster Spiritual Care: Practical Clergy Responses to Community, Regional and National Tragedy.* Woodstock, VT: Sky Lights Path Publishing.

Robertson, Ian N., H. Ronald Riggs, Solomon C. S. Yim, and Yin Lu Young. 2007. "Lessons from Hurricane Katrina Storm Surge on Bridges and Buildings." *Journal of Waterway, Port, Coastal, and Ocean Engineering* 130: 463–483.

Rogers Richard. 1996. "The Effects of Family Composition, Health, and Social Support Linkages on Mortality." *Journal of Health and Social Behavior* 37: 326–38.

Ross, Alexander. 1980. "The Emergence of Organizational Sets in Three Ecumenical Disaster Recovery Organizations." *Human Relations* 33: 23–29.

Ross, Alexander and Smith, S. 1974. "The Emergence of an Organizational and an Organization Set: a Study of an Interfaith Disaster Recovery Group." Preliminary Paper #16, University of Delaware, Disaster Research Center.

Ruiter, Stijn and Nan Dirk De Graaf. 2006. "National Context, Religiosity, and Volunteering: Results from 53 Countries." *American Sociological Review* 71/2: 191–210.

Schwartz, David R. 2004. "Mista Midnights: Mennonites and Race in Mississippi."*Mennonite Quarterly Review*, Volume 4. Available at http://www.goshen.edu/mqr/pastissues/oct04swartz.html, last accessed December 3, 2010.

Sharkey, Peter. 2007. "Survival and Death in New Orleans." *Journal of Black Studies* 37/4: 482–501.

Shearer, Tobin Miller. 2010. *Daily Demonstrators: the Civil Rights Movement in Mennonite Homes and Sanctuaries.* Baltimore, MD: John Hopkins Press.

Smith, Bruce W., Kenneth I. Pargament, Curtis Brant, and Joan Oliver. 2000. "Noah Revisited: Religious Coping by Church Members and the Impact of the 1993 Midwest flood." *Journal of Community Psychology* 28/2: 169–186.

Smith, M. H. 1978. "American Religious Organizations in Disaster: a study of congregational response to disaster." *Mass Emergencies* 3: 133–142.

Spence, Patric, Kenneth A. Lachlan, and Jennifer M. Burke. 2007. "Adjusting to Uncertainty: Coping Strategies Among the Displaced after Hurricane Katrina." *Sociological Spectrum* 27: 653–678.

Spradley, James P. 1980. *Participant Observation.* NY: Holt, Rinehart and Winston.

Stallings, Robert, editor. 2002. *Methods of Disaster Research.* Philadelphia: Xlibris.

Stallings, Robert and E. L. Quarantelli. 1985. "Emergent Citizen Groups and Emergency Management." *Public Administration Review* 45: 93–100.

Stough, Laura and Sharp, Amy. 2008. *An Evaluation of the National Disability Rights Network Participation in the Katrina Today Project.* Washington D.C.: The National Disability Rights Network.

Sutton, Jeanette. 2003. "A Complex Organizational Adaptation to the World Trade Center disaster: An Analysis of Faith-based Organizations. Pp. 405–428 in *Beyond September 11th: An Account of Post-disaster Research*, edited by Jacque Monday. Boulder, CO: Natural Hazards Applications and Information Research Center.

Szabo, Liz. 2007. "Faith Rebuilds House and Soul." *USA Today*, July 18, 2007, Pages 1–2.

Texas Division of Emergency Management. 2005. Situation Report #29, October 22, 2005. Austin, Texas: Department of Emergency Management.

Texas Division of Emergency Management. 2008. "Hurricane Ike: Impact Report." Available at http://www.fema.gov/pdf/hazard/hurricane/2008/ike/impact_report.pdf, last accessed August 3, 2011.

Texas Division of Emergency Management. 2005. "Hurricane Rita." Available at http://www.disastercenter.com/Tropi-cal%20Storm%20–%20Hurricane%20–%20Rita.html, last accessed August 29, 2005.

Thoits, Peggy and Lyndi. Hewitt. 2001. "Volunteer work and well-being." *Journal of Health and Social Behavior* 42/2: 115–131.

Thomas, Deborah, et al., editors. 2013. *Social Vulnerability to Disasters.* Boca Raton, FL: CRC Press.

Tomeh, Aida K. 1973. "Formal Voluntary Organizations: participation, correlates and interrelationships." *Sociological Inquiry* 43/3–4: 89–122.

Tootle, Deborah M. 2007. "Disaster Recovery in Rural Communities: a case study of Southwest Louisiana." *Southern Rural Sociology* 22/2: 6–27.

United States Army Corps of Engineers. 2007. *Performance Evaluation of the New Orleans and Southeast Louisiana Hurricane Protection System.* Washington D.C.: U.S. Army Corps of Engineers.

United States Congress. 2006. *A Failure of Initiative.* Washington D.C.: U.S. Congress. Available at http://www.gpoaccess.gov/serialset/creports/katrina.html, last accessed January 7, 2011.

United States Fish and Wildlife Service. No date. "Cameron Prairie National Wildlife Refuge." Available at http://www.fws.gov/swlarefugecomplex/cameronprairie/, last accessed August 2, 2011.

Waltner, Willard and Elma. No date. "Six months after Camille." From the MDS Archive files on Hurricane Camille.

Waugh, William. 2006. *Shelter from the Storm: Repairing the National Emergency Management System after Katrina.* The ANNALS of the American Academy of Political and Social Science Series.

Weber, Lynn and Lori Peek, editors. 2012. *Displaced: Life in the Katrina Diaspora.* Austin, TX: University of Texas Press.

Webb, Gary, Kathleen Tierney, and James Dahlhamer. 2000. "Businesses and Disasters: empirical patterns and unanswered questions." *Natural Hazards Review* 1/3:83–90.

Weaver, J. Denny. 2005. *Becoming Anabaptist: the origin and significance of Sixteenth-century Anabaptism,* 2nd edition. Scottdale, PA: Herald Press.

Weiss, Robert S. 1994. *Learning from Strangers: the art and method of qualitative interview Studies.* NY: Free Press.

White House, The. 2006. *The Federal Response to Hurricane Katrina: Lessons Learned.* Washington D.C.: The White House. Available at http://georgewbush-whitehouse.archives.gov/reports/katrina-lessons-learned/letter.html, last accessed January 7, 2011.

Wiebe, Katie Funk. 1979. *Day of Disaster.* Scottdale, PA: Herald Press.

Wiegand, Bill. No date. "The Charlot Sisters on Second Street." Available at http://pc.danellis.net/index.htm, last accessed July 1, 2010.

Wilson, Jennifer, Brenda Phillips and David M . Neal. 1997. "Domestic Violence after Disaster." Pp. 115–122 in The Gendered Terrain of Disaster: Through Women's Eyes, ed. Elaine Enarson and Betty Hearn Morrow. Miami: Laboratory for Social and Behavioral Research, Florida International University.

Wilson, John and Marc Musick. 1997. "Who Cares? Toward an Integrated Theory of Volunteer Work." *American Sociological Review* 62: 694–713.

Wilson, John. 2000. "Volunteering." *Annual Review of Sociology* 26: 215–40.

Wisner, Ben et al. 2004. *At Risk.* London: Routledge.

Witt, James Lee and James Morgan. 2002. *Stronger in the Broken Places.* NY: Times Books.

Wilson, John and Marc Musick. 2000. "Effects of Volunteering on the Volunteer." *Law and Contemporary Problems* 62/4: 141–168.

Zhang, Yang and Walter Peacock. 2010. "Planning for Housing Recovery: Lessons Learned from Hurricane Andrew." *Journal of the American Planning Association* 76/1: 5–24.

RESOURCES

- For photos of Hurricane Camille, visit the Harrison County Library website at http://www.harrison.lib.ms.us/library_services/camille_pics.htm, last accessed January 10, 2010.
- For information about Mennonite Disaster Service, visit www.mennonite.mds.net.
- For information on the Southern Mutual Help Association, visit http://www.southernmutualhelp.org/.

Index

About the Author

Brenda Phillips is the Associate Dean at Ohio University in Chillicothe. In 2013, she was inducted into the International Network of Women in Emergency Management's Hall of Fame. Dr. Phillips is a recipient of the Mary Fran Myers Award for Gender and Disaster Research and the Blanchard Award for excellence in emergency management education. She co-edited *Women and Disasters: From Theory to Practice* with Betty Hearn Morrow and *Social Vulnerability to Disasters* with Deborah Thomas, Alice Fothergill, and Lynn Blinn-Pike. She is the author of *Disaster Recovery* and the lead researcher for a National Council on Disability project titled *Effective Emergency Management: Making Improvements for Communities and People with Disabilities.* Her published research can be found in a variety of journals including the *International Journal of Mass Emergencies and Disasters, Emergency Management,* the *Journal of Black Studies, Disaster Prevention and Management, Disasters, Humanity and Society,* the *Journal of Emergency Management, Natural Hazards Review,* and *Environmental Hazards.* She is a graduate of Bluffton University (Ohio) and The Ohio State University.